Edward Dunbar Dunbar

Social Life in Former Days, Chiefly in the Province of Moray

Edward Dunbar Dunbar

Social Life in Former Days, Chiefly in the Province of Moray

ISBN/EAN: 9783337861537

Printed in Europe, USA, Canada, Australia, Japan

Cover: Foto ©Suzi / pixelio.de

More available books at **www.hansebooks.com**

SOCIAL LIFE IN FORMER DAYS.

EDINBURGH : PRINTED BY THOMAS CONSTABLE,

FOR

EDMONSTON AND DOUGLAS.

LONDON, . .   HAMILTON, ADAMS, AND CO.

CAMBRIDGE, . .   MACMILLAN AND CO.

DUBLIN,   . . . M'GLASHAN AND GILL.

GLASGOW, . . . JAMES MACLEHOSE.

SOCIAL LIFE IN FORMER DAYS,

Chiefly in the Province of Moray.

ILLUSTRATED BY LETTERS AND FAMILY PAPERS.

BY E. DUNBAR DUNBAR,

(LATE) CAPTAIN 21ST FUSILIERS.

THUNDERTON HOUSE.

EDINBURGH: EDMONSTON & DOUGLAS.

MDCCCLXV.

PREFACE.

WHEN arranging the family papers at Duffus House, Gordonston, and Lesmurdie Cottage, the residences respectively of my brother, Sir Archibald Dunbar, my cousin, Sir Alexander Gordon Cumming, and my kinsman, Captain James Stewart, I occasionally found documents which appeared to me to throw considerable light on old social life, or to be otherwise interesting, and which I therefore sent to the local press.

Wishing to give them a more extensive circulation, I now venture to offer them, systematically arranged, to the public.

E. DUNBAR DUNBAR.

SEA PARK, *July* 1865.

TABLE OF CONTENTS.

PAGES

I. EDUCATION, 1-16

II. MEDICAL, 17-29

III. PRICES OF PROVISIONS, 30-32

IV. POSTAL ARRANGEMENTS, . 33-34

V. TRAVELLING, 35-37

VI. TAVERN BILLS, 38-41

VII. FIELD SPORTS, 42-46

VIII. QUARANTINE, 47-51

IX. FISHINGS, 52-60

X. IMPRESSING FOR THE NAVY, 61-63

XI. SMUGGLING, . 64-70

XII. THE FAMILIES OF BURGIE AND OF GRANGE, 71-76

XIII. AN EXTRAVAGANT AND UNDUTIFUL WIFE, 77-79

XIV. OFFICE OF HERITABLE SHERIFF OF MORAY, 80-86

XV. TRANSPORT OF A PRISONER, AND JAIL OF
INVERNESS, 87-92

XVI. COUNTRY MATTERS, . 93-100

XVII. EDINBURGH GOSSIP, 101-104

XVIII. LETTERS FROM LADIES OF RANK, 105-127

XIX. GENIAL LETTERS, 128-137

PAGES

XX. YOUNGER SONS,   138-143

XXI. WHOLESALE MERCHANTS,   144-152

XXII. DRINKING-SONG,   153-158

XXIII. ELGIN TOWN-COUNCIL,   159-174

XXIV. INCORPORATED TRADES OF ELGIN,   175-178

XXV. AN INVERNESS BAILIE'S ADVICE AND
        ASSISTANCE,   179-184

XXVI. MERCHANTS' LETTERS,   185-191

XXVII. RECEIPTS AND ACCOUNTS,   192-199

XXVIII. POETIC EFFUSIONS AND BEGGING LETTERS, 200-204

XXIX. INVENTORY OF HOUSEHOLD FURNITURE,   205-213

XXX. PARLIAMENTARY EXPENSES AND POLITICS,   214-231

XXXI. ECCLESIASTICAL,   232-260

XXXII. WITCHES,   261-273

XXXIII. FUNERALS AND FUNERAL LETTERS,   274-283

XXXIV. WILL OF THE DEAN OF SALISBURY, 1618,   284-291

XXXV. CATTLE-STEALING, .   292-296

XXXVI. JOHN, EARL OF SUTHERLAND: HIS IN-
         FLUENCE AND POWER,   297-304

XXXVII. MILITARY,   305-322

XXXVIII. REBELLION, 1715-1716,   323-335

XXXIX. REBELLION, 1745-1746,   336-388

XL. CORONATION OF GEORGE III.: SUBMISSION
       TO HIS GOVERNMENT,   389-392

I. EDUCATION.

KING'S COLLEGE, Aberdeen, was the University most frequented by the youth of Moray; and students of the first, second, third, and fourth years' regular attendance were known respectively as Bajans, Semies, Tertians, and Magistrands,—designations which, we believe, are still applied.

" To Master ARCHBALD DUNBAR, of Thundertoun :
      " To ye care of the Postmaster of Elgin.
                  " KING'S COLLEGE, *Octr. ye* 16*th*, 1702.

"SIR,—If this shall chance to find you out when you ar wandering through the north, it is sent to inform you, that (because the Bajan class is fixed in our college) I am to enter with the Semies this ensueing winter; if therfor in the course of your peregrinations you chance to meet with any who have a mind to save themselves a yeares time and expense at the college, pray be carefull to advise or recomend them to me, who (according to the late laudable custom of other universities) can receive them for Semies, although they have never been Bajans in any college. Particularly I am informed that at the school of Elgin ther

A

is a son of Logic Cumin's and two others who have
learned the Greek, but because I have no acquaintance of thier parents, and Mr. Tod the schoolmaster is
unfriendly to our college, I must recomend them to
your management.   In a word your Alma Mater and
old Master do be thir presents constitute and ordain
you their Factor, sole Actor, and speciall Errand-
bearer as to the premisses in all partes and places
where you pass in your northern precinct.   And if
you wil be so kind to let us see you as you go south,
you shall have the thanks of the whole house, as weel
as the gratefull acknowledgments of, Sir, your most
obsequious servant,   WIL. BLAK.

"James Keith and his wife who ar presently with
me drinking your good health, send their service to
you, and therwith also my wife bids me give you
hers."

———

"KING'S COLLEGE, *Nor. ye* 16*th*, 1705.

"SIR,--I have yours and shall carefully look after
that boy you recomend.   If in your peregrination
through the north you will be pleased to inquire
amongst your acquaintance for such as ar ready to
enter Semies this winter and advise them our way,
you will do a kindness both to your Alma Mater and
old Master, whom upon all occasions you shall ever
find, Sir, your most obsequious humble servant,

"WIL. BLAK."

" My brother James is not com north, nor (tho' he sayes it) do I expect him this winter.

" I hear that Dr. Forbes at Elgin has a son who might be in my Semic class this winter : but I have not the fortun to be acquainted with the Doctor, and therfor must put you to the trouble to speak to him.

"If any you meet with have Latine enough, tho' they have but a small begining in the Greek, I shall see they can compleat theire courses, give them as much (and if they please mor) Greek than ever probably they may have use for, and that without any hindrance to theire other studies. For my schollars all this winter ar to have one lesson (viz., from the evening to the morning) each day in the Greek, and two each week through all the succeeding yeares."

" KING's COLLEGE, *May ye* 10*th*, 1708.

" SIR,—I have yours of the 1st current and in answer therunto am concerned to acquaint you, that, by ane Act of the last Comission of parliament for visiteing our universities, and the practise of all the colleges in this kingdom (in each whereof one master is now fixed to the Greek class) any student is, and wil be permitted to enter Semic, without being obleidged to enter Bajan, if he understand the Latine tongue, and have a competencie of the Greek, *i.e.* (as it is everywhere now understood), can read the Greek, and

expound a litle of the Greek New Testament, and
have allowance and approbation of the Greek Regent
so to do : which a small compliment for his consent
does never and nowhere fail to procure.

"If therfore any of your acquaintance in your coun-
trie about you, have a mind to save theire children's
time and expense at colleges the first year, they may
cause teach them a litle Greek at home, and so enter
them Semies in any college within this kingdom,
who will not (nor can legally) refuse them with the
qualifications and conditions for said.

"And seing matters ar now caryed so in all the
colleges of north as well as south Britan ; pray take
the paines to advise some of your acquaintance to, Sir,
your faithfull comerade and most obedient servant,

"WIL. BLAK.

"The bearer has imployed his time to very good
purpose at our college : and I have made him Master
of Arts."

Dr. Thomas Reid, the eminent metaphysician, and
author of the *Inquiry into the Human Mind, Essays
on the Intellectual Powers,* etc., was educated at
Marischal College, and in 1752 was elected Professor
of Moral Philosophy at King's College, Aberdeen.
The Professor gives an account of the admirable arrangements which he helped to introduce into the

latter university, and which ought never to have
been discontinued :—

" To ARCHIBALD DUNBAR, Esq.,
    " of Newton, at Duffus.

" KING'S COLLEGE, *Septr. 4th*, 1755.

" SIR,—I did indeed intend, both last vacation and
this, to have seen a little of the north country, and
in that case should certainly have done myself the
honour to wait of you at Duffus ; but sometimes
sickness in my family, and sometimes other accidents,
have hindred me hitherto.

" Some ambiguity that has happened in a word of
the letter you favour me with, makes me uncertain
whether your intention is to put Bob to my class this
session, which happens to be the Magistrand class ;
or whether you intend that both your sons should
enter with the Greek Professor. Give me leave, therefore, to acquaint you what my class is to be employed
in, that you may the better judge how it will answer
your intention with regard to Bob, and the progress
he has made. One hour in the day, for about two
months, in the beginning of the session, will be employed upon Optics and some branches of Mathematicks, which I could not overtake last session.
All the rest will be employed in the Philosophy of
the Mind, Logic, Morals, and Politics. If this is
what you intend for Bob, you may depend upon it
that I shall faithfully and timeously acquaint you

what progress he makes. If you propose to put him
in the Greek class with his brother, this is not at all
an unusual thing at this college of late. You may
please, in that event, to acquaint him that Charlie
M'Ever, his class-fellow, being sensible that he was
not well founded in Greek and Latin, and finding the
Mathematicks a little too hard for his age, went back
last session to the Humanity class, and enters the
Greek class this session, and I believe will make a
fine scholar ; and Captain Fraser's son went back to
the Bajan class last session.

" Your concern that the behaviour of your sons be
narowly looked after is most natural, and what every
one that knows the heart of a parent must approve of.
I can assure you that in this society we have for
some years past been using our best skill and application for this purpose. While the students were
scattered over the town in private quarters, and might
dispose of themselves as they pleased but at school
hours, we found it impossible to keep them from low
or bad company, if they were so disposed. But they
are on a very different footing since they lived within
the college : we need but look out at our windows to
see when they rise and when they go to bed. They
are seen nine or ten times throughout the day statedly
by one or other of the masters—at publick prayers,
school hours, meals, and in their rooms ; besides occa-
sional visits, which we can make with little trouble to

ourselves. They are shut up within walls at nine at
night. We charge those that are known to be trusty
and diligent with the oversight of such as we suspect
to be otherwise ; and I verily believe there are few
boys so narrowly lookt after, or so little exposed to
temptations to vice, at home as with us at present.
This discipline hath indeed taken some pains and
resolution, as well as some expense to establish it.
It makes our work laborious during the session, and
must meet with the common prejudices that every
new thing does. We behoved to be somewhat diffi-
dent of it ourselves till we tried it. But now, after
the experience of two sessions, we are not only satisfied that it is practicable ; but have already seen such
effects of it, both upon the morals and proficiency of
our students, as we hope will at last justify us to the
world, in sticking so obstinately to it in opposition to
such an union of the two colleges as behoved to have
altogether undone it. You may rest assured that I
will take a particular concern in your sons, and shall
take it upon me to acquaint you of the opinion their
masters have of them.

"The board at the first table is 50 merks per
quarter ; at the second 40 shillings. Some one of
the masters dines always at the second table, as well
as at the first. The rent of a room is from seven to
twenty shillings in the session. There is no furniture
in their rooms, but bedstead, tables, chimney grate,

and fender—the rest, viz., feather-bed, bed-cloaths, chairs, tongs, and bed-hangings, if they chuse any, they must buy or hire, for the session, and indeed the people that let those things are very apt to exact upon them, so that it is much better, especially if one is to be some sessions at the college, to have them of their own, and dispose of them when they leave the college. Whatever they leave in their rooms is taken care of till next session. They provide fire, and candle, and washing to themselves. The other dues are—two guineas to the Master; to the Professors of Greek and Humanity for their publick teaching, five shillings each. All other perquisites not named, from twelve shillings to seventeen and sixpence, as near as I can remember; the greatest part of which goes to four Oeconomy servants, and four College servants. The Professor of Medicine orders the diet and regimen of those that are valetudinary, and attends the Bursars and poorer sort in case of sickness, gratis. Others who are in good circumstances, if they should need the attendance of a physician, may either employ him or any other their parents recommend.

"There is an advertisement from this college in the Aberdeen's Papers of Tuesday last, which contains a recommendation to the parents of students. You may please to look into it. I think it would not be amiss if your son should be begun to the Greek Grammar before he comes to town. For every one here has a place in his class according to his proficiency, from the first to the last ; and when one sets out in an advanced post, it proves a great spur to diligence, that he may at least keep the rank he has got. I am, with great respect, Sir, your most obedient and most humble servant, THO. REID."

The Rev. Lauchlan Shaw, the historian of Moray, considered St. Andrews the best place in many respects for a young student :—

" To ARCHIBALD DUNBAR, Esqr.,
      " of Newton at Duffus.
                              " ELGIN, *Sept.* 17, 1763.

" DEAR SIR,—Since the time I was at Duffus I have been some days at Rafford for my health, which has been lately very much broken—and this was the reason why I did not before now let you know the issue of the commission you gave me.

" Mr. Cook (who goes to Forres at Martinmass) has, I find, given you his thoughts about sending your son to the university this ensuing winter. By being in the Greek class he can have no time to improve in the Latin during the session, and he will need a proper Governor next summer to revise his Latin and Greek. In my opinion its a loss (and I found it so), to enter into the university before one is well advanced in the Latin, which is the dead language most

useful and necessary to be understood. With respect
to the place—Aberdeen or St. Andrews—if he goes
to the first, the Old Town is preferable to the New,
a more free air, fewer avocations, and more strict
academical regulations, and very sufficient masters,
but it is too near to the vanities and diversions of
the New Town.

" St. Andrews is wholsome, private, far from diversions, but they study more the Greek than the Latin.
Professor Shaw is dayly expected here, if he comes
I shall acquaint you.   I sincerely wish that your son
may meet with all encouragement in his studies, and
may make progress in learning and virtue, and with
compliments to your lady and children, I ever am,
dear Sir, your obedient obliged servant,

" LACH. SHAW."

William Falconar, Bishop of Moray, could not conscientiously recommend a Presbyterian pedagogue,
showed how the oath required by the Hanoverian
Government could be avoided, and stated the salary
of his Episcopalian protégé :—

" For ARCHIBALD DUNBAR of Newton, Esq.,
        " at Duffus, near Elgin.
                        "EDINR., *April 23rd*, 1754.

" SIR,—I would have wrote you by Mr. Baldie, but
when he called at my lodgings, I happened to be
abroad.   After I received your last, I had laid myself

out to find a proper pedagogue for your sons, and intended, as you proposed, to have sent him along with Baldie, and for that reason Baldie was detained here some days ; but as I could not, in so short a time, hit upon a sufficient young man, I thought it was better to allow your son to take his journey than to spend his time and money here doing nothing. There is a young man, Mr. Alexr. Diack, just now governour to the Master of Elphinston's sons, who is well and fully recommended to me by those who are perfectly well acquainted with him, and, as Mr. Elphinston's sons have finished their home education, Mr. Diack leaves the family at Whitsunday next. He is a good scholar, of modest behaviour, and of a virtuous character. He understands the learned languages, the French, Mathematicks, and writes a fine hand ; so that so far, I think, he will fit your purpose. I believe he has not, nor, as I am informed, will he take the oaths ; but I think you need not mind that qualification, as Mr. Elphinston, who is an officer in the army, made no scruple as to that point, nor does indeed any gentleman in this country heed it at all, as they make these gentlemen, who perform the part of pedagogues, pass under the name of factor or clerk, or comerade, or what they please. If you like this proposal, you have no more to do but write me directly, and I shall, without loss of time, secure Mr. Diack. He has twelve guineas a year where he

now serves, and if he answers the good character I
have of him, it will be money well laid out. I cannot
in conscience recommend any of our new-fashioned
Blades, nor do I think them proper instructors for
young gentlemen, and, therefore, if what I have proposed is not agreeable to you, I hope you will not
take it amiss if I decline the providing you in a
Presbyterian dominie or a libertin Whig; I wish you
and your family too well to do you such an ill office.
I hope Baldie will do very well. He is young and
good-natured, and therefore you must overlook, in
some measure, former faults, in hopes of better behaviour, which time, experience, and good instruction
will bring about.   With my usual compliments to all
your family, I am, dear Sir, your most humble servant,

" WIL. FALCONAR."

Certificate in favour of a French master,—his
terms, etc. :—

" This serves to certifie and inform any gentleman
or community, who may have taste or inclination for
the French language, that the bearer heirof, Mr. John
Brulet, a Native of France, near the City of Rheims,
the M : of Champaigne, has lived in my family above
three months, with great decency and behaviour, as a
French-master.

" From his knowledge in the English, as well as his

skill and method in the French, he has in the first place, taught his scholars not only to read and thoroughly understand the French grammar, but also, to get by heart such parts thereof, as are necessary for their daily improvement.

"And in the second place, he has taught them not only to read and explain many Books of Telemachus, but even to pronounce the French in the most proper manner, ane attainment not to be acquired at the hands of any, but those of a true Native of France, which is the peculiar excellence of this man above other French teachers, and had not a seperation in my family, been necessary at this juncture, Mr. Brulet had not been parted with so soon.

" His fees are of the common sort. Seven shillings per month, or a guinea per quarter, is what I have paid, but as I had but five scholars to give ; for their sake, and the constant benefit of his conversation with them, I entertained him here, which was no bad part of the bargain for him or them. The pains and attention he gives, and the particular pleasure he takes in the progress made by his scholars, is apparently such, that he, or she, who does not proffit, must be an absolute dunce or a careless idiot.

" In short, it is obvious to any person of but tollerable skill or taste in the French language, that there never was, and perhaps never will be, such another man, in his way, in our country, which, at Duffus,

the 20th Day of Octor. 1755 years, is declared to be
the humble opinion of   ARCHD. DUNBAR."

A dancing-master's discharge and obligation in
1704, to Mr. James Sutherland, second son of James
Lord Duffus :—

" I, William Badhame, danceing master in Edinburgh, be the tenor hereof, grant me to have received
ffrom Master James Sutherland, Advocat, the sum of
ffiftie punds Scots money, in full contentation and
satisfaction of all due me for danceing, upon acompt of
Mistris Elizabeth Sutherland, his sister, preceeding the
date of thir presents. And, in like maner by thir presents it's provyded that in case the said Mistris Elizabeth Sutherland shall at any tyme here after happin
to come where I the said William Badhame teaches
danceing, I oblidge my selfe upon the payment of
sixteen pund Scots to perfect her, oblidgeing me and
my heirs, &c., to warrand thir presents good valid
and effectuall of all that I can ask or clame of the
said Mrs. Elizabeth Sutherland, any manner of way,
at all hands and against all deadly as law will; con-
sentin thir presents be insert and restrat in the books
of Councill and Session, or in any other Judges court
books compitent within this realme, therein to remain
ad ffuturam rei memoriam, and constituts,

my prors, &c. In witnes wherof (wrytin be George Keith wryter in Edinburgh,) I have subscribed thir presents at Edinburgh, the eighteent day of Septer., Javij and ffour years. Before witnesss James Donaldson, merchant in Edinburgh, and the said George Keith, wryter hereof. WM. BADHAM.

"J. Donaldson, *witnes.*

"Geo : Keith, *witnes.*"

The qualifications and salary of a governess :—

" To the much Honoured the LADY THUNDERTON—These :

" RANES, HUNTLY, *Jan.* 30*th* 1710.

" MADAM,—Robert Gordon has writ now twice to my father as (by your Ladyship's desire as I suppose) concerning me, if I be willing and fit for your service. In his last he desires I should writ to your Ladyship to show that I can sow white and colourd seam ; dress head suits, play on the Treble and Gambo, Viol, Virginelles and Manicords, which I can do, but on no other. He desires to let know what fie I wold have, which is threttie pound and Gown and Coat, or then fourtie pound and Shoes and Linnens, which is for a year. If those terms please your Ladyship, I am content to serve for half-a-year conform, to try if I please your Ladyship. I expect an answer with the first occassion, and I am, Madam, your most humble servant,

" JEAN CHEIN."

Expenses of the board and education of two young ladies whose father was serving in the Low Countries under Marlborough :—

" Received from Joseph Brodie of Milntown in name and behalf of Archbald Dunbar of Thundertoun, the soum of four pund Scots, and that for Alexr. Dunbar of Belmuckedie his two daughters (Meg[1] and Ket) their current quarter colledge fie, as witness my hand at Dyke the twentie-second of Decr. 1709.

" ALEXR. NICOLSON."

" Received from the said Millntoun in name and behalf of the said Mr. Archbald Dunbar of Thundertoun two pound sterline, and that for Alexr. Dunbar of Bermuckitre his two daughters Meg : and Kett : ther quarterly buird, and that by me Janet Dunbar. In witnes wherof I have subscrybed day and date above written.

JANET DUNBAR."

---

[1] " Meg" married Lieut.-Colonel Whitney, of Ligonier's dragoons, who was afterwards killed at the battle of Falkirk when charging at the head of his regiment.

II. MEDICAL.

In the early part of the eighteenth century, Dr. Robert Innes appears to have been the principal physician in Elgin, of which town he was also a magistrate. Gilded pills with ale for the miss, snuff for the lady in an interesting situation, and plum-cakes to celebrate (we trust) the safe arrival of the babe, must not make us forget that the doctor imported his drugs direct from London, and professionally attended the Chancellor's (Seafield) Countess.

" Memorandum—Baillie Innes, in Elgin, to Mr. Archbald Dunbar of Thundertoune, May 28, 1705.

" WHEN it pleases God you arrive safely at Edinburgh (and at leasure) please remitt the thirtie-eight pounds sterling twelve shillings, heirwith delivered you, to Mr. Edmund Sheepherd, drugist, at the Rose and Croune on Ludegate-hill, London, and cause gett ane acquittance or discharge for the same to me ; and whatever the current exchange is, I hereby oblidge me to remitt the same to you, on advertisement. Withall,

B

when your conveniencie allowes, mynd the bill, like-
wyes given you now, upon the Countess of Seafield,
and gett payment thereof, all which will be verie
oblidging to dear Sir, yours verie affectionatly,

" ROB : INNES."

" ELGIN, Sept. 22, 1705.

"DEAR SIR,—After my humble dutie to your lady
and sweet self, I presume to give you the trouble to
bestowe the inclosed thre shillings on ane book for my
Jamie's use, which cannot be had nearer than Edinburgh. Its neam is John Leusden's Collections of the
New Testament in Greek, done into thirty-six lessons,
with the Analysis. I am told its pryce is twixt half
ane croune and fourtie pence ; but although it be
some more, pray send it; withall, if you have recovered payment of the Countess of Seafield, of the
twentie shilling she owed me, be pleased likewayes to
buye for me, and send me by the bearer, Etmullerus,
his works Compendised and Englished, the last
editione, which I am told is ane most excellent mar-
rowish piece of phisik, and is bought for about seven
shillings English. I return you most heartie thanks
for your last favor done me. Your readiness to serve
your freinds is the occasion of this trouble. All your
freinds here are in health, and mynd you as oft as we
meet ; and I am truelie, dear Sir, your affectionat
cussen and comrad,   ROB. INNES."

" To The Laird of Thundertoun,
"att Duffus.
" Elgin, *Aprile* 1711.

"Sir,- . . . if your lady's true and full tym be come. I have sent ane hysterik cordiall julep which is provoking and whereof she may take a third pairt when it comes, and the other third pairt (if she is not delivered in the tym) two hours thereafter, and what remains two hours after that; in the meintym lett her walk and take snuff or what may provoke snezing. I wish her ane happie hour and safe deliverie, and continues still, Sir, yours affectionatly,

"Rob. Innes."

" Elgin, 3*d May*, 1711.

"Sir,—I have sent the two plumbcakes, with two small boxes with the suggar bisket by the bearer, as alsoe the mutton; and the baker comes alongst with them, but the plumbcakes, especially the upper, must be carefullie taken out, least the glasing or garnishing be spoyled. The baker will assist and direct in this; and how soon they and the bisket are taken out, they may be put near a fyre, least they grow wett by the dampness of the weather. They are all well done, and will please all concerned. I shall be with you, Godwilling, once this afternoon, and see them rightly sett doune to-morrow morning, all the workmen have promised to be with you by thrie this afternoon, I am, Sir, your most oblidged servant,   Rob: Innes."

"ELGIN, *June* 28, 1713.

"SIR,—Please receive seven small gilded pills in ane little box, whereof your daughter Bettie is to swallow five in the morning by themselves, tumbling them doune her throat with ane mouthful of cold ale, either one by one or two together as she best can ; and if this begin not to work two hours after taking them, lett her swallow doun the other two—observing ane phisical dyet all day, I mein keeping warm and dyning on fresh broath, and when disposed to drink, let it be table ale warmed ; And I am, Sir, yours affectionately,   ROB: INNES."

This account is in Scots money :—

" Accompt Laird off Thundertown, since Jan. 22th, 1719. To Kenneth Mackenzie, Chyr Aporie (Surgeon Apothecary) in Elgin.

		lb.	ss.	d.
Janr. 22.	To ane plaister for his cook,		10	0
1719.	To phlebotomie of him, .		12	0
Febr. 27.	To ane bottle bitters for his lady,		10	0
Mar. 12.	To ane bole for his lady, . .		6	0
	To halfe ane ounce balsam for her,		13	0
	To ane cephalick powder for her,		2	0
	To ane pott of liniment for her,		6	0
15.	To the bole repeated for her, . .		6	0
28.	To two ounce calamus aromaticus for your selfe, ...		4	0
	To two ounces centaury for him, . .		4	0
May 13.	To ane vomitory for your sister-in-law,		10	0

	To ane stomachick mixture for her,	.	J	3 0
	To halfe ane ounce oyle of mace for her,	J		4 0
	To ane stomachick plaister for her,	.		18 0
14.	To ane lottion for her,	. . .	J	19 0
	To three ounces hungary water cam-			
	phorat for yourselfe,	. . .	J	14 0
	To ane ounce spirit of win, camphorat			
	for yourselfe, .	. . . .		8 0
19.	To ane mixture for your servant, Robert			
	Kinach,	. . .		8 0
	To phlebotomie of him,	. .		12 0
Janr. 29.	To materials for wine for your lady,			18 0
1720.	To ane morning mixture for her, .	.		6 0
	To therty morning powders for her,	.	J5	00 0
	To two pound tincture for her,		6	6 0
31.	To ane box pills for her,	.	J	4 0
	To ane anodyn for her,	. . .		6 0
ffebr. 23.	To two pound bitter tincture for Mrs.			
	Rebecca,	. . . . .	2	18 0
	To ane ounce tincture of antimony for			
	her,	. . . .		12 0
	To ane cosmetick for her,	. . .		18 0
Mar. 7.	To materials for ane diet drink for Collin			
	Menzies,	. . . . .	6	6 0
Apr. 15.	To ane bottle julep for your lady,		3	4 0
	To ane pott of ane elecuary for her,			14 0
	To three masticatory balls for her,			7 6
	To ane bottle juices for her,	.		4 0
22.	To ane hypnotick for her,	.		7 0
	To ane gargarism for her,	. . .	J	16 0
	To ane box gilded pills for your daughter			18 0
	To two ounces oxycroceon, .	.	1	00 0 ·
			39	13 0"

Lord Reay encloses two prescriptions :[1]—

" To Archibald Dunbar, of Thunderton, Esqr.

"Tongue, 15*th* *Nov*: 1727.

"Sir,—I send you on the other side Dr. Boorehaves receipt for any pain in the head, eyes, toothack, &c. :—Make a litle basket like a small beehive, open above, and put under it some live coal in a shovel, on which put a snuff-pen full of the powder, covering it with a coarse napkin well warmed at the fire ; the smoak will pierce it, and how soon the smoak is over rub your forehead and temples pretty well with the napkin, both at morning and bed-time. I found much benefit by it. I have no fault to the Bishop, he is of the true kind, a little headstrong and willfull. If you send the swine to Mr. Gordon of Haughes, in spring, he will get them sent me, and if you think them too deir a ffie for the present advice, and curing your former dullness of hearing, ask anything I have you want, the more freedom the welcomer.—I am, Sir, your very humble servant,   Reay.

" Sp. Benzoni.
 Mastichæ.
 Olibani.
 Styrae, Calamit, ad Drach. IV.
 M. Sp. pro Thymiamate cujus
 parum simull prunce insparsum
 fumet, et pannos evaparandos.

---

[1] The prescriptions are difficult to decipher ; and may not therefore be correctly copied.

"I shall add from the same hand the best thing I ever tryed for my teeth and gums, with which I rub them after dinner and supper,—

" Sp. Aqua stillatit Rosae, .	une.	xv.
Sp. Matricalis Bynlis,	une.	ij.
Salis dulcis, .	une.	ij.
Tinct. gummis Laccae,	une.	.j.
Myrrae drach . . .	une.	ij.
M. F. Liquer ad dentes gengioasque.		

"N.B.—If you can't get the Spn. Mat. Bynlis, take Sp. of Scurygrass as a Sunedauay."

———

Dr. Graham would have doubtless advocated Hydro pathy had it been established in his time.

" To Sir ALEXANDER DUNBAR,
   " at Thunderton, by Elgin.

   " EDINBURGH, *July* 11*th* 1778.

"Six days of TOTAL abstinence! you are a man—an angel, Sir Alexander—the worst is now over—you vindicate the dignity of your rational nature— you transform human into divine !—

" I speak from experience Sir ; I have a double right to speak as a physician and as a man, most heartily to congratulate you. It is many years since I tasted one drop of any thing stronger than water—not even in sickness do I allow myself a vinous or spiritous medicine : what did I say ? sickness ! I am

never sick—I am never sorry, I am about your own
age.

"Go on, Sir Alexander! as you do. Such little
variations as are or may be necessary, your own good
sense and observation will point out to you. Take
care that the bath is only milk warm.

" Yes, eat as many greens boiled and raw, and as
much ripe fruit, as you find agrees with you. Let no
medical rascal lace you up too tight.

" Let beef and mutton, kept long after they are
killed, be your principal meat. Eat few soups or
broth—prefer, roasting on the spit, and broiling on
the gridiron. Yes, yes Sir! you may eat fish, and
roasted fowls, tame and wild, full grown.

" Eat strawberries and sugar, but no milk.

" Bathe, now, every *other* day. Let sweet music
— cordial friendship — virtuous love ! engage your
time and attention. Project and pursue with moderation some great, useful, or honourable work. Set
up some delightful—some mighty object to your
view ; and say *I will attain to it*—I will finish the
work—I will reach the goal !

" Go on, too, observing the directions and using the
means I had the honour of prescribing to you Sir
Alexander, from the first—and if your body and your
mind don't sing and dance and rejoice together soon,
come to Edinburgh, to   JAS. GRAHAM."

Dr. James Walker not only practised in Elgin and its neighbourhood, but was also an enthusiastic agriculturist; and having married the widow of the last hereditary Sheriff of Moray, he carried on extensive farm operations at Westfield, in which property she ("the old gentlewoman") was life rented.

"19th May 1778.

"Doctor Walker's most respectful compliments.

"Shall hope the happiness of knowing that Sir Alexander, and Lady Dunbar and ffamily are in good health.

"Understands that the widow of John Gordon of Auchinereath is to dwell in a house of Sir Alexander's, which, after months, remains in disrepair.

"The Doctor was not asked to accost Sir Alexander, and hopes this freedom will be ascribed to the genuin natural motive, and not to the genius of meadling. The Doctor knows the Knight's humanity, and he well knows Mrs. Gordon's puny state, and that plaister and whitewash quite fresh must deeply affect her.

"People say that the joiner he employs, chooses to act by a deputy, and the deputy by many substitutes—the thing is undone. They also say the plaisterer would attentively see the whole done.

"It is requested the Knight may not take the trouble to write to the Doctor on this subject. The

Doctor only suggests to the Knight what he sup-
poses his humanity will draw him to consider as
truly as he does the rent.

" Deeds of Humanity are never repented."

" The Doctor's respectful compliments.

" Intended, to-morrow, to have sent Sir Alexander
a formal accusation, a sour one, concluding neglect of
performance upon his own proposals, that the Doctor
should hear from him once a week ; but still the sloth
of a Lochside Knight cannot allow the mentioning
better or less better of headache, pained sides, weari-
ness of back, &c., or of ails the good Lady complains
of. Is not the plan an easy one, my dear Sir ? If all
complaints are easier, we are better.

" But, in earnest, the Doctor may be bewildered in
this general observation. The Doctor finds himself
deeply serious. If Sir Alexander thinks that a few
shillings excites all this concern, shall not attempt to
undeceive him in theory nor scratches of a quill.

" This weather persuades the Doctor to change the
medicine for the time. It feels rigid.

" Sends a box of small balls. Recommends that
three be swallowed in the morning—fasting; three
at mid-day ; and three at bed-time—nine a day.
Requests particulars in next that, at least, earnest
tryal may be made to mend a habit of body which

vexes the Doctor. It is easy to loath it, and say one is well; but the Doctor can commend no such doings."

———

"*Sunday, 25th August* 1779.

" Doctor Walker's respects.

" Has a right to forgiveness (whether the Knight acknowledges or denys), for giving the trouble of enquiring how Sir Alexander and Lady Dunbar are in this drenching, and now blustering, weather.

" Shall be glad to know that the Lady bore her late journy better than is said, and that the Knight has weathered this soaking state, which threatens to bring animal life to a state of slubber.

" The Doctor feels it—the old gentle-woman deeply —and only wariness keeps off extreme hardship.

" It is like we have still more to bear, therefore caution."

———

" . . . If you broil over the fire and fry the backs of your hams, he who mends your chilliness must change the comodians of natural things, so far as you are concerned.

" Particular accounts of drugs I always decline. My only interest in them being loss of money. Therefore, request my friends may hereafter excuse it; but for your satisfaction have caused draw out the parti

culars furnished for you.   Most respectfull compliments to your Lady."

" The broken vial refurnished.   The morning tincture to be continued.

" Broths to be prepared *secundum artem* of the
cooks, with beef, mutton, or fowls.

" Leck pottage may be read—' Cock-a-leekie.' . . ."

" *27th April* 1780.

" . . . Suffer me to enquire how market offers
for grain.   My acquaintances and the dealers are
wondrous wise and deep   I think you may rely on
me ; I shall blabb nothing from you.

" A little stirring offers just now ; but (as you word
it) they are very costive.

" Do advise me.   I have half bear, half oats, in the
small parcel."

" *Wedy., 25th Sepr.*, 1782.

" Doctor Walker's respectful compliments.

" The butter-kitt came here, for which attention the
Doctor's thanks to good Lady Dunbar ; but no notice
of the price.

" A verbal message bade the Doctor have the cask
weighed—why ? as it seems it was weighed by the
owner.

" But such are the various numbers of pounds
assigned to a stone weight (from fourteen to thirty-
four), the Doctor must beg leave to ask what number
of pounds to a stone weight at Thundertown—and
what is the price of said stone weight—that he may
do himself the pleasure to make thankful payment.

" The Doctor proposes to kill a full-fed cow in the
beginning of next week. If beef so firm is oft seen,
he is imposed on.

" Is Sir Alexander disposed to send for a quarter,
and which quarter? price threepence per pound, without discount ;—a quarter may weigh 80lb.

" Notice may be sent, if he chooses it, 'twixt and
Tuesday first."

III. PRICES OF PROVISIONS.

DEALERS in grain, meat, etc., were not allowed to charge except at such rates as had been fixed by legal authority.

" Att fforres the sevinteinth day of May 1699. - The Comissioners of Supply of the Sherifdome of Elgin, appoynted by Act of Council, of the date the last day of March last by past, for stateing and setling the pryces of victual within the said shyre, having several tymes met and conveened at Elgin and fforres, and last of all at fforres, this present day having taken true and exact tryall of the pryces of victual for five weeks space preceeding the date of the said Act, and duly considered the said pryces, the forsaid Comissioners, by virtue of the power given and comitted to them by the forsaid Act of Council, have stated and setled, and hereby states and setles, the highest pryces of the best victual and meal to be as follows, viz. :-- The best wheat at eighteen pound scots per boll : the best bear at twelve pound scots per boll : the best oats at ten pound per boll : the boll of pise at twelve

pound : the best oatmeall by weight, being eight stone,
at twelve pound per boll : the best bearmeall at
threitein merks four shillings six penies per boll : and
the forsaid pryces, so setled, are appointed by the said
Act of Privie Council to be the feer and setled pryces
until the first day of September nixt : and none are
to presume to sell at higher rates either in mercats,
girnels, or otherwayes, within the said sheriffdome of
Elgin, under the certification of being pursued as
Occurrers or Userers, as the said Act bears. And to
the end the above writen pryces may be published,
the said Comissioners ordained, and ordains, thir presents to be published at all the parish kirks of the said
shyre, to be read this nixt Lord's day after devine service ; and doubles therof to be sent to the Magistrates
of the burghs within the shyre, to be by them proclaimed at their mercat-croces : and this present setle-
ment of the pryces of the said victuals to be binding
and take effect after the publication and intimation
herof : and ordains the same to be recorded in the
sederunt-book of the said Comissioners, that none
pretend ignorance."

" Wee, Sir Thomas Calder of Muirton, Knight
Baronet, and Robert Dunbar of Newton, Esquire,
Justices of Peace within the shire of Elgin, do here-
by testify and declare to all concerned that the way

of living in the town of Elgin, within the said shire,
for merchandise of all sorts of vivers, victuals, and
other necessaries for families, being to be had at low
rates is as follows, viz. :—ane carcass of best beef, in
the shambles, at eight pund scotts ; Item—ane mutton
bulk, at two merks scotts of the best sort ; ane good hen
at two shilling scotts, and two shilling sixpenies scotts
the dearest ; ffourteen egs for ane shilling scotts ;
ffourteen haddocks for ane shilling sixpenies scotts,
or two shillings at most ; ffourteen whitings for ane
shilling scotts ; ane large cod-fish for four shilling
scotts ; ane stone of butter of the best sort at three
pund scotts, wherof ther goes twenty-two pund to
the stone ; ane stone of the best chese, of the north
country make, two merks scotts, or thirty shillings
scotts at most, wherof ther is given twenty-two pund
to the stone ; ane pint of milk for sixteen peneis
scots ; muirfowl and partridge at two shilling scotts
the pair ; waterfowl as follows, viz. :—ane goose at
eight shilling scotts ; duck and drake, wild or tame, at
four shilling ; and we declare that the above rates are
the comon and ordinarie mercat prices, except in cases
of dearth and scarcity : By these given under our
hands, at Elgin, the thirtieth of December, one thousand seven hundred and ten years.

" THOMAS CALDER.
RO. DUNBAR."

IV. POSTAL ARRANGEMENTS.

POSTMASTER-GENERAL's obligation :—

" I, Alex. Smith, post-master generall of this kingdom, doe hereby oblidge myselfe to send to Mr.
Archibald Dunbarr of Thundertown ane Flying Post,
and Edinburgh Gazette, tuice a week from the date
hereof untill Candlemass one thousand seven hundreth and one years.   In witnes whereof I have
written and subscrived ther presents with my hand
at Edinburgh, the nynth day of December 1700.

"ALEXR. SMITH."

Before the era of naming streets or numbering
houses, recourse was had to very grotesque and
often complicated addresses.   The following are, respectively, of dates 1702-3-4 :—

" ffor

" Mr. Archbald Dumbarr of Thundertoune to be
left at Capt. Dumbar's writing Chamber at the Iron
revell third storie below the Cross north end of the
close at Edinr."

" For

" Captain Philip Anstruther off Newgrange att his lodgeing a litle above the fountain-well south side of the street Edenbrough."

————

" ffor

" Mrs. Mary Stowel at Whiteakers in St Andrew Street next door save one to the blew balcony near the sun dyall near long aiker London."

————

The clerks in the General Post-Office must have been a careless set of fellows.   Extract from a letter sent to a Morayshire gentleman :—

"EDINBURGH, 15th Aug., 1755.

" There is no news, our Edinburgh mail being returned in a mistake for the London mail, and *vice versa*."

V. TRAVELLING.

A JOURNEY from Morayshire to Edinburgh must have been, especially in winter, a very arduous undertaking ; it generally occupied five or six days.

"ffor Mrs. DUNBAR of Thundertoun,
　　　　" Att Duffus.

　　　"NEWTOUN OF ABERDEEN, 17 ffebry., 1708.

" MY DEAR,—After I came to Keith I found bothe road and the weather so bad that I chosed rather to stay ther Saturday all day than venture the hills allone on Sabath-day. By good providence there came three or four gentlemen who designed the same jurney, and after deliberation it was concluded wee should not goe by the Cairn, but by this place, where through both evil way and weather wee are, blessed by God, saifely come this night. We disyne sex milles farder, and so on, as the weather will allow. Through all the hills nothing but storm appears, and in the valeys, great rains and impetous watter runns. This only wee have left us for comfort, that in this road wee are now in, we have both boats and bridges, so that we will not be put to any necessity of rideing of watters. I wrote you ane memorandam from Keith, to give ffaskan what salt he calls for. Give him likewise the one half of the barell of figgs, which let be sawn in the midst, which is the best way of devisione. This, with ducty, being from, dear Beckie, your

" A. DUNBAR."

" 2 of the cloak, afternoon. We came here about 12.

" Adiu."

The writer of the following extract flourished in 1783. He seems to have been a bit of a philosopher :—

" You will be astonished when I tell you that for as many chaises and horses as are in and about Edinburgh, and for as high as the duty is, that you must bespeak your chaise eight or ten days at least before you intend setting out, otherwise you can have none, especially when you are going a long journey like mine. But the fulness of luxury, like the corpulency of the body, is a symptom of approaching decay; and as everything in nature has its different periods as well as the animal and vegetable world, namely, infancy, maturity, and decay, I am very much afraid that our poor country is at least at the middle period, for you will not know a shoemaker's or a tailor's daughter by her dress, from a lady of the first rank in this place."

The fare from Aberdeen to Edinburgh by "The Fly" was two pounds two shillings, as we find by a ticket, dated 25th August 1789, on the back of which there is this printed notice :—

NEW BLACK-BULL INN, *North Side of the* REGISTER OFFICE, Edinburgh.

THE FLY, sets out from the above Inn, for LON-DON, NEWCASTLE, and GLASGOW, every day, and from Mr. IBBERSON's, George and Blue Boar, Holborn, London, Mr. BROADIE's, Turk's Head, Newcastle, and Mr. DURIE's, Black-Bull, Glasgow, every day for Edinburgh—For ABERDEEN, by way of PERTH, every Tuesday, Thursday, and Saturday ; and from Mr. WILKIE's New-Inn, Aberdeen, every Monday, Wednesday, and Friday, for Edinburgh.— Fresh horses every stage.

N.B.—SETS OUT, as above by way of Cornhill, Newcastle and Borrowbridge, at least twenty miles nearer than by Berwick and York, The ROYAL CHARLOTTE LIGHT POST COACH, which, for accommodation and expedition, is not inferior to any that ply the road ; goes from Edinburgh to London in two days and one half, with the agreeable advantage (by setting out in the morning) of travelling mostly in day-light.

Performed by J. ROBERTSON & Co.

Mr. Dunbar of Kincorth was a younger son of Sir William Dunbar of Durn, Baronet, and a brother of Anne Countess of Findlater and Seafield. He would be treated as an honoured guest. The money is Scots.

" Accompt Wm. Dunbar of Kincorth to Margaret Stewart, spouse to Wm. Brodie, merchant in Elgin.

22d Decer. 1699.	Imprimis by ane subscribed oblige-ment, . .	26	12	6
	By another obligement, . . .	08	05	0
Janry. 1700.	Item with ffaskin, Mr. Archbald Dunbar, and John Chalmer four pynts brunt wine, . . .	06	16	0
	Item with Bishopmiln, Newtoun, and Mr. Archbald Dunbar three pynts brunt wine, . . .	05	02	0
	Item four ounce of sugar to a pynt of sack, ...	00	04	0
	Item a pynt of brunt wine with Mr. Archbald Dunbar and Mr. Read, ...	01	17	0
	Item for his part of sevin pynts Jaugo is	01	05	0
	Item a pynt that he called for after-wards,	00	15	0

Item when he went at that tyme
to the west, for his own, and his
servant and horse, meat and drink,   02 00   0
Item for his horse therafter for corn
and strae, ...   00 13   0
Item his own and his servant's dyet
then, ...   02 00   0
Item two seckpossets is   .   .   04 16   0
When at your court for meat to
yourself and servant, and horse
corn and strae, .   .   .   04 10   0
Item four pynts brunt aquavite,   .   06 13   4
Item for corn and strae to your
horse, ...   01 04   0
Item meat and drink to yourself
and servant,   .   01 10   0
                                     ——————
                                     74 02 10
Item for the cess accompt which I
took of £7 11 8,   .   .   07 11   8
                                     ——————
                                     81 14 06
Item for your horse sevintein dayes
when last here, ...   05 02   0
Item for twenty dayes dyet to your
self and servant,   .   .   .   07 08   0
Item one pynt brunt acquavite with
Bailie Stewart, James Wiseman,
and others,   .   .   01 13   4
                                     ——————
                                     95 17 10
Whereof receaved per recept,   16 00   0
                                     ——————
                                     79 17 10"

Copy of a bill paid in 1769 to Robert Gordon, Landlord of the "British Arms:"—

BRITISH ARMS, To	MAGNUM BONUMS,			
ELGIN.[1]	To 35 bottles Claret,	4	7	6
	To bottles Champaign, .			
	To bottles Rhenish,			
	To 1 bottles Oporto,	0	2	0
	To bottles Zerry, .			
	To bottles Frontiniac, .			
	To bottles Mountain,			
	To bottles Madeira,			
	To bottles Malaga,			
	To 1 bottles Lisbon,	0	2	0
	To bottles Orange-wine,			
	To 3 mutchkins Punch, .	0	3	0
	To extraordinary fruit and sugar,			
	To 3 mugs porter, .	0	1	0
	To arrack, .			
	To cyder,			
	To negus, .			
	To sack-whey, . .			
	To tea and coffee, marmalade, etc,			
	To drams, .			
	To small-beer, .	0	0	3
	To pipes and tobacco,			
	To entertainment,	0	4	0
	To paper, .			
	To cards,			

[1] The Royal Arms are slightly different in the original, which is a printed form, with the numbers and prices written.

		£	s	d
To cadies, .				
To hay,				
To corn,				
To drink to servants, .		0	6	0
To the saddler, .				
To the smith,				
To the barber, .	.			
To grease to the horses feet,				
To the laundress,				
To broken,		0	5	0
To more wine,				
To more punch, .				

VII. FIELD SPORTS.

HAWKING was long a favourite sport in the North. The Earl of Buchan appears to have replenished his falconry from the Gordonston stock.

" To my honorabel and loving frinde
    " SIR ROBERT GORDON, geve this.

                        " BAMFE *the* 10 *May*, 1619.

    " SIR,—I have wryten thir fewe lynes to deseir you to doe me the favor as to send me ane facon of this yeir, with this berer, and wharin I can doe you anny pleseur or service you sall find me ever redie to obay your imployments, so hoping you will grant me this my first sent, I tak my leive and rests your loving frind, to my pouer,   BUCHANE."

Having received a couple of hawks from the Earl of Seaforth, the Laird of Brodie asks his friend to get them trained.

" To Mr. ARCHIBALD DUNBAR,
    " of Thundertone.

                     " FFORRES 6*th Aug.* 1712.

    " SIR,—I am glade to hear that you are weell, and that you are nothing the worse of your fatigue att the

Runns of Lossie, I am also rejoysed to hear that you are clever and can voltige and waltt a litle as to your former way, in the meantime this serves to acquant you that I have two halks sent me by my Lord Seafort, to witt a ffalcone and a Terfle ffalcone of the best aire of the Lewis, and they are full and weell feathered, so if you please take them and breed them by your ffalconar, and when they are bredd I shall give you your choyse or both, tho I was oblidged to give a great deall of drink-money. I know Kilravock and others would take them, but I incline to give you the first offerr, so you will send me ane answer by this express, whither you will send for them or not. If I hade a ffalconar I would have bredd them myselfe, which is all from, Sir, your affectionate and humble servant,   GEO : BRODIE."

The Laird of Newton intimates that he intends to "blode" two young dogs ; that is, let them have their first taste of blood.

" To Mr. ARCHIBALD DUNBAR,
          " of Thundertoun.

                    "NEWTOWN, 24th Sept. 1702.

" LOVING BROTHER,—I am gleade ye ar cum saife to the cuntrie, but expected ye would haive been here befor this time. I desined to haive blode two young doges this day, but shall delay sport till Satur-

day expecting your cumming, I hoop ye will bring
Capt. Dunbar alonge, to whom give my servise. My
wife will quarall you at meeting ffor unkindnes,
wherfor she has sent no comendations. I containou,
as formarly, your most affectionat brother,

"R. DUNBAR."

"CLOAVS, 29th Janr. 1703.

"AFFECTIONAT BROTHER,—Cloavs and I shall met
you the morou in the Spinle moore, betwixt eight
and nine in the morning, where ye canot miss good
sporte twixt that and the sea. ffaile not to bring ane
bottle of brandie along, ffor I asheure you ye will lose
the wadger. In the mean time we drink your health,
and am your affectionat brother,

"R. DUNBAR."

Sir Harrie Innes, of Innes, evidently alludes to the
Loch of Spynie, then undrained, and the rendezvous
of all sorts of wild fowl.

" To Mr. ARCHIBALD DUNBAR,
" off Thunderton, att Elgin.

"INNES, ffeb. 2d, 1703.

"DEAR ARCHIE,—It is good ffor a man to pay his
debt while he has gear. I send you your swan's skin,
but least you have a Highland man's appetite ffor

annual rentt ffor your loan of that I had of you, I
send another, which I slew yesterday. I shall be glad
to play with you att hunting or shooting any day
you are att leisure. If the dayes post bring you any
news, I shall be glad to know what they are. Mean-
tyme, I still continue, dear Archie, your oblidged
ffriend and most humble servantt,

                              " HARIE INNES."

  " If you have but use ffor one skin, the doctor will
thank you ffor the other.'

The Loch of Spynie had attractions even for the
Marquis of Huntly.

" To the much honored
        " Mr. ARCHIBALD DUNBAR,
            " off Thunderstoune—These :

                    " LEUCHARS, October, 1707.
                        " Wednesday.

  " MUCH HONORED,—My Lord Marquesse off Huntly
has been att sporte this day att the Loch off Cottise,
and to-morrow desynes to be att the Loche off
Spynye, therefore we your humble supplicants order
you to repair in your pinace, most honoured, by to-
morow, be eleven, at the mouth off the Rindes, or the
gray ston off Pittgeviny. Your personall presence is
nott doubted, iff leisure allow; however, order smookes
to be putt on att Duffus, Crookmoor, &c., ffull of

Leuchar's strong ale, betwixt eleven and twelve this
night. We are your humble servants,

> " ALEXR. INNES :
> GEO. INNES :
> WILL. SUTHERLAND."

Extract from a letter, dated 16th March 1704, from
Mr. Wiseman, commissary clerk of Elgin, to the same
address.

" Receive Grossie, and if he play tricks whip him
weel for his paines, and that is the only way for him;
he has not bein in a feild, nor sett a foull since you
saw it upon a Sabbath day. If I come up I will require some days for acquainting you with Grossie's
hunting, *which I think the kingdome will not match.*"

A dear dog! The animal must have been valuable
and worth the price, as Sir Robert knew well how to
make a good bargain.

> " ELGIN, *March* 1749.

" Then received ffrom Sir Robert Gordon of Gordonstown the quantity of ffive bolls bear, as the
agreed price of a dog, called Spottie Boug."

VIII. QUARANTINE.

THE annexed document is docqueted "Comittee concerning the boats of Causy, 1647." The Commissioners of Supply, we presume, now represent "The Comitte of the shyre:"—

" ELGIN, 7 *July*, 1647.

"The Comitte of the shyre having mett, and it being represented to them that certaine boats, laden with goods and passengars, war com from Aberdeen, and that a cours might be taken for saving the countree from infection, they ordained that the goods should remaine on the shore untill the merchants com hom to whom they belong, and that thereafter thos merchants should goe to Causi and receav the goods, and open them and cleanse them thoroughli by the advis of the Town or Magistrats of Elgin, or such as they appoint ; and that the said merchants or any persons that cleans, handls, or receaves the goods should be separat for the space of twenti thre dayes or a month, and should be admitted to noe hous or societie within the countree untill they be tried, and found free of infection : and if any of them shal fail therin to bee punished by death.

"Lykas, the Comitte and Barons of the shyre ordained that the persons who cam in the four boats, should be separat, and kept up from al societie, untill they be cleansd and tried, and for this effect that ther should bee a guard of   persons appointed and entertained to keip them from straying through the countree untill the tym of the triall pass, and they receave a testimonial from the comitte. And it should be intimated to the passengers and others suspected persons, that ther is warrand given to the guard to provyd for them, and in cace they offer to break out by force, and by that means infect the countree, they have ordour and warrand to shoot them or put them to death.

"The Laird of Dufus, Sherif of Muray, Spyni, Provest of Elgin, Kirtoun, James Dunbar, appointed to meit at Duffus Kirktown, for this effect, on Tuisday be eight hours.

"The Sheriff has undertaken to bring twenty-four men here to see ther arms taken from them and thes ordours execute.

"The Comitte ordains the parishes of Forres, Dyke, Rafert, and the Laird of Tarbet's land in Alves, to secur ffindorn as they wil be answerable, and that a guard bee put in the town to remaine ther constantlie, that noe barques or boats upon any pass bee par-

mitted to land without the notice given and consent
of Robert Dunbar of Burgie, Bailies of Forres, Grang-
hill, Kincorth, Coubin, Brodie, Esterbin, Woodhead,
or any five of them being present, giving them the
full powar of the comitee to that effect, and adds to
them the Sherif of Murray, Tanachi, Kilbyoak, Mr.
James Campbell of Moye.

"The Comittee thinks fitt that the parishes of
Alves, Duffus, King Edward, Spynie, guard the Causi
two nights about, 24 men or 30 men apiece, and every
guard to stay two dayes and two nights, till they be
releived ; and the special heritours in the parishes, or
their doers, to come with ther parishouers.

"The Laird of Innes undertakes for the water-
mouth of Spey to the boat of Bogg, and that he shall
deal with the rest of the heritours to secure from Bogg
to Skirdastan and Fiddich.

"The Comittee ordains every threti chalder of
victuall to give a hors to carie malt and salt to
Badenoch.   ROBERT GORDON, *Preses.*"

Letters from the Clerk of the Justice of Peace
Court, and from an officer stationed at Burghead :—

" Mr. ARCHBALD DUNBAR of Thundertoune.

" ELGIN, *Septer*. 22*d*, 1709.

"SIR,—By this dayes post ther is come a letter from
her Majesties Advocat to the Justices of the Peace

of this shire, desireing that on receipt of the said
letter they may meet in order to consert measures
for preventing any ships bound from Danzick, or any
seaport of the Baltick, for this Kingdom, to land any
men or goods upon this shores, or any mens goeing
from the shoar aboard of them.   The Advocat has
sent print instructions for this end, and since (as he
terms it) it is of the very last consequence to our
lyves and safeties, it ought to quicken your diligence.   Therefor it is proper you meet here to-
morrow, be ten acloak, for the end aforsaid, I am
Sir, your most humble servant,

"JA: WISEMAN.

"Receive, inclosed, ane letter from Major Colt,
which my too much anxietic for news made me open
—which I beg you will excuse.   I have wrote to the
most of all the Justices of the Peace."

"To the much Honored Mr. ARCHBALD DUNBAR, of Thunderton ;
"and in his absence to the LAIRD OF MYRLAND—heast.

"BROUGHEAD, 24th Septr. 1709.

"MUCH HONORED,—By her Majesties comands, wee,
the Offeshers in this presinct, is ordered to call for
asistance in caice aney ships should atemp to cume
ashor, or land ther men with long boats.   There is
tuo ships ryding at ankor forgainst this place, and

is just nou sending ther boats ashor. Ther is men heir that is willing to wacth, but ther is neather armes nor amonitione heir. Your help and asist-ance, both for men and armes, is requered by, much honored, your humbbel servant,

" ALEXR. PHILP."

IX. FISHINGS.

LANDED proprietors who had sea-coast or river attached to their estates, employed fishermen, whom they paid at certain rates for the fish, after deducting the price of the curing-salt which they imported, and the fish was sent in large quantities to continental towns, where it found a ready sale among the Roman Catholics.

Sir Harrie unfortunately does not give the year. "The Raick" and "The Pott" are celebrated pools in the Spey, near Garmouth :—

" To the LAIRD OFF THUNDERTON—Heast, heast.

"INNES, *June* 25, 5 *at night.*

" SIR,—You will not (I hope) be displeased when I tell you that Wat. Stronoch, this forenoon, killed *eighteen hundred Salmon and Grilses.* But it is my misfortune that the boat is not returned yet from Inverness, and I want salt. Therefore by all the tyes of friendship send me on your own horses eight barrels of salt, or more. When my boat returns, none, particularly Coxton, shall want what I have. This in great heast from, dear Archie, yours,

" HARRIE INNES.

" I know not but they may kill as many before two in the morning, for till then I have the Raick, and to-morrow the Pott. These twenty years past such a run was not as has been these two past days in so short a time, therefore heast, heast ; spare not horse hyre. 1 would have sent my own horses, but they are all in the hill for peatts. Adieu, dear Archie."

" To the LAIRD OFF THUNDERTON.

" INNES, *Aug.* 20, 1716.

" SIR,—I am so unweil that now near two o'clock I am gott from bed.

" There is betwixt four and five last of Grilses and Salmon packed yesterday.

" I know the price att Bamffe is above forty merks for Grilses.

" I expectt no harm from your hands. If ye be to writte to Holland, cause bring home one thousand weight of twyne ffor next years fishing. Also, two or three pieces of holland musline I want, but I understand nott how to commission for itt.

" Good wyne I love, such as I drunk last with you, but I want money. A barrell or two of cucumbers and capers my wife speaks of, butt I know not the value. Do on the whole as you please, and I shall pay you most thankfully, and ever remain, dear Archie, yours, HARRIE INNES."

Letter from the fishermen in Burghead to those in Findhorn, relative to the prices given for fish, etc. The reply shows that a salted (cod) fish cost a fraction under threepence :—

" For —THOMAS FINDLAY, Skipper, in Findhorn, or to anie other
    " Skeipper in the toune, in his absence—Thes are :

            " *Att* BROUGH, *the* 30 *of Januarie*, 1713.

" Kynd freinds, this is to let you know that Thundertoun and Roshaugh was in this town this day, and is to cleire with us for our fish on the last day of this instant, and desired us to wreit Wast to you what you got for your fish, and how manie you gave to the hunder. Wreit East ane positive account, and oblidge all your freinds and weill-wishers in this toune, young and old. Pray you doe not feall to wreit to us, and this is all at present, with all having ther serwice to you all.

                            " WILLIAM GEDDES.
                            JOHN PROT."

Answer to the above :—

" ffor WILLIAM GEDDES and JOHN PROT,
        " Skippers in Burgh Sea—These :

            " FFINDHORN, *January the* 30*th*, 1713.

" We receaved your letter, and in answer therto we hav goten but an pairt of our moey, and as for the prise, we are informed by Andrew Adam that our prise is not to be broken of what we got formirly, which was nintin pound Scots the hunder, and we pay twelve shiling Scots for the peck of salt, and we giv six scor and twelve for each hunder. This is all we can show you as to that mater. This being the nedfull from your frends and well-wishers,

" GILBERT THOM.

JOHN MARNOCH."

"The Seven Brethren" was chartered by the Lairds of Kilravock, Clava, Thunderton, Kinsterie, and Muirtown. The Captain, William Dawson, afterwards Provost of Forres, also had a share of the cargo :—

" FINDHORN, *the* 17*th November* 1708.

" Accompt of the first cost and charges of ane loading of Bear, Salmond, Hareing, and Cod-fish, shipped aboard the shipp, the Seven Brethren, for Lisbone, viz. :—

	Scotts.		
To 791½ bolls of bear, at £3, 6s. 8d. per boll,	£2,638	6	8
To 3 last hareings, at £96 per last, .	288	0	0
To 6500 dryed codd-fish, at £14 per 100,	910	0	0
To 6 barrels salmond, at £38 per barrell, .	228	0	0
To 18 barrells of grilses at 1-5th rebate of salmond price, .	547	4	0
	£4,611	10	8

CHARGES.

To 300 dales for bugdaline, stelline, and bulkes-head, .	£100	0	0
To trees for stools and bearers, .	10	0	0
To nailes for bugdaline, &c.,	10	0	0
To carpentares for bugdaline, .	12	0	0
To receiveing of 791½ bolls bear, at 1s. per boll, . . .	39	11	6
To shippeing of said bear, at 8d. per boll, ...	26	7	8
To shippeing salmond, hareing, and cod-fish, . . .	5	12	0
To ⅔ of averadge in and out to Findhorn, ...	8	0	0
To cockett, bill of health, sufferance, &c., to Custom-hous, .	9	0	0
To cash given the surveyor for attendance, ...	12	16	0
To cash for towing the dales out at the end, ...	5	12	2
To personall charges and horse-hyr hence to Inverness,	10	2	0

£249 1 4

£4,860 12 0"

"Invoice of the Jannet of Belfast, John Mackmichan, master, for Diepe—

Sterling.

To 121 barrell grilsess, at £2 per barrell, .	£242	0	0
To 35 barrell salmon, at £2, 10s. per barrell, .	87	10	0
To 31 barrell herreings, at 10s. per barrell is .	15	10	0

£345 0 0"

Here are a few items from a long account of the
disbursements connected with the "securing" of four
whales, which were stranded in November 1729 on
the sands of Burghead. In this enterprise were concerned Brodie of Brodie, Lord Lyon King-at-Arms,
Sir Robert Gordon of Gordonston, Premier Baronet of
Scotland, and Dunbar of Thunderton, formerly Sheriff
of the County, all of whom thus became dealers in
spermaceti and whale's blubber!

" To two hundred and sixty horse loads
   of speck, from ebb to high water, att
   1 peny each, ... £1   1   8
To two hundred and sixty horse loads
   of speck from the shoar to the Corf
   house, att 1sh. st. per load,   .   . 13   0   0
To two hundred men employed att
   different tides for turning and tear-
   ing the whales, att 8sh. per tide,   6 13 4
                            —————£20 15 0
To carriage of 78 hhds. 1 turce. from
   different places to the Corf-house,
   being thirty-nine horse loads, att
   1sh. st. per load, ... 1 19 0
To fraught of 36 hhds. from Cromarty
   to Burgh-head,   .   .   .   2   2   8
To fraught of 12 hhds. from Chanry
   to Findhorn, ...   0 10 0
To carriage of six loads of herring casks
   from Findhorn to Outlet, for floating the whales, att 1sh. st. per
   load,   0   6   0

To returning the same,   .   .   . 0 6 0
To nine herring casks bought att Find-
    horn, for containing the sperma and
    blubber,   .   . £1 2 6
                                    ————— £6 6 2

To five drag ropes, bought from the
    skippers of Burghead for securing
    the said whales on the shoar,   . 5 0 0
To cash paid the five skippers of Burgh-
    head, with their crews, for their
    pains and diligence in killing and
    securing the whales, being fifty men
    in number, ... 10 0 0
To Anne Sutherland in Burgh-head
    her account of all charges,   .   . 7 0 0
To Skipper Geddess's account of ale
    and brandy, ... 1 0 0
To a blacksmith in Coutfield for mak-
    ing seven knives, ... 0 10 6
To the coupers for tighting, heading,
    and packing the sperma on the
    shoar,   0 5 0
                                    ————— £23 15 6

To ten loads of peats burnt on the
    shoar, att 6d. per load, by the
    watchmen, ... 0 5 0
To nine days work, of eight men, bar-
    relling the blubber, at 5sh. 4d. st.
    per diem, ... 2 8 0
To thirty-two days attendance by Wm.
    Naughty on the coupers and cutters
    in the Corf-house, att 1sh. st. per
    diem,   1 12 0
                                    ————— £4 5 0

A ship, called "Susana of Burlingtown, of the burden of fforty tuns, then lying in the harbour of Lossie—ffrancis Bulson, master," was chartered, at sixteen shillings per ton, to carry the "blubber and spermaceti" to London. It was there disposed of by Peter Machattie, factor for the parties. The unskilful manner in which the "speck" was separated from the "flock" reduced the expected quantity of oil. Mr. Machattie's communication must have brought down the ardour of the blubber co-partnery to the freezing-point !

" To ARCHD DUNBARR off Newton, Youngar,
         " per Ednbr. to Elgin.

                              " LONDON, 11th Jully, 1730.

" SIR,—Referring to mine of 25th and the 27th past, since have yours of 20th do., with Thundarton's account of chearges, amounting to £85, 19s. 5½d., upon the whales blobber and spermacetta, which sum is more, I am afraid, than will be made of the subject in some time. The blobber is all oyled, and the quan-tity thereoff will not exceed six or seven tuns, as is beleived by the boyler, who cannot, as yett, give the true account—it being upon the water in fatts, ready to be run off in casks, which I hope will be in a day or two's time ; and for the spermacetta it is very littell in quantity, the most of the casks being oyll, and the spermacetta is at present low. However, I am informed it is giving a better price in Holland, to

which place I have sent ovar a trayall, and att the
return of my lettar shall, I hope, be cabell to give a
satisfactory account thereoff. The reason which is
given for the small produce of the blobber is that a
great deall of the flock was cut in with the speck,
which has consumed the oyll and wested the substance
thereoff. There has been such propar measures taken
with it, which I hope will appear to be most advan-
tagious for the propreiators thereoff, and shall endeavour to dispose of the same to the best account.
Referring till next post, I am, with perfound respectt
to Sir Robert and Thundarton, Sir, your most obedient
humbell servant,   PET. MACHATTIE."

An abstract of account shows that Thunderton's
outlay was £85, 19s. 5½d.; Sir Robert's, £55, 8s. 2d.;
Brodie's, £27, 2s. 3d.—total money laid out, £168,
8s. 10½d. The net proceeds are stated at £112,
15s. 11½d.; showing a dead loss of £55, 13s. 11d.
sterling. Whatever profit may have accrued from
cod sales to Morayshire lairds, it is evident that
whales were not in their particular line!

X. IMPRESSING FOR THE NAVY.

In time of war, every sea-coast proprietor was obliged to furnish a certain quota of men to the navy :—

" To ARCHIBALD DUNBAR, Esqr., of Duffus.

" ELIZABETH TENDER, *att Speymouth*,
28*th Sep'r.* 1761.

" SIR,—Being appointed by the Honble. Captain George Falconer to receive the quotas of fishermen, for this district, agreeable to his letter to you, I hope you will be so kind as forward this service as fast as possible.

" As it is far against my inclination to distress the fisheries of this country, I beg you will favour me with a list of your fishermen, with their age and descriptions, and your method of delivering up your quota, that I may immediately grant protections to the remaining fishermen, and the Government not be long under the expense of a vessel and forty men attending this duty that is wanted in another station. I am, Sir, your most obedient and most humble servant, A. BAILLIE."

Captain Falconer's printed circular, to which Lieutenant Baillie called attention, intimates, that by authority of the Commissioners of the Admiralty, the fishermen would be protected from impressment during the present war on this condition, " that you immediately furnish one man to the navy out of every six of them, and deliver them to the naval officer of your district to be approved." The circular proceeds thus :—

" Upon delivering your proportion, you will please give in to the said Naval Officer a full list of the remainder of your fishers, subscribed by you as Proprietor, containing their Names, Ages, Size, Complexion, or other description, so as five Protections may be delivered for every man so furnished to the Navy ; and which Protections, by the aforesaid Authority, I do assure you, will effectually prevent the possessors of them from being impressed during the present war ; or if, through mistake, they should at any time be impressed, upon application to me, or the commanding Officer for the time, they will be immediately discharged.

" This moderate demand, on such assurances of security for the future, I flatter myself will be chearfully and immediately complied with by all concerned. But if, contrary to expectation, the proposal should be rejected by any, they may depend on it, their fisher-

men, where ever found, either on sea or land, will be
impressed ; nor will any solicitations on their behalf
be listened to by their Lordships, and much less by
your most obedient humble servant,

"GEORGE FALCONER.

"*Edinburgh*,___ ___

"This will be forwarded you by___
to whom please send your answer."

There was difficulty both at Findhorn and Burghead
in getting men to serve.

"(*On His Majesty's Service.*)
"To ARCHIBALD DUNBAR of Newton, Esq.,
"at his house at Duffus.

"FORRES, 2*d March* 1757.

"SIR,—I am surprised you have neither performed
your own promise nor complyed with my orders and
advice. I know, and am informed your number of
fishers (distinctly from Sir Robert Gordon's) is not
under twenty men, out of which the King must have
three young men ; and I know as well as yourself
that those that are fittest for me are Alexr. Sutor,
Andrew Grote, and James Neilson, and if you do not
quickly send me those men, the Brough shall quickly
run the same fate with Findhorn ; and I am, Sir, your
humble servant,

"R. HAY, *Lieutenant.*"

XI. SMUGGLING.

THE duty on wine and brandy was thought so high, that constant attempts were made to smuggle them into the country. Extract from a letter to Dunbar of Thunderton, in 1710, written by William Sutherland, merchant in Elgin :—

" . . . I have ventured to order Skipper Watt, how soon it pleases God he comes to the firth, to call at Caussie, and cruise betwixt that and Burgh-head, until you order boats to waite him. He is to give the half of what I have of the same sort with his last cargoe, to any having your order. Its not amiss you secure one boat at Caussie as well as the burgh boats. The signall he makes will be all sails furled, except his main topsaile ; and the boats you order to him are to lower their saile when within muskett shott, and then hoise it again : this, least he should be surprised with catch-poles. He is to write you before he sails from Bordeaux, per Elgin post." . . .

When the chief magistrate countenanced such proceedings, we cannot blame the " Vintner :"—

" 27th *Aprile* 1716.

" Alexr. Erskine, Collector of the Customs att Inverness, protests against Archbald Dunbar of Thunderton, Provost of Elgine, ffor all damage and loss
that has happened to seven hogsheads of rede wine,
imbezled without payment of duty, and seized by
Alexr. Cummine, tydsurveyor att Inverness, in the
sellar of William Crombie, vintner in Elgine, one of
the keys of the said sellar being in custody of the
said Archbald Dunbar, and delivered to him by Alexr.
Cummine fforesaid, which key he refused to me, the
said Alexr. Erskine, on the 26th att night, and next
morning the hanging lock of the said sellar of which
the said collector had the key, was brock off, and the
other lock of which Thunderton had the key was
intire and close lockt up, which he himself opened,
and upon tapping, the fforesaid seven casks was found
with nothing in them but water, a little colloured with
wine, whereas they were all left by the fforsaid Alexr.
Cummine ffull of good and sufficient rede wine upon
his delivering up the key to the said Archbald Dunbar,
and thereffor protests that he shall be lyable in the
ffull value of the fforsaid seven hogsheads of rede
wine, conforme to eighteen pound per hogshead ; and
also protests against the fforsaid William Crombie,

E

vintner, ffor the value of said wine being imbezled
by him and taken in without paying the duty, and
also carried out of his said sellar and the cask ffilled
up with water.   ALEXR. ERSKINE."

" Alexr. Erskine, Collector of the Customs att Inverness, protests against Archbald Dunbar of Thunderton, Provost of Elgine, and Justice of the Peac of the
County of Murray, ffor refusing to me a warrant to
search such houses, kilns, barns, &c., of the town of
Elgine and adjacent places in that countie, and refusing to giv me a constable to goe along with me to
search ffor wine imbezled out of the sellar of William
Crombie, vintner in Elgine, and other uncostomed
goods, confforme to a write of assistance produced
to him.   ALEXR. ERSKINE."

———

Charles Eyre, Esq., Solicitor for H.M. Customs in
Scotland, took the matter up, but as he was fond
of good wine, it was agreeably settled by Ludovic
Brodie, W.S., who writes thus :—

" . . . Your affair with the Exchequer has bein
advysed, and the bills are ordered to be re-delyvered,
you peaying the officiers' costs who seized the wynes.
Now the costs to them, according to the rules of
Court, will be but about three or four guineas, besyde

what may be claimed for information getting, as to
which Mr Erskin seems not to demand anything for
himself; but to referr himself to your discretion. . . .
This matter has stood the most drinking (and also
some considerable charges) that ever I drunk in any
other, for tho Eyre be a gentlemanie prettie litle
fellow, yet he drinks lyke a d——l, and I have had
many sore heads with him. . . . Wyseman will not
deny but I desyred him to cause buy or make such
a brydle as would please you : if you do not plague
him with your tongue, you are in wrong to yourself
and me, for he would not loose ane hour's drinking
for all the bussieness in the world."

In November 1744, William Gordon, Master of the
ship "Betty," belonging to Portsoy, ran a cargo of
wine, brandy, tobacco, etc., into the harbour of Spey,
and from thence sent boats which landed part at
various places along the Moray Firth. The Commissioners of Customs ordered a procognition to be taken
by the local Justices, and a report to be sent to them.
The majority of the Justices, however, said they could
not legally compel parties to depone by way of precognition, especially when they refused to say anything in a matter which might eventually be brought
against them. At an adjourned meeting of the

Justices, held at Elgin on 13th January 1745, the chairman read the following letter from Duncan Forbes, Lord President of the Court of Session :—

" DEAR SIR,—The Christmas holy-days, which have emptied the town, and adjourned the Board of Customs, have prevented my being able to write you on the subject of your smuggling, as I once thought I should ; but lest what I may write upon consultation with others should come too late for your meeting on the 15th inst., I have taken the part in the mean time of dropping you this line.

" I have not been more surprized for a great while, than when I heard that a majority of Justices, at your last meeting, putt off the precognition on a doubt whether they lawfully could take information from the witnesses upon oath, and thereby, however innocent their intentions were, flung some cold water at least upon the inquiry.

" As to the doubt itself, I confess I am at a loss to guess on what it is founded ; precognitions have at all times been taken on oath in Scotland, and hence the established practice in the Court of Justiciary, of cancelling, at the trial, the oath formerly emitted on the precognition, before the witness emit his deposition in Court, if he desire it. No occult crime, however dangerous to the common weal, or to the Crown, could be detected or punished, if witnesses were in

the least backward, without a power, in those whose
duty it is to enquire, to examine upon oath.   And
if the practice of England is enquired into, no Justice
can commit, as they may in Scotland, upon a signed
information only.   The Justice must examine the
informant upon oath before he can issue his warrant,
so that, as I apprehend the scruple is without any
just foundation, I doubt not at your next meeting,
after gentlemen have had time to inform themselves
duely, it will evanish.

" I cannot suffer myself to suspect that, considering
the notoriety of the mischief that smuggling does to
this poor unhappy country, and the forwardness lately
shown, by all ranks of men, to express their detesta-
tion of it, and to bind themselves to one another and
to the publick, by resolutions and engagements of
honour, to discourage that villanious traffick, any
gentleman or number of gentlemen, will in broad day
light, and in an open Court (whatever their connection with, or tenderness for the unhappy smuggler be),
be so impudently profligate as to attempt to screen
the cut throats of their country, and thereby expose
themselves to the universal contempt and abhorrence
of mankind.   Such an attempt requires more than
an ordinary degree of courage and wickedness ; the
guilty person cannot hope to remain unknown, the
Minutes of the Court must record his infamy, nor is
it to be expected by him that the character, which by

such practices he may purchase, shall remain confined
to his own country : the common post can, by an
Extract of the Minutes, convey his fame to Edinburgh, from whence it may be communicated to the
whole kingdom.

" Now tho', for these reasons, I hope you will be
unanimous at your next meeting, yet, if contrary to
my expectations, and very much against my wish, the
smugglers should find protection, and the national
justice, as well as interest, should be defeated, I hope
you will be so good as to transmit the Minutes, dis-
tinguishing how each Justice voted, that, besides furnishing me as a private gentleman with information
who I ought to detest and avoid as a scoundrell, I
may be able to inform my fellow-subjects, as far as
that may be done within the laws, whom they ought to
look upon as enemies to their country. Other rebukes
they may possibly meet with, but it is not necessary
to speak of that at present. I write, you see, with
great freedom, as I am very much in earnest; but
what I have said are the dictates of my heart, and
you are at full liberty to make what use you please
of what I have wrote. This mean, shameful course
to destruction must be prevented, or our unhappy
country must be undone. Make my compliments to
every one who can lay his hand on his heart and say
he does not deserve the title of Rascal, and believe me
to be, &c., DUN. FORBES."

XII. THE FAMILIES OF BURGIE AND OF GRANGE.

ROBERT DUNBAR sold the estate of Burgie, about the year 1660, to his cousin, Thomas Dunbar of Grange, in whose family it continued until the death, in 1827, of his descendant and male representative, Lewis Dunbar Brodie. Although he had parted with the *estate*, Robert still retained the *designation* " of Burgie," which was also assumed by his descendants, who, on subsequently acquiring property near Elgin, made the Dean's manse, now North College, their chief seat. The last so designated Laird of Burgie, John Dunbar, got into difficulties, sold his estates, which we have shown were in the vicinity of Elgin, and is supposed to have emigrated about 1756 to Carolina, where his brother Robert had previously settled.

These particulars are given, because, on a competition by claimants for the estate of Burgie, in 1827, time and money were wasted by persons who did not attend to the fact, that the later proprietors of that estate were not the " Dunbars of Burgie," but the " Dunbars of Grange."

The Earl of Moray's letter had the desired effect. The King's authority was vindicated by the expulsion of " young Burgie."

" For the Right Honorable my LORD CHANCELLOR, and remanent LORDS of his Majesties most honorable PRIVIE COUNSELL :

" CASTLE STEWART, 28th May, 1668.

" RIGHT HONORABLE,—I am treuly sory that ther should such a necessity ly upon me as to give your Lordship notice of any rude and illegal disorders falling out in the place of my residence ; but that your Lordship in your wisedome may both punish and redress this and obviat the lyke, I find myself oblidged to give your Lordship ane accompt of what has past upon some civil transactions betwixt the Lairds of Grange and Burgy. Burgy did give Grange possession of his hous and estate, and did dispone the same unto him for very onerous causes ; and whilst Grange, his wife, and family were settled and living in the hous of Burgy, young Burgy did, on the sixteenth day of May inst., with armed men, enter the hous, and eject Grange, his servants and family, and possess himself of the hous, plenishing, trunks, papers, and whatever was in the hous, and plants a garrisone in it. Upon notice whereof I wrot to the actor by a messenger, and required him in the King's Majesties name, and your Lordship's, to disband these armed men, and retire himself, repossess Grange to the hous

and goods which he had wrongfully invaded; but
instead of yielding, he did with great contumacy refuse either to render the hous or restore the goods,
as the letters and instruments thereupon will make
appear to your Lordship. Upon which high contempt
and violation of his Majesty's laws and peace of the
kingdom I could not be silent, but give your Lordship an accompt theirof, that you may in your justice
vindicate the King's authority and laws from such
barbarous contempt, and tak some speedy and sum-
mare way to reduce and punish this insolency, to
the terror of others, and encouragement of his Majesties good subjects, who place ther safety from violence
in the shaddow of his Majesties laws and Goverment.
The partie grieved will apply himself to your Lordship for redress, whose just cause and the peace of the
countrey I crave leave to present to your Lordship's
favour; and that his Majesties service may prosper in
your hands is the constant desyre of, Right Honorable,
your most humble servant,   MORRAY."

"These are to empower macers of the Justice Court,
or messengers of arms, or town officers, within the
town of Edinburgh, to apprehend the persons of
Robert Dunbar of Burgie, elder, and of Alex. Petrie,
and to require all Magistrates to concurre with them,

and to seize the saids persons till they find caution to appeare when they shall be cited, and that they shall demean themselves in the interval peaceablie. Given at Edinburgh the sixteenth day of June sixteen hundred thrie score eight.   ROTHES, *Chancellor.*"

———

" I, Sir Charles Araskine of Cambo, Knight Baronet, Lyon King at Armes, Wheras be ane act of the Privie Counsell, dated the eighteinth day of June instant, given in favours of Thomas Dunbar of Grainge against Robert Dunbars elder and younger of Burgie and their complices, wherupon letters ar raised direct to me, you, and our remanent brethren heraulds, to pass with ane coat of armes displayed and sound of trumpet, and in our Soveraigne Lord's name and authoritie to charge the said Robert Dunbar, younger of Burgie,[1] and his complices speciallie named in the said act, to compear beforr the Lords of Privie Counsell upon the threttie day of July next to come, for the causses at length contained in the said act and

[1] In tracing the history of north country families, it were well to bear in mind that the designation of an estate added to a person's name, does not necessarily prove the ownership of such estate ; of this we could give numerous examples, let one, however, suffice. Archibald Dunbar sold the lands of Thunderton, in Aberdeenshire, in 1712, to Charles Gordon of Buthlaw, yet during the remainder of his life, he (Archibald) was designed " of Thunderton ;" and his successors in the estate of Duffus, though never possessed of an acre of the Thunderton estate, were for upwards of a century commonly so designated.

letters : These ar therforr ordaineing you, Herome
Spence, Rothsay Herauld, with ane trumpeter in
your companie, conform to the tenor of the said act
and letters, to cite and charge the said Robert
Dunbar, younger of Burgie, and his complices, and to
do all other things requisit and necessar prescrybed
be the said act and letters, conform to the tenor of
the samen, and this my order and warrant to you for
that effect in all points. Given under my hand at
Edinburgh the tuentie third day of July 1668, and
sealled with my seal[1] of office.

"CHAR. ASKINE, *Lyon.*"

The Laird of Burgie's License, 1665.

"We, William Lord Bellenden of Broughton, Lord
Thesourer Deputt of the Kingdom of Scotland, dooth
hearby give libertie and lisence to Robert Dumbear of
Burgie, and all such as ar of his family, or shall accom-
pany him att table, to catt flesh in this forbidden
tym of Lent, and on all other forbidden dayes, till
Lent nixt, in the yeir 1666, without any trouble or
penaltie to be incurred be him or them for the samyen,
notwithstanding of any Acts made, or to be made,
in the contrary. Dated Edinburgh the 20th daye of
Febuary.   BELLENDEN."

---

[1] A copy of this seal will be found in Mr. Laing's *Catalogue of Scottish
Seals*, about to issue from the press.

The widow of Ross of Pitcalnie was proud of her descent from the house of Burgie.

" To ALEX. DUNBAR, Esq.
                        "EDINBURGH, 20th July, 1761.

"SIR,—In answer to yours of the 13th, threatening me with caption, I can only repeat what I wrote when you acquainted me in yours of the 4th, that you was obliged to raise horning on my bill. Therefore I refer to what I then wrote, and shall only add that your father may put his caption in execution against me. I can go to prison ; the affront won't be mine, and before I come out, the Fifteen Lords shall know the merits of the cause that laid Burgie's daughter and Pitcalnie's widow in such quarters.

"Not in the least finding fault with your conduct, which I verily believe is much against your inclination, I am, dear Sir, your affectionate cousin, and very humble servant,   NAOMI ROSS."

XIII. AN EXTRAVAGANT AND UNDUTIFUL WIFE.

INHIBITION proclaimed at the market-crosses of Elgin and Forres :—

"Charles, be the Grace of God, King of Great Brittane, ffrance, and Irland, Defendar of the faith, to our Lovits,
Messingers, our Shrefs in that pairt, conjunctlie and severalie specialie constitute, greiting. fforsnameikle as it is humblie meined and shown to us be our lovit James Dunbar of Inshbrok, that where Katharine M'Kenzie, his spous, having casten off the fear of God and that conjugall respect and reverence that she owes to the said complainer, her lawfull husband ; and having betaken hirselfe to the councill and advyce of certain evill disposed and ungodlie persones, who haunts with hir, she daylie spends, abuses, and waists, the said complainer his substance with the said persones ; and contracts and takes on debts and sowmes of money, which the said complainer is altogither unable to pay ; and makes, blocks, and bargains for merchand weir ; sels and hypothecats his houshold plenishing, inshight goods and geir ; and ther are some persones who furnish hir with merchand wair, aill,

wine, bread, baken meats, and lend hir money, which
the said complainer is altogither unable to pay, and
whilk will tend to the ruine of him, his wife, and
children, and the litle fortune whilk it has pleased
God to bestow upon him, without remeid be provyded.
as is alledged.

OUR WILL IS THEIRFOR, and we charge you straitlie
and comand that, incontinent thir our letters seen, ye
pass, and in our name and authoritie, inhibite and
discharge the said Katherine M'Kenzie, the said com-
pliner his spous, that she on nawayes sell, analyie,
dispone, hypothecat, nor put away any of his said
houshold plenishing, goods, geir, inshight, abulziements, nor others pertaining to him ; nor yet contract
nor ontake debts, sowmes of money for merchand
wair, wine, aill, bread, baiken meats, or others, whereby the said complainer may be driven in debt or
compelled to pay the same ; nor yet contract, block,
nor bargin with any persone for that effect ; and
sicklyke, that ye, in our said name and authoritie,
inhibite and discharge all and sundrie, our leidges
and all others whom it effeirs, be open proclimation
at the mercat croses of our burghs of Elgin and
Forres, and other places neidfull, within this our
kingdome, that they, nor none of them presume, nor
take upon hand, to take or receave, be dispositione or
hypothecatione, nor pledge, fra the said Katharine
M'Kenzie, any of the said complainer's houshold plen-

ishing, goods, geir, inshight, abulziements, or others
pertaining and belonging to him; nor yet lend to
hir sowmes of money upon band, ticket, acompt, or
otherwayes; nor yet furnish to hir merchand wair,
wine, aill, aquavitæ, brandie, baiken meat, nor other
liquors, whereby the said complainer may be driven
in debt; nor yet contract, block, nor bargin with hir,
any maner of way, to the said complainer his prejudice : certifieing them, and ilk of them that failzies
and does in the contrair, the samen shall be decerned
to be null and of no availl. And the said complainer
shall not be holdin to pay any debts, sowmes of
money, or others, furnished to his said spous, eftir
the publicatione of thir presents conform to the lawes
and practiqe of this kingdome in all points. And
that ye cause registrat thir our letters, with the execution therof, within fourtie dayes nixt eftir the
execution of the samen, conform to the act of parliament, according to justice, as ye will answear to
us therupon : the whilk to do we committ to you,
conjunctlie and severalie, our full power be thir our
letters, delyvering them be you, duelie execute and
indorsit again to the bearer. Given under our signet,
at Edinburgh the third day of September, and of our
reigne the threttie fift yeir, 1683.

"*Ex deliberatione dominorum Concilij.*

"AND : YOUNG."

XIV. OFFICE OF HERITABLE SHERIFF
OF MORAY.

SIR ALEXANDER DUNBAR of Westfield was, about the year 1446, created Heritable Sheriff of Moray, and the office continued with the descendants of his eldest son, who either acted themselves or by depute, for nearly three hundred years.

Order to the Sheriff regarding the County Member :—

" To THE HIGH SHERIFF of the Shire of Elgin,
    " Free.

            " FROM THE HOUSE OF COMMONS,
                " *the* 22*d of May* 1721.

" SIR,—-I am commanded by the House of Commons to acquaint you that you are immediately, upon receipt of this, to summon the Representative of your Shire to attend his service in Parliament on Monday the ffifth day of June next, and you are to give me an account of the receipt of this, and what you have done thereupon, upon pain of incurring the displeasure of the said House.—I am, Sir, your humble servant,

"SP: COMPTON, *Speaker.*"

Even the ducal house of Gordon paid deference
to the Sheriff of Moray. Thomas Miller had been
assaulted by dependants of the Duke, who wished to
settle the matter in his own Regality Court. The
delinquents were, however, seized and imprisoned by
the Sheriff :—

"Mr. James ffRASER, Sriff-Clrk. of
   "Elgine and fforres,
     "Elgine.
        "GORDON CASTLE, 23d June, 1720.

"SIR,—The Sheriffs of Murray have always observed
a strict decorum and a neighbourly way with the
Duke of Gordon, with reguaird to his and their juris-
dictions, which is cumulative. The present Duke, my
master, will cultivat frindshyp and good correspondence with the present Sheriff of Murray, not doubting
but he will receive just returns.

"A little, fantastick, nonsolvent, and troublesome
animal, Thomas Miller, no weaver, no prentise, no
inhabitant, yet maliciously takes upon him to raise
vexatious processes against some of my master's servants : I humbly expect my Lord Sheriff will deal
tenderly in this matter. I dare not pre-limit his judgment, but I say to you that the matter pursued ought
to be remitted to the judge ordinary of the place.—I
am your most humble servant,
        "ALEXR. ABERCROMBY."

F

Ludovic Dunbar of Westfield, in 1724, being in
reduced circumstances, sold the jurisdiction for two
thousand pounds to the Earl of Moray. Against this
sale Thomas Dunbar, D.D., Vicar of Little Bustead,
Essex, the nearest heir-male, had entered an inhibition, but it was found that " Westfield," the seller,
was "absolute ffiar, and under no prohibitory, irritant,
or resolutive clauses, by the rights and infeftments of
the estate and office, to bar him from selling." To
his kinsmen in Moray, who wished him to redeem
the property and to prevent a sale, Thomas Dunbar
sent an answer which proves that he could feel, act,
and write like a scholar and a gentleman :—

" LONDON, *July* 29, 1723.

" GENTLEMEN,—I received your favour of the 20th
of May, by the hands of the Right Honble. the Lord
Lovat, for whose generous condescention and kind
concern and endeavours I have the greatest defference
and regard. But as to the subject matter of your
letter, (not to trouble you with the unkind treatment
I mett with from those of your name I had the honnor
to be presented to, and particularly from the present
Shereff's father when I was in that countrey,) I must
beg leave to enquire what power the late Sheriffe
James, or his brother, had to lay so great a burthen of
debts, as you mention, upon an entailed estate ; and
who they were that encouraged, countenanced, or con-
nived att their so doing ; for I have seen an instru-

ment of resignation by which their father, Alexr.
Dunbar of Westfield, seems to limite that estate, and
the inheritance of it, to his heirs male, and for each of
such to his heirs female, with certain conditions and
restrictions, as the kind bearer hereof will inform you
more at large. Now, if your law, (to which I am
pretty much a stranger,) notwithstanding such entail,
leaves it in the power of every prodigal or extravagant
heir to confound an estate which has been so long in
a family, and descended to him in a regular line of
succession, surely this can be no inducement to any
tollerrably discreet person to improve or augment, but
much less to redeem such an estate. But this you
seem to have intirely given up, or to acquiesse in, and
I doe confess it is not now my business, but the present Sheriffe's, to consider, and I wish it may long be
so. Tho' if it should be my fate to survive, which I
by no means desire, the purchasers must expect to be
called to account. But that the office should be liable
to the same fate, is so prodigiously shocking that I
hardly know how to declare myself upon that head
with any tollerable temper and decency (*obstupui,
steteruntque comæ, et vox faucibus hæsit*).[1] That it
should be in the power of any one sheriffe, without
the consent of heires presumptive or in reversion, to
dispose of, or allienate, an office which, in all the in-

[1] "I was amazed, and my hair stood on end, and my voice clung to
my jaws."

struments I have seen, and by what I have heard, was
ever called and esteemed hereditary. The argument
you are pleased to make use of, in justification of so
rash and bold an attempt, is that without the sale of
this valuable branch of the Sheriffe's inheritance, his
family must want subsistence. But I pray, gentlemen, give me leave to aske how his family would
have been subsisted if his predecessor had lived. And
can you thinke it reasonable, that I (who am threatened to be excluded, disinherited, and finally cut off,
from a reversion to which, in my turn, I am entitled
by birth, by blood, and by all the laws of God, of
nature, and I hope of my countrey) should straiten
myselfe or lessen that small fortune, which, by the
blessing of God, I owe entirely to my own industry
and application, to the affluence of a person who has
so shamefully prostituted all the rules of honour and
justice? That I have a due regard to the character
and dignity of that ancient family, you will observe
by the steps and measures I have taken, and (by God's
permission) am steadfastly purposed to maintain, and
pursue at the expence of all I am worth, even to the
dernier resort,[1] and therefore, *caveat emptor*.[2]

"And now, gentlemen, though I have expressed myselfe with some warmth in an affair which not only
affects me, but yourselves, and, as you justly observe,
ought to have very great weight with all that bear the

---

[1] The last resort.   [2] Let the purchaser beware.

name of Dunbar, or that have the remotest connection with it; yet I doe most sincerely acknowledge your goodness, in the kind concern you express for the support of an ancient family, and all the honour you have done me in this application. I pray God have you all in his good care and protection, and am, with greatest regard and esteem, your affectionate kinsman and most obedient humble servant,

"THO. DUNBAR.

"I had once some thoughts of giving my selfe the pleasure of visiting my native country this summer; but the loss of my dear and only brother, and the difficulties I have been involved in on that account, render such an absence impracticable att present. But if it should please God to spare my life and health another year, I will not despair of that satisfaction, nor of an opportunity of waiting upon you att your several seats, and making a personal acknowledgement of this favour and condescention."

It is remarkable that of the Westfield family, which for centuries was of great importance, there should be difficulty in finding out the heir-male. The Vicar of Little Bustead predeceased Ludovic Dunbar, whose death and succession are thus alluded to in letters

from Ludovic Brodie, W.S., to William King of Newmiln, Elgin :—

" EDINBURGH, 25 Aprile 1744.

" I return you many thanks for your early intelligence of that unhappy and melancholy accident which
terminated the life of poor Dunbar of Westfield. I
should be glad to know whether he hath left, signed
by him, any deed of settlement of his estate in favours
of the Lady Hemprigs, nearest heir of line, for otherwise I am afraid, as it is provided to heirs male whatsoever, it may be difficult to find them out ; and if
they are found out, that Lady, who is the heir of line,
may be in a great measure cut off."

" EDINBURGH, 5th May 1744.

" I see by a letter from Sir William Dunbar of
Hemprigs to Baillie George Dunbar, merchant here,
that he hath found among Westfield's papers a dispo-
sition of his estate in favours of Sir William's Lady,
daughter to Alexander Dunbar of Westfield, which
will prevent disputes about the succession."

XV. TRANSPORT OF A PRISONER, AND JAIL OF INVERNESS.

COUNTRY people, such as farmers and their servants, had to act as guards in the transport of prisoners. The unhappy woman was accused of child-murder :—

" A list of the guard for conveying the person of Jean Mill from the Tolbooth of Elgin to Nairn, to be delivered over to the Sheriff of Nairn there, in terms of the principall warrand from the Lords of Justiciary herewith sent :—

> " Alexr. M'Kimmie, in Overtown, *g.*
> John Allan there, *ab.*
> George Ogilvie in Houme, *g.*
> John Cook in Barnhill, *g.*
> 5 Thomas Murdoch in Westhill, *g.*
> Alexr. Murdoch in Achtirtyre, *ab.*
> Duncan Grant in Green of Manbean, *g.*
> Alexr. Grant in Coxtown, *g.*
> James Gallan in Insharnach, *g.*
> 10 Andrew Couban in Mostowie, *g.*
> George Kynnoch in Inerlochty, *g.*
> John Allan in Mostowie, *g.*
> William Murdoch in Crossley, *g.*
> James Brander, elder in Miltown, *g.*

15 James Brander, younger there, *g*.
   George Imlach there, or his servant, *g*.
   James Sim in Miltown, *g*.
   Alexr. Gilzean in Inverlochty, *g*.
   John Skeen, there, *g*.
20 John Robb, there, *g*.
   James Douglas, there, or a servant, *g*.
   Alexander Glass in the Coledge of Elgin, *g*.

" These are warranting Alexander Pitriken, officer, to summond the above persons to compear before the Shirriff of Murray, his deputes or substitutes, within the Tolbooth of Elgin, upon Thursday next, the twenty-fifth of Aprile instant, at nine o'clock in the morning, to carry and convey the person of Jean Miln, presently prisoner in the Tolbooth of Elgin, from the said Tolbooth to the town of Nairn, to be delivered to the Shirriff of the shire of Nairn, and from thence to be carried by a party from the said shire to the Shirriff of Inverness, to be incarcerated within the Tolbooth of Inverness untill the tryall of the said Jean Miln before the Lords Commissioners of Justiciary at their Circuit, the first of May next, conforme to the warrand directed to me, Shirriff-Depute of this shire of Elgin and fforres : And I hereby nominate and apoint the said John Grant to be Captain of this Guard, and each person to appear, under the penalty of twenty punds Scots money.   Given at Elgin the twenty-third day of Aprile 1745 years.

                                      " WILL. KING."

"ELGIN, 25 *Aprile* 1745.—The Sheriff-Depute fines and amerciates John Allan and Alexander Murdoch, two absents, marked in the within list, in the sum contained in the within warrant, each of them payable to the ffiscal of Court.

"WILL. KING."

"NAIRN, 26*th* *Aprile* 1745.—Then received by me, Sherriff Deput of Nairn Shire, the person of therein named Jean Mill, in order to be transported to Inverness, as the Lords' warrand under mentioned directs, together with the said Act and warrand it self, and that from Alexander Grant, Captain, appointed by the Sheriff of Elgin and fforres, for commanding the party that brought her, the said Jean Mill, here.

"DA. CUMYNG."

The Court-house and the "holes" in which prisoners were incarcerated at Inverness, were truly disgraceful :—

" INVERNESS, 17*th* *March*, 1786.

"Memorial for the Provost, Magistrates, and Town Council of Inverness, for themselves and the community, to the Heritors and Commissioners of Supply, and Magistrates of Burghs, in the Counties of Inverness, Ross, Moray, Sutherland,

Caithness, Nairn, Cromarty, Orkney, and Zetland :

" *Sheweth,*

" That the Circuit Court of Justiciary for the northern district, comprehending the above-mentioned counties, has been invariably held at Inverness.

" That the present court-house, which is very antient, having been built only for the town and county, is very inadequate to the proper accommodation of the Lords of Justiciary and other members of the court, the sheriffs, and the number of gentlemen who are called upon to attend as assizers.

" That the jail, which is adjoining to the court-house, consists only of two small cells for criminals, and one miserable room for civil debtors, and is often so crowded with prisoners from the different counties as to render their situation truly deplorable ; to give some idea of which it is only necessary to mention that there are at present, and generally, about thirty persons confined in these holes, none of which is above thirteen feet square.

" That the court-house and jail are now so much decayed as to render it necessary immediately to repair or rebuild them.

" That the memorialists have long anxiously wished to rebuild them on an enlarged plan, so as to afford ample accommodation for the Circuit Court, and to

soften the rigour of confinement to unfortunate prisoners, by removing the necessity of having them so
crowded together as they are at present.

"That with this view they have lately purchased,
at a considerable expense, a piece of ground, adjoining to the present jail, fully equal to the purpose,
and have procured a proper plan and estimates to
be made.

"That the sum necessary for carrying their plan
into execution will be about fifteen hundred pounds
sterling, which they are utterly unable to advance
from the funds of the community over which they
preside, and must, of course, abandon the idea, unless
liberally assisted by the different counties and burghs
connected with the Northern Circuit, and who are so
very materially interested in promoting this necessary
work.

"The memorialists, therefore, relying on the public
spirit, generosity, and humanity of the gentlemen of
the northern counties and burghs, do now call upon
them for liberal aid towards erecting a Court-house,
in which their accommodation as assizers will be a
principal object, and providing for such criminals as
they may send for trial: a prison decent and secure
will be particularly attended to.

"The memorialists, while soliciting the assistance
of others, think it incumbent on them to declare the
extent to which they will go for carrying this useful

work into execution, and they have resolved on *five hundred pounds sterling*, being a sum equal to the utmost stretch of their ability as a community. If, then, contrary to their hopes, the present application should fail of success, they claim that the want of accommodation in their Court-house, or smallness of their jail, may never be charged against them in future.

" Signed by appointment of the Magistrates and Council,

" WILLIAM MACINTOSH, *Provost.*"

XVI. COUNTRY MATTERS.

BEFORE the general introduction of coal into Moray, so necessary was a supply of peat, that it almost invariably formed an item in the rent of farms.

" 11th July, 1732.

" Wee, John Watson, William Gilzean, and John Laing, all tennents in Ardgy, do hereby certify and declare that sixty loads of peats or therby (when filled by our own servants, and lede by our own horses), was usually applyed for makeing up a leet of peats, fourteen foots square, carried up seven foots high, and rooffed in to fourteen foot from top to bottom ; and, accordingly, wee the declarants, and the other tennents of Ardgy, were in use to cast, winn, lead, and stack, for behoof of the heretors of the lands and barronie of Duffus, upon their and our proper charges and expences, certain leets of peats, conform to our respectif possessions at the dimentions above-writen, and that yearly ; and failzieing of the saids peats, we paid ten pounds Scots money for each leet.

" I. W.
WILLIAM GILZEAN.
JOHN LAING."

From Sir Harie Innes, Convener of the County :—

" To Archibald Dunbar, Esq.,
    " of Newton, at Duffus.

"Elgin, *Febry.* 21*st*, 1747.

"Sir,—Provost Duff wrote me this morning com-
plaining of the distress the inhabitants of this town,
and military, are reduced to for want of peats being
brought to town : that the soldiers must be supplied
some how or other is without doubt, and to do without ground of complaint there is a necessity of a
meeting of the Justices of Peace.   I wrote Sir Robert
Gordon to this purpose, and if Monday will suit both
your conveniences, you will be expected that day to
concert what is proper to be done.   I am, Sir, your
most humble servant,   Harie Innes."

———

Many estates, and even royal burghs, were, to a
recent date, "thirled" to particular mills,—that is,
the tenants and inhabitants were obliged to send
their grain to the established mill of the barony or
burgh, to be ground, and to pay a proportion of it
as "multure."   The town of Elgin was "thirled" to
"Oldmilns," which had formerly belonged to the
Prior of Pluscardine.   Greyfriars was the seat of
Mr. King of Newmiln ; it is now within the Parliamentary bounds of Elgin.

" ARCHBALD DUNBAR, Esquire,
" of Newtoun, Duffus.

"GRAYFFRIARS, *near* ELGIN, 30 *Decer.* 1736.

" SIR,—I had your's this day, inquireing me anent what multure I payed att Oldmilns. ffor answer, know that I am not thirled to that miln, or doe I live, or have I any land within the thirlage; but being informed that they ground wheat better att the Oldmilns than att my own miln, I sent my servant, the last year, with two boles of wheat to the Oldmilns, and after he returned I asked him what multure they had taken from him. He told me a peck out of each bole, and that they would take noe less, although he scrupled the giveing it. And when John Naughtie, one of the millers, came asking me ten shileing Scots for each bole of the wheat I had ground att the Old milns, as the millers wages, which I payed him, and quarrelled him for taking so much multure, and so much money from me that was out sucken, and noe wayes bound to them, he told me they made noe distinction, but tooke the same multure from evrie one that came to them whither out or insucken; upon which I told him that I should take care of ever grinding afterwards att their miln—which is all I know of their multures, and am yours W. KING."

Just as poultry now belongs to the lady's department in the management of a country house, so in

former days did the breeding and rearing of young
horses. *Honi soit qui mal y pense.*

" To ARCHIBALD DUNBAR,
      " of Newton, Esquire, at Duffes.

                          " ARNDILLY, 17*th June* 1756.

"DEAR SIR,—You may think I have been ungrate,
as I have not thanked you before this time, for the
use of your fine stalion to one of my chaise mares
last year, and that you was at so great trouble as to
keep the mare and servant for some days.   That
mare has this year a pretty stood fole from your
horse.   I cannot at present tell how I can return so
great a favour, but when it falls in my husband's
power or mine, our inclination is great, and the im-
ploying us will be a compliment.   I would gladly
have a pair of horses from your fine horse, therefore
I have ventured to send my other mare to be served
by him, if you will be so good as to grant me this
second favour.   My husband is pretty much recovered.   I am heartily sorry I did not see the young
gentlemen as they went to Edinburgh.   My husband
and I present you, Lady Newtown, and all the young
family with our deutie, and intreats you will allow me
the honour to be, dear Sir, your most affectionate
cousin and obedient humble servant,

                          " JEAN GRANTT."

    " *P.S.*—We was made happy by Mr. Coban's information that your lady designs to see us at Arndilly this summer. Tam intends you a visite, in a week or two, that she may deliver the Cairngorm stone she promised."

The wages of servants, as given in a document dated 1760.

"Regulations of Fees for Servants in the county of Bainff :—

	£	s.	d
That the best man servant who drags the ware, and is capable to big and sow corns, shall have	27	0	0
That the second man servant who fills the side of the ware horse, threshes the side of the barn, lays on loads, and is a good hook in harvest, shall have	25	0	0
That the third man who likewise fills the ware horse, is capable to thresh the side of the barn, and can shear in harvest, shall have . .	20	0	0
That the first best man servant where there are no waring, who can big the corns, and hold the plough, shall have	23	0	0
That the second man servant who works the horse, and holds the horse plough, shall have .	19	4	0
That the third man servant who drives the plough, shears in hervest, and threshes in the barn, shall have	13	6	8
That the best woman servant who can beke, brew, and miln, shall have	12	0	0
That the second woman servant who is capable to shear in hervest, but otherwise not so capable, shall have .	10	0	0

	£	s.	d.
That the best man hook who can big and bind corns, shall have	16	10	4
That the second sort of men hooks shall have	6	0	0
That the best woman hook, who stays out the harvest, shall have	5	0	0
That the second sort of woman hooks shall have	4	10	0

That hirds according to their charge shall have from £6 to £1, 10s. every half-year.

"And which respective fees are declared to be in satisfaction to men and women servants, of all that can be asked or given to them for their year's services above inscribed, in name of fees, shoes, or any other bounties whatever ; and where the master gives, or where the servant receives, any higher or greater fees, under any pretence whatsoever, such feeing shall not only be void, but the master and servant who shall contraveen the premesses be fined therefor."

———

The moral Grieve got, when at Kilcoy, "five pounds in money, twenty shillings for shoes, eight bolls of meal, and a cow's grass annually:"—

"Wee, the Justices of the Peace hereto subscribing, do certify and declare, that the bearer hereof, George Calder, from the county of Aberdeen, served Lady Kilcowie in station of a grieve, behaved himself honestly and moraly for the course of ffive years in her

service, and may be received into any Christian society;
and the same is attested by us, two of the Justices of
Peace of the county of Ross, and united parishes of
Suddie and Kilmuir Wester, where the said George
Calder resided for the time above mentioned. At
Allangrange, this 1st of June 1767.

> "ROD. MACKENZIE, *J.P.*
> GEO. MACKENZIE, *J.P.*"

The certificate by the Minister of Langbryde is of
recent date, but too amusing to be omitted :—

" To all his Majesty's loving subjects who can feel
for a fellow-sinner in distress, I beg to certify that
the bearer, W. J——, is the son of my old bellman, a
man well known in this neighbourhood for his honest
poverty and excessive sloth, and the son has inherited
a full share of the father's poverty and a double portion of his indolence. I cannot say that the bearer
has many active virtues to boast of; but he is not
altogether unmindful of scriptural injunctions, having
striven, and with no small success, to 'replenish the
earth,' though he has done but little to subdue the
same. It was his misfortune to lose his cow lately,
from too little care and too much bere chaff; and that
walking skeleton, which he calls his 'horse,' having

ceased to 'hear the oppressor's voice, or dread the tyrant's *load*,' the poor man has now no means of repairing his loss but the skins of the defunct and the generosity of a benevolent public, whom he expects to be stimulated to greater liberality by this testimonial from– theirs, with respect, &c.,

" WILL. LESLIE."

XVII. EDINBURGH GOSSIP.

John Sutherland was the Edinburgh agent of the gentleman to whom he wrote :—

" Archibald Dunbar, Esqr., of Newton,
" at Duffus.

" Edinburgh, 2d Feby. 1749.

" Dear Sir,—I hope you receive your news papers safe. Receive enclosed this weeks three Mercuries.

" There is nothing here new, only a very comical piece of humour, said to be done by the Duke of Montague. It was advertised in London that a man was to go into a chopin bottle and there play on the fiddle! —a curious piece of necromancy, you will say ; but lo ! when a numerous cloud of spectators are convened, at half-a-crown each ticket, a man appears on the stage, and, addressing himself to the audience, says, ' If you will but double the above sum, the man will appear in a pint (that is a mutchkin) bottle ; ' upon which they discovered the trick : among the rest the Duke of Cumberland, who in a furious passion drew his sword, which was presented by the Queen of Hungary,

valued at ten thousand pounds, and Montague alone
took the deceiver's part, but yet he was not able to
withstand the fury of the spectators, who were now
turned actors, and they tore and broke everything in
the house and set fire to it.   During the squabble the
Duke's sword was thwarted out of his hand, and he,
thinking it to be some of his friends, did not mind it
during the fray, but upon enquiry for the sword it
was gone, and now one hundred pounds premium is
offered for restoring it.

" A few nights after, the same man is alleged to
have, at a masquerade, employed another to go through
the masquerade with a sheath and sword, and call, in
a hurry, near where the Duke was, ' A fine sword ; a
fine sword ; who lost a fine sword ?'   The Duke,
comming in a surprise to look at it, said, ' It was the
Duke,' meaning himself, and upon looking at it, it was
found to be a piece of stick in a white paper sheath.
I wish you would be so friendly as to signify if such
collections be troublesome or agreeable to you, and I
shall continue or desist, as you please.   I am, dear
Sir, your much obliged and obedient servant,

" JOHN SUTHERLAND."

Such collections being " agreeable," Mr. Sutherland
was requested to continue them.   We give extracts :--

" 23*d Feby.* 1749.—We are here in a great hubbub about settling the poors'-rates. The Merchant Company have agreed to pay seven per cent., and the Faculty of Advocates have refused to assess themselves with anything, after a long debate, when it carried, *No*—seventy-two against five."

" 20*th Aprile* 1749.—You will observe a letter in this day's paper anent a ploy which was occasioned by about thirty or forty officers jumping on the stage, when in the last part of the act King Henry says, ' Hence, let rebellion be for ever quashed.' Upon this one of the officers called to the fiddlers to play ' Culloden Reel,' and then the gallery people hissed, and threw potatoes, &c., at them, which is to let you into the rise of that stir."

" 1*st June* 1756.—The Edinburgh Banks have sent some of their directors with twenty-five thousand pounds of Glasgow notes to get specie for them, which may crack some of them."

" 13*th March* 1759.—The Duke and Dutchess of Douglass are, alas ! parted, through faults on both sides, as is alledged. Two very handsome fellows were this day found guilty of a robbery, and will probably string, and the only defence their councill urged, it were better send them to Martinico or Guardulope than to the gallows."

" 9*th October* 1759.—George Baillie, your cousine, married 29th September last, and from superabund-

ance of complaisance set out next day with another
lady for this place, where he presently is, and I had
the pleasure of saluting him on the happy event this
day."

"15th Octr. 1759.—I congratulate you upon the
reduction of Quebeck, and consequently the empire of
North America ; but amidst our joy we are enjoined
prudence and caution, for it is certain Thurot is sailed,
and the Solebay Man of War says he sailed through
his fleet (under French colors), consisting of six war
ships and twelve transports, and Admiral Boyes with
eleven ships in quest of him, steering northwards,
either to the Murray (where I pray God Thurot may
never come) or Pentland firths. This afternoon Boyes
is anchored in Leith road, drove up by a nore-east
gale, and, so soon as the wind permits, and he provided with a little provisions and pilots, is to proceed
on towards the north. We have expresses from England, two or three a day, and it is rumoured the Brest
fleet is out. May Hawk fly and catch him."

"2d July 1760.—By this night's news Mineer
Dutchman seems to try us in that country ; but, in
the true sense of the word, they 'catched a Tartar,'
for their seven ships of war are all taken, six hundred
of twelve hundred are killed, the rest prisoners, and
the Governor of Batavia, who sent them, acknowledges
his fault, and pays, beside begging pardon, a hundred
and twenty thousand pounds."

XVIII. LETTERS FROM LADIES OF RANK.

ISOBELL, Countess of Seaforth, widow of Kenneth, third Earl, was daughter of Sir John Mackenzie of Tarbat, and sister of George, first Earl of Cromarty. Her Ladyship's daughter, Margaret, married James, second Lord Duffus, who, having killed William Ross of Little Kindeace in the year 1688, fled to England, where he remained until influential friends purchased a remission from the Crown. The writing of the Countess is large and well formed; that of Lady Duffus is very inferior.

" For my LORD DUFFUS
" They :
" CHANORI, 8 *Apryll* 1688.

" MY DEAR DUFFUS,—We are mightily afrayed of your health, and has sent this expres to conjure you to be cairfull of yourself. As for what is done, Lord pardon you the sin of it ; but no man thinks ye could have done less, or that ye could have born with what ye met with. I pray you have a cair of yourself, and goe on to doe your business, and let us know wher or

to whom we shal derect your leters whil ye are at
Court; I think to my Keny,[1] when ye are at London.
Ye may writ to Megg with every ocation, to give her
asurance of your health, which she will still be doubting. We all think, and Siddy,[2] who has better skill in
such afairs, that after al the provocations ye met with,
yet that it was in your own defence what ye did, for
certinly ye had been killed if it had not fallen out as
it did; so your busines will not cost you much trubel
to get it don. Be cairfull of yourself for Megg's caws
and the babys. Many a man has falen in such ane
accedent warse than your circumstances was, yet has
bein at peace with God and all the world, and lived
very happily for all that. The Lord's peace be with
you, and derect you and preserve you from all ill.—I
am your affectionat mother,

" ISOBELL SEAFORT."

" CHANORI, the 13th of Apraill 1688.

" DEAREST HERT,—I can slip no ocation but I most
wrait you, knowing you will be earnest always to hear
how I am, which, I blis the Lord for it, is very well,
and so is all your childrin and all frinds heare; and
now it is my greatest trubill the fear of your wrong-
ing your own helth, which I hop you will considir
how much it will ofend God, and what a gref it will

---

[1] Her son Kenneth, fourth Earl.   [2] Mackenzie of Suddy.

be to me, so I expek to hear good neuse from you,
and writ to me ase oft as you have ocation. No mor
at the taim, but that the Lord may blis you, and direk
you and protek you, is the earnest prayer of your own
till death. M. DUFFUS.

" My Lady presents hir respecs to you."

Henrietta Duchess of Gordon, wife of the second
Duke, was a daughter of the celebrated Earl of Peter-
borough. Her Grace had sufficient influence to induce
the ducal family to renounce Popery and embrace the
Protestant faith. The writing of the Duchess is par-
ticularly good and distinct. The lady to whom her
Grace sent the following letters was then unmarried.
She was daughter of the deceased Alexander Dunbar
of Westfield, and she resided with her maternal uncle,
Sir Thomas Calder of Muirton, Baronet :—

" To Mrs. ELIZABETH DUNBAR at Muirton.
                    "GORDON CASTLE, *August the* 20*th*, 1722.

" MY DEARE FREIND,—It being now just ten days
since I had the pleasure of hearing from you, which to
me is a tedious age, I send the bearer on purpose to
bring me acounts of your health, and of all I have
a consern for with you ; and I send you and Lady
Muirton sum of the flowered painted satin which you
commended in the winter, having had an occasion to

Holland. I belive the thirty yards will make each a
night gownd, and the tea is, I belive, a litle better
than the ordinary that is sold ; the imperiale will doe
well to mix with the green. You will, I hope, forgive
me this libertie I take in hopeing you will, without
any uneasiness, except from your freind such a trifle,
since I hope you are truly convinced that nothing can
be so agreable to me as the hopes I have of enjoying
the vast satisfaction in the most entire freindshipp
that is possible for two hearts so sincere and so
simpathising as, I belive and hope, ours are.

" This is all the July flowers that are as yet blown,
and the very first, which I belive are the best ; but if
Lady Muirton wants more, next week she may have
as many as she pleases.

" I have also sent two more trajedies. There is
two lady's and one man's character in the ' Imperial
Captives,' that I belive will please you ; and also I am
sure the oddness of the lives of the misfortunate paire
in this litle book will move your pity, as it did mine.
It is a strange mixture of prodigeous love and penitence
for a fault, where the strugle of our frail nature, and
the glimerings of divine grace, apear in a very naturale
manner ; and though it is not quite so well as in the
French, yet, if you have not already seen it, you cannot
but be entertained with it, for it is a litle out of the
common method of our days, where vice hardly makes
sutch a penitent end. I hope it will not be many days

before I have the pleasure of seeing you ; and belive
me, where ever I am, my kindest thoughts will ever
be with you, and I shall never be so well pleased as
when I enjoy the charming company of my dearest
freind, from whoes and your aunt's aquaintance I shall
ever begin the date of my satisfaction and happyness
in this country.

"Wishing you all the prosperity that this world
can aford, I continue with the greatest esteem, my
dearest, your most faithfull and most affectionate
freind and sarvant,　　　　　　　　　H. GORDON.

"Just now I hear Generale Sabin and the Earle of
Rothes are gone back to the south, so that as soon as
my Lord returns from Badenoch, I hope to see you.
My kind sarvice to Lady Muirton and Sir Thomas.
Henri and Betsy offer ther kind sarvice to you all."

"GORDON CASTLE, *Octbr. 9th.*

"MY DEAREST FREIND, . . . I am glad the Art of
Love pleases you ; I thought it very prety, and did
not imagine a subject of that nature could have been
quite so modestly expressed as to be of so good use to
us ladys as it realy is.　You may keep any book of
mine that is in your hands as long as you please, and
be asured nothing will ever be more agreable to me
than to have any oportunity to contribute, any manner

of ways, to your fellicity and pleasure. I have a good many late editions, with sum additions, of sum books that may please you, particularly sum translated out of the French, which I sent for on purpose for you ; but I belive, with what you have already, and the time you are so justly to employ in the care of your good aunt, you will want no more, till we have the pleasure and happyness to meet here, and then you shall chuce what ever pleasses you best. Since I knew you I cannot find the way to make my houres fly but in your charming dear companey, although you are always present in my kindest thoughts, which makes up the most agreable time of, my dearest, your most faithfull and ever affectionate freind and sarvant,

" H. GORDON.

" My most kind sarvice to all at Muirton. I shall shortly answer Sir Thomas's letter."

———

"GORDON CASTLE, *fryday noon.*

" MY DEAREST FREIND,—This morning I had the favour of your oblidgeing letter by which I was very sorry to hear of good Lady Muirton's loss. My two godchildren have had such badd luck that I can scars expect Lady Muirton will venture to make choice of me for a third, but if she does me that favour, I hope I shall have better fortune, since none can be better pleased to have any opportunity of

doeing her any kind of sarvice. I was once fearing Sir
Thomas's absence would oblidge Lady Muirton to goe
and oversee the hering feshing, and so our cumming
on Teusday might be unseasonable; but now since you
expect him so soon, I hope nothing will happen to me
to deprive me of that pleasure which I long very much
for. As to the mariages talked of, I belive this day,
by Sir Thomas or Walter Hamilton, we shall know if
there is any truth in them. I saw lately two letters
from Brodie, since his return from Berwick, wherein
he says his jorney there was only to make a visit to
the Earle of Deloraine, but tells they had him at Edinburgh maried one week to Mrs. Stuart of Camila, and
the next, to Mrs. Slye, but adds that he was then
confined to his chamber, his eye being almost as badd
as when at London, and the same kind of operations
to be again made, except the boreing his nose ; so I
fear it will be yet a time before he enter the state of
matrimony. By what he says of Sir Robert Gordon,
it looks very probable his affair may succeed since it
apears he is in earnest, but how farr the lady's father
may be engaged will take a litle time to know, for it
is possible there may in time be a very great fortune,
if Innernighty make his peace. I hear nothing of Sir
Hary's progress, but we are every minute expecting
to see Sir Thomas, who will tell us all the news.

" By all those who pretend to skill, I hear the
herring fishing has all apearance of being very good,

which I most heartily wish for the good of all concerned, but more particularly for my freind Sir
Thomas. When that affair is over, I hope you will all
be at leisure to cum here for sum days, which will
be a very great pleasure to me, who always am, with
utmost esteem, my dearest, your most faithfull and
most affectionate freind and sarvaut,

" H. GORDON.

" All here make their compliments to you and Lady
Muirton."

———

" March 28th.

"MY DEAREST FREIND,—It is impossible for you to
imagine how very great my disapointment was on
Tuesday night, when I had with so much pleasure
expected to hear from my dear friend, and found
myself balked, the cause of which I could not com-
prehend, and in my heart I can never suspect you
of the very smallest neglect or unkindness to auy,
but specialy to one who, next my own, will ever
love and value you above all things in the world ;
so after passing some anxious hours, my Lord in the
morning sent my charming freind's letter to me, which
he had forgot, which gave me unspeakable pleasure,
and I shall promise you hereafter never to trouble you
again with any excuse of any kind ; but I truly was so
hurried and balled upon by my Lord, to see a dyeing

gentleman, that I realy fancy I writte nonsense, but kind nonsense I hope it was.

"You will now, I belive, my dearest, be very agreably surprized to hear from Lady Muirton the particulars of a treaty of peace, formarly proposed sum houres after we parted with Sir Thomas on Sunday last, which was happyly concluded last night. I term it my forth wedding night, and am hopefull it will be the last I shall ever have. As there are many good things, I hope, may attend this reconcilement, there is none, I asure you, more agreable to me than two persons being united who, I am sure, wish you as well as it is possible ; for my part, ther is no pleasure to me that surpasses what I enjoy in the very hopes of being sum time in a possibility of doeing you the least sarvice — judge you then, my dearest, what would be the effects if my wishes could turn to a reality.

"I have just dune with these two vollumes of novells. You will, I asure you, find the most of them very prety, and as I fancy you will not have mutch time to spare that way before Easter, I shall only disier you to read, till that is over, The Force of Freindshipp, which I am sure you will like. I read with great pleasure all I can com at upon that subject, that I may know if any surpasses me in the notions I have of that happy state I am so deeply engaged in with you, without which I always must

think life a great burden. The next I would recomend
to your reading is The Princess of Cleaves, which you
will be charmed with, and where there is admirable
examples for all the maried ladys who live in the
temptations of this corrupted age. The heroine of
this novell goes through all the strugles, and I think
more, than ever Heloise did, and made not the least
fallen stepp; and her husband's is also a most admirable charactar. The next that should follow should
be Don Carlos, it being a part of the historys of
France and Spain of the same ages. When you have
had the pleasure of reading these, I think you will
have a mind to begin and read them in course. The
first is very prety, but there being many adventures,
perhapps you would think it a litle tedious at the first,
so I have recomended those I fancy will please your
tast, and be a litle diverting, which is what I belive all
of uss, in this part of the world, want at times; but I
asure you, as odd as a good part of my life has been
since I came to this contrey, I never thought the
time apeared tedious to me till I had the happyness
of your acquaintance, and the charming satisfaction of
enjoying so dear a freindshipp. But judge how it is
possible in nature to be content with so very litle of
what one loves so very much, but as providence has,
no doubt for sum wise and nessesary end, alloted to
me a life of mortifications, so belive me this last is a
most sensible one; but I must still live in hopes the

time will shortly come when we may with more ease
and fredom enjoy the pleasures that must flow from
so entire a freindshipp, which will be, my dearest, a
happyness beyond expresstion to your most affectionate and ever faithfull freind and humble sarvant,

" H. GORDON."

" GORDON CASTLE, *September* 1*st*.

" MY DEAREST FRIEND,—You will easily belive how
sensibly I regret any thing that prevents our meeting,
which I find is put off, I believe, to this day fortnight,
if you can at that time part with Lady Muirton for
a litle start, or else it must be sooner, but Lady Thunderton will be pleased to hear a sermon, and her peats
and harvest will be prety well over by that time.   By
her servant, the bearer of this, I send the King of
Sweden's picture frame, and a litle box with two
fidleing new fashioned tipits and a faun, which I hope
you will doe me the favour to except.   I have sent
Mrs. Elizabeth Dunbar of Duffus a faun a litle more
gaudy, but I like the Godess Diana best, so sent it to
you : had you been here, you should have chose yourself.   You know, my dearest, what must always please
me best, when you are absent from the person who
loves and values as I doe, so be kind and fail not to
lett me hear from you, as often as it is not troublesum
to you.   I also think Lady Muirton, if she has occa

stion to writte, must use the fredom to make use of
you for her secretary ; for it is not convenient she
doe any thing now that is the least trouble to her. I
fancy, before now, you have heard the comicall adventure that had like to have happened to us, a litle after
I parted from you, occastioned by Captain Cumming
haveing made Ned drink at King Edward :[1] he came
home in the chaise with Arundele in it, to hold him,
and his soun to drive, and we ride home in the dark
at great leasure, but, thank God, no accident happened ; but when you come here you will laughf at a
more particular acount, since I was very like to have
had my lodgeing in the fine green place that night.
My dearest, you must know with what kindness and
tenderness I shall always think of you and look upon
your picture : till we meet next I fear I shall not, with
my will, part with it, till I get Mr. Alexander to draw
an other.   I continue, as long as life, my dear, your
most faithfull and ever affectionate freind and sarvant,

" H. GORDON.

" My kind sarvice to Sir Thomas. All here send
there complements to you all at Muirton."

Miss Anne Stuart, niece of Charles, fifth Earl of
Moray, dates her letters from Dunibristle, Fifeshire.

---

[1] Now called Kinnedar.

She was probably daughter of Francis, who succeeded, as sixth Earl, on the death of his brother Charles. Lady Anne Stuart, daughter of the sixth Earl, married Stewart of Blairhall, so, on our hypothesis, the lady did not change her name,—a subject on which she had expressed doubts when writing to her friend.

" To Mrs. DUNBAR, at Muirton :
　　" To the care of the Postmaster of Forres.

　　　　　　　　" DUNIBRISTLE, *Jan.* 28, 1723.

　" MY DEAR SPOUSE,—You needed not have given me half so many reasons for your long silence, for I was perswaded it was not forgetfullness in you, but some cause which I waited with impatience to know, and I am so rejoiced when I get a letter from you, that it takes all thoughts away of accuseing you of un-kindness. My Lord has had a fit of the gout, and is not perfictly recovered yet. I hear nothing of our going north this summer, which I am very sorry for. Duke Hamilton is to be married the 6th of February, it being Lady Anne Cochran's birthday ; she is to be married in white velvet trimed with silver. I hear Bracco is going to be married to Lady Mary Mont-gomery, but some say he is going to London. Earle Rothes, it is said, is to marry Lady Isabella Scot, and is to get thirty thousand pounds sterling with her : I wish it may be true, for he wants the money and very well deserves it. Lord Deskford's marriage with

Drummelier's daughter is still talked of. They have
got an assembley at Edinburgh, where every Thursday
they meet and dance from four o'clock to eleven at
night ; it is half a crown the ticket, and whatever tea,
coffee, chocalate, biscuit, &c., they call for, they must
pay as the managers direct ; and they are the Countess
of Panmure, Lady Newhall, the President's Lady, and
the Lady Drummelier. The ministers are preaching
against it, and say it will be another horn order : it is
an assembley for dancing only. Lord Crighton gave
a ball lately, where there was a vast many ladys—
Peggie Bell was queen. My fingers are so cold that
I cannot hold the pen, as you may see by my write ;
so I add no more but that I am, my dear spouse,
your most faithfull affectionate humble servant,

                    " ANNE STUART.

    " My mother gives her humble service to my Lady
Calder. I do the same to all friends at Muirtoun,
especially Jamie, my young lover."

                    — — —

                    " DUNIBRISTLE, May 1, 1723.
    " MY DEAR SPOUSE,— I doubt not but by this time
you think me very much to blame that has not
answered the kind and oblidging letter you write to
me about a moneth since, but I declaire solemnly I
received it only a few days ago. It is, I believe, the

carelessness of the post at Aberdeen that occasions
our letters to be so long ere we get them. I reckon,
my dear spouse, all the ladys in the north have got
cocades of willow green for the rich laird : were I not
in mourning for Earl Panmure, I would certainly give
good example to those in our neighbourhood. This
marriage will make me very cautious who I talk
slightingly of, least they fall in my own lap, for you
may remember I told you what past betwixt that
young lady and I at Castle Grant. She did indeed
use a good deal of freedom with his person, but I
fancy London has given him a better air, together
with the possesion of seven thousand pounds a year,
which is a very genteel thing, and has a great deal of
beauty in it. I suppose you have heard of the death
of Earl Linlithgow, Countess of Errol, and Countess
of Strathmore. Earl Panmure dyed of a plurasie,
which is not ordinary for a man of his age—he was
sixty-eight. The Duchess of Hamilton is with child,
so is the Countess of Wigton. Lord Crichtoun is
making his adresses to Lady Susan Hamilton, but the
Duke does not seem to favour it. Lord Blantire is
to be married to Lady Catherine Cochran. I am extreamly glad of the good agreement in the Duke of
Gordon's family ; I wish it may be always so. One
would think a man could not wish greater happyness than he may find in that fine lady ; and the
Duke, in conversation, seems very agreable, but, alais !

they don't see the charms that is in one another. My
Lord and Lady Moray gives you their most kind ser-
vice. Pray let me know what is become of Mrs.
Cummin. Give my humble service to all friends at
Muirtoun. I ever am, my dear spouse, your's most
affectionately,   ANNE STUART."

" Jan. 10, 1725.

" MY DEAR SPOUSE,—Your kind letters are always
most acceptable to me, but none was ever more so
than the last, for I very much wanted such a cordial.
My spirits were as low as you can immagin, which
you will not be surprised at when I tell you my Lady
Morray was so ill at the time, I knew not whether she
would dye or live. I am sure you would pitty me on
such occasions, did you know my anxiety, and I flatter
myself you would sympathize with me, not only out
of regard to my Lady, but from friendship to myself.
Blissed be God, she is now perfictly well, but she was
for many weeks she did not stirr out of her room ;
and I must do her the justice to say she never complains without reason, nor keeps her room longer than
is absolutely necessary : her greatest fault is that she
is not carefull enough of her self. There arises great
vexations to me from my Lady's bad state of health.
The long tract of years she has enjoyed without the
lest indisposition, till within this little time, gives me

the greatest fear when she takes this fitts of illness,
and I were the most ungratefull creature on earth if
my conscern for her were not prodigeously great, for
she has been to me, from my cradle, liker a mother
than ane uncle's wife ; and the fears of my being disapointed of my so much wishd for journey to the
north is a vast affliction.   I dare not let myself expect that journey will hold unless my Lady's health
were better established, though still my Lord talks of
it as a thing certain. · You see, my dear, I tell you all
my grievances, but I hope it will go no farther, for it
is a subject I would write on to no mortal but yourself.   Any news I have, I doubt not but you have
heard before now, unless it be Mr. Hay Drummelier's
marriage with my Lord Blantire's sister.   The Master
of Stormont and Innernity's daughter are to be married
this week ; so of four of five Anne Stuarts that were
last winter in town, there remains but me, and I know
not whither to be ashamed of being behind with those
ladys, or proud of keeping memory of that name ;
some say the latter, and that I ought to continue so
to do, and not follow the example given me, but I am
not as yet positive to follow that advice, and I believe
you will think I should not be rash in my resolutions.
I rekon you have got a particulare acount of Major
Erskin's marriage, which was the most magnificent
that has been in Edinburgh of a great while.   The
most remarkable of the bride's cloaths were a crimson

velvet smoke petecoat, trimed with a silver or gold
arras (I have forgot which), and a cherry sattin hoop.
She had three sute of cloaths, viz., a white sattin, a
blue podesoy trimmed with scollopt open silver lace
above the knee, and a green stuff with gold flower, all
very pretty. At Lady Cristian Hamilton's marriage
with Sir James Dalrymple, they were all prodigeously
fine : Lord Binny's cloaths were fine yellow cloath,
richly laced with open silver, which was, I think, a
comical choice. Mr. Keith, Colonel Keith's son, and
Mrs. Peggy Cunninghame have made a runaway marriage. I am affraid his fortune is not so good as she
might have got. I have been longer in writing to
you than I designed, but I waited for Mr. Russle's
being the bearer, because that was a surer way than
the post. I heartily wish you, and all the good company where you are, a happy new year, and am, my
dear Spouse, most sincerely your's,

" ANNE STUART."

Mrs. Ann Dunbar was known as " Lady Dykeside."
Her husband's father had sold Dykeside, in the parish
of Birnie, but the family retained the designation.

" The LADY THUNDERTON.
    " att Duffus House.
                " FORRISS, 17 Sept. 1745.

" MADAM,—I hope the tea came safe as ordered,
three pound bohea, one green. The rock indigo was

all sold to a man in this town before I knew it was
come home. There is no news in town. Now for
trifels. Mrs. Carltown and I are very great already.
It was a mistake when I wrote you no new fashions;
she has severals, all of which I am to have the looking att, and patterns when next we meet. The morning caps are worn extremely full in the border, and
full behind. The hair and wiggs still curled. Lady
Force's cap, last from Edinburgh, the flowered lawn,
the very newest fashion att London. All plain silk
night-gowns, worn with different coloured sattens
sewed on the breast and sleves, almost like Miss
Brodie's yallow gown, but not pucked. Velvet
clokes, laced round with black lace, and made a little
longer than they are here, and newer than capuhins.
Lady Force, Miss Brody, Captain Cumming, and Mr.
Sinclair was in this kirk Sunday. They called here,
spent an hour agreeably, and all remembered you.
The Lady is to be to visit Mrs. Carltown soon. I
continue to be, with great regard, dear Madam, your
Ladyship's most obedient humble servant,

"ANN DUNBAR."

" To Miss NELLY DUNBAR,
" att Duffus House.
"FORRIS, 25 December.

" MY DEAR MISS,—I rejoice to hear you and all
the family are well, and that you are happy in having

your brother with you this holydays. I long to see
every one of you, and assure you, when I have not
that pleasure, I often think of you. May every one
of you be as happy as I wish you, and your Papa
live to see itt. We shall drink all your health att
eating the fine goose and pears you send; in the
mean time accept our thanks. Tell your papa that
Miss Brodie is to be married, on New Year's day, to
Maclod younger, whoe she seems really to be fond of,
which surprises every body, as he is not the most
charming person in the world, and, till folks saw with
their own eyes, everybody supposed itt a match that
had more of prudence than love. He is absolutely
the ugliest chield I ever saw. They were in town in
company with the Lyon, his lady, Sir William Dunbar,
and all the Roses, Miss Forbes, the Master of Forbes,
Captain Cumming, Jack Sutherland, Grange, Birdsyards, his familie, Tannachie and his, Kinsteary and
his, Captain Beckworth and his, and your humble
servant, att a grand ball given by an officer here.
Miss Brodie looked at her intended spous, not only
with liking, but with rapture, which all the company
observed, pleased to see her happy against their expectations. Ask papa if he will even do us the favour
to take a ride this lenth, and tell him none would
be fonder to see him. Make offer of our joyned compliments to him and all the familie. Deliver the enclosed paper carefully to him, and return him thanks

in Mr. Dunbar's name and mine for all his favours.
Say we wish him, and every individual he has any
concern with, a series of happy New Years, and believe me to be, with the greatest affection, my dear
little Elfe, your most obedient humble servant,

"ANN DUNBAR."

Margaret Countess of Moray, wife of James, seventh
Earl, was daughter of the Earl of Wemyss, and sister
of the Countess of Sutherland.

" To Miss DUNBAR,
    " at Mrs. Glase's, Edinburgh.
        "DUNIBRISTLE, 27th May 1763.

"DEAR NELLY,—You have been much more mind-
full of my commissions than I have been, for which I
thank you, for I did not say a word to you by Lady
Jane to-day, who is by this time in town; but my
woman Jenny will be in town this week, and then I
shall rectifie all mistakes. In the meantime bespeak
from Mrs. Fife as much of the green and purple as
will trim a gown. She will know the usual quantity,
but as I am of the broad and tall growth, she will
make and send six yeards more than the comen
quantity, with a dozen and a half or two dozen of
tassels. I would not have any gimp in them, but
just the green and purple silk mixed. Now the
sooner this is done the better; and as I will have

frequent opertunityes of folks in town, I shall always
make them call at you. My Lord was quite vexed
about the very bad day you got. He and I hopes you
felt no bad effects from it, and will be glad to hear
that all at Duffus are well ; and mind our compliments to your brother Sandy, who we hope to see
when he is at leisure.

"I hope Lady Jane Home and Mrs. Ratterie and
you will continue your acquaintance. They are sensible good people both of them ; their cleverness in
conversation, and little turn to railerie, has given
them some enymies, but every body that knows them
as I do, must like them and will be their friends ; for
their smartness is more for funn than mischief, but
every body has not good nature enough to understand
them on the right side. A long long intimacie makes
me speak from experience of their merits, and the
longer you know them you will have the better opinion of them. I assure you I have not failed in
recommending you to them.

"I remember, when here, you mentioned about rideing cloaths, and I have made inquirie what has the
preference amongst the young ladys that are really
riders. I find it is a plain cloth with a small rope or
twist of gold or silver, for tho' the white fustion is
cool and pretty for summer they soon loose their good
looks, and to have as manny as to wash other, which
is the way necessary, comes to more expense than the

price of the plain cloath one. If I hear of any body
that wants a maid I shall certainly not forget Mrs.
Glase's friend. The character you gave me of her, and
the good esteem the world allows her, shall always
make me very willing to do anything that is obliging
to Mrs. Glass, and I shall thank you for puting it in
my power. You tell me of another strong claim to
my civillitys, in being related to the Sinclair family,
for I assure you I am as clanish as if I had been born
be-north the Grampion hills.

" I have returned the pretty patterns. They are
very neat and well done. I have keept a very little
bit of each, in case of any further whims about this
said triming.

" Now, dear Nell, adieu, and bellieve me ever your
sincere friend,   M : MORAY.

" Now if my two good friends takes more libertie
with you than would come in the way of strangers,
remember it is in and through me, for I always think
young folks the better of being in an intimate state
with elder folks than themselves, even though they
do not spare their complexions sometimes.

" If your flower-maker has any flowers on hand
that you think would suit my wild taste, I will be
glad to purchase a few. You may send me a sight of
them by the carrier, and the prices, for the incourage-
ment of industry."

XIX. GENIAL LETTERS.

ONE of the Presbyterian ministers of Elgin was such an enemy to keeping holidays that he searched houses, to prevent the owners from having a Christmas goose—to this Sir Harrie alludes. Mess Jon was probably the Episcopalian clergyman.

" Mr. ARCHIBALD DUNBAR,
      " off Thunderton, att Elgin.

"INNES, *Decr.* 23, 1702.

" DEAR ARCHIE,—I am not so greatt a fooll as to make ffeasts that wise men may eat them, nor yet so greatt a presbeterian but I can eatt a leg of a goose, and play at umber on yool-day. If you will come out here on Thursday's night, the doctor and you and I shall be as merry as we can, and if you bring Mess Jon with you to be ffool in the ffamilie, and make us laugh, you shall have a revenge off your lost fifteen shillings, and mightily oblidge, your obliged friend and humbell servant,   HARRIE INNES.[1]

" Send me your news by this days post.

[1] The Duke of Roxburghe is the direct male descendent of Sir Harrie. The hospitalities of Innes have been transferred to Floors.

" If you have any commands ffor Edinburgh, I am to send ane expresse which will be dispatht this night."

John Forbes, of Culloden, elder brother of the cele- brated President, was familiarly known as "Squire Bumper."

"*Sept.* 20*th*, 1705.

" DEAR THOUNDERTOUN,—I pray God be with you and your distrest lady, which I am fforced to do in this maner, being straitnd with tyme—tyde being be- twixt nyne and ten aclock. If you intend I should have your horse att the pryce I offered you last night, viz., a ginea dead arles, and my note ffor ffive hunder marks, payable att Whitesenday seventeen hundred and six, you may take my horse ffrom my boy and send doun yours to Leith, and if other wayes you desyre to dispose off him I wish you good markett, being your intyrely affectionate comrade and most humble servant, Jo. FORBES."

"INNES, *August* 1*st*, 1711.

" DEAR ARCHIE,—Culloden and I bid you heartyly welcome home.

" I thank you ffor your care of my letters, but wish you had made this your rod. Were my side reco- vered of my horse-fall, and my own, I had seen you

this day ; which also hindered my seeing your children when I designed.

" Colloden and I do most earnestlie beg you to take
your morning drams with us here Monday morning ;
and it is hard to say but either, or both of us, will
convey you a pairt of the way home, if both be able,
and perhaps the whole length home.   In the mean-
tyme satisfie us if there be a battle in fflanders, or
not, because it is so told, and, if so, who won, and
what other of news you please.   We are, dear Archie,
your obliged and affectionatt comrades to serve you,

" HARRIE INNES.

JO. FORBES."

William Dunbar, W.S., was a younger son of the
Laird of Boath, Nairnshire.

" To ALEXANDER DUNBAR, Esquire, Advocate,
    " To the care of Rhind and Warren,
        " Merchants, London.

"BOATH, Wednesday, 7th September 1768.

" Tho' I have been days in the country, yet an un-
interrupted course of visits and card-playing has put
it beyond my power to pay that tribute which I owe
to you, not only in virtue of a solemn promise, but
from the ties of gratitude and esteem which I shall
always endeavour to hold sacred.   It is true, indeed, I
might have scrawled a few lines in the interval of a
rubber when I happened to cut out, but I know that

would not be such a letter as you would expect; besides, it would be shamefully overrated at the value of
tenpence. I am afraid even this one will fall under
that condemnation, for I am not vain enough to
imagine that anything, the produce of this Northern
clime, can so much as engage the attention of a gentleman encircled by the splendid allurements of a
capital where pleasure springs under every footstep.
My sober ambition is to know that you pass your
time agreeably, and allow me to assure you I shall
feel very sensible satisfaction to learn that your purposes are fully answered.

" Mr. Cosmo Gordon, Jock Innes, and I travelled
together. I parted from them at the Bridge of Dy,
and prosecuted my intentions of joining my friends at
Kemnay. During the course of our journey I made
repeated observations of the learned counsel, which
would not be in any degree new to you, as they were
only such as I have often heard you remark formerly.
They confirmed my opinion that the designation in
the list of jurymen was no less true than droll. The
remaining part of my journey furnished nothing
worthy of notice, except Miss Mary Burnett, who, I
will venture to say, would be accounted handsome
even at Vauxhall or ' Raneleigh'—(I fear not right
spelled). At Hatton Lodge I fell in with young
Knockando, accompanied by an old college acquaintance of your's called Bean. This gentleman went out

to India in 1761, and is already said to have accumu-
lated ten thousand pounds sterling; notwithstanding
of which I thought him a puppie, and d—— forward
in prating. We found the noble family at Cullen
House emerged from the cloud of melancholy which
lately hung upon them. Lord Deskford appeared to
me like the ghost of Tenducie—tall, meagre, feeble.
Were he like the Italian in every respect, Te Deum
might be sung in *Erse* along the banks of the Spey;
but that prospect seems to have evanished, as it is
thought a short while will restore the young Lord to
health and vigour, after which it will be necessary
that he marry. I had the honour of a second inter-
view with our Advocate-Depute on my getting on to
Fochabers. I touched the lips of his fair sisters, and
ate some very good bread and butter. Dr. Levingston
of Aberdeen is in attendance at Gordon Castle to introduce to the world a young Marquis or a Lady,
perhaps both—for the Duchess is prodigiously big.
The young Commissary and his Clerk were the only
acquaintances I saw at Elgin. Many enquiries were
made about you. Chittock's fame and intrepidity
were extoled at great length by the young Provost,
and he said his father had no doubt but that your's
would be restored to perfect health, and return to
pass his days in tranquility at Duffus.

　" I saw George Ogilvie, Advocate, at Nairn yesterday, on his way to Inverness. There is no other

youngster upon this Circuit, and for ought that I can learn, very little business. All the prisoners made their escape from the jail at Inverness, so the Lord Pitfour will have the trouble only of ffugitation, and reprimanding the magistrates. Ogilvie told me there would be one trial on criminal letters, where it seems the prisoner had been liberate on bail. He is to figure away to the jury, and begged I might go with him, but I declined. Never were such speeches, it is said, as this young counsel made about the end of last Session, and yet you or I heard nothing of them, although then upon the spot. However, they were echoed to the North by the Lords Kaims and Pitfour in letters to Lord Finlater. His Lordship asked me at Cullen what I thought of Mr. Ogilvie's appearance. I answered I had heard of no public appearance, but defending his *annexa*. My Lord looked surprised. I was no less so. How the hero behaves at Inverness shall be the subject of another letter, as I intend to go in to-morrow.

" I hope it is quite unnecessary for me to assure you with what readiness I would execute any commands you may have in this or the eastern part of the country. I have time and horses at command, and you know I will not be wanting in inclination. Believe me to be, with the greatest regard and affection, my dear Sandie, your sincere friend and obedient servant,   WILL. DUNBAR.

" *N.B.*—Might you not give me an order for one or other of your pointers ? I will not make a demand on Brodie, not even for the privilege of shooting. Pray can you lend him seven thousand pounds sterling, at four and a half per cent. ? 'apply to Robert Donaldson, writer, Covenant Close.'—*Ed: Ev: Courant.*"

Sir William Gordon endeavoured to prevent the proprietor of an adjoining estate, who was also a wealthy London merchant, from draining part of the Loch of Spynie :—

" Sir ALEXANDER DUNBAR,
        " of Northfield, Bart.

                    " GORDONSTOWN, *8th June* 1782.

" DEAR SIR,—Be so good to inform me how it fares with you and the Lady. It will be some time before I recover from my late fatigue, so as to be able to pay you and her Ladyship my personal respects. But, if I live, I am determined it shall not be full three years.

" I have at last read over the proof, and am obliged to allow our friend, the bailie, all possible merit as a partisan in the predatory war, which he has had the conduct of, and in which, had not Providence been upon our side, I plainly perceive my Regulars must have been totally discomfitted, both from the natural difficulty of the ground, and their not having so thorough a knowledge of the country. Indeed, by

my health not permitting me to be present, my opo-
nents had every advantage they could have wished or
desired, though after all, I think it will not much
avail them, as the main points I go for, are fully established, and I cannot help thinking that Mr. —— will
find, in the end, that before he broke ground he should
have sent me a friendly summons to capitulate, in
which case I would have surrendered upon much
easier terms than can now be expected.

> ' I grant his foreign imports ffresh and fair,
> What I complain of is his homespun ware—
> His manners, principles, and length of ear,
> Which make him prey on those he should revere.
> To take a goose or duck were no great matter ;
> But this marauder steals both land and water.
> If such a fox your toils should come within,
> Would you not hang him first—then stuff his skin ?
> When thus prepar'd—he—we a nuisance call—
> Might serve to grace the portal of a hall.'

" I thought these few lines, which I lately found in
an old manuscript, were not inapplicable to the present subject, and might help to warm and divert my
friend in one of his cold fits.

" Wishing to know that Lady Dunbar is on the way
of recovery, I remain, dear Sir, your most obedient
and much obliged humble servant,

"WILL. GORDON."

Glowing description :—

" Sir ALEXANDER DUNBAR, Bart.

" BANFF, 29th *Decr.* 1783.

"SIR,—Mr. Reid called on me this evening with a
proposal of letting you see my violin, and on terms of
parting with her. I have sent her, per the bearer,
from the consideration that it were pity not to gratify
a musical genius of your extensive knowledge with
such an easy granted request.

" She is an old one—Italian—and the original price,
as I am informed, was ten pounds. She has been well
cared for. The breast has been off, from what cause I
know not—but ever since, she has sustained a very
good character. From Wales I got her for another
violin, and a considerable balance, as he stood in need
of a little ready cash. Perhaps the new tenor and
treble may not (merely on account of the newness) at
first touch emit such a fine body of tone, but a few
strokes of the bow will remove that inconveniency.
The counter has never pleased me like the counter I
first got her with, which was very mellow. We have
no assortment of strings here. Her present counter
is mis-sized, but you can try her with another size if
you have any by you.

" I shall say nothing more as to the merits of the
instrument ; your own knowledge of music will perfectly well enable you to ascertain her value ;—and
tho' I would not choose to part with her under value,

yet if you wish to have her, you would let me know
what you would willingly give for her. I own she
came to me under her original value, but not a very
great deal ; and as I esteem her for being well-
toned and mellow, as well as for being easy to stop,
you may believe I will be the more reluctant to part
with her.

"I fancy you play the psaltery too, Sir. I have got
an uncommon (I believe I may call it new invented,
as I was the first in this country who thought of getting such an instrument made,) instrument, which, by
partaking both of the nature of the violin and psaltery,
becomes a kind of psaltero-violin. Its strings are
therm—tuned thus—

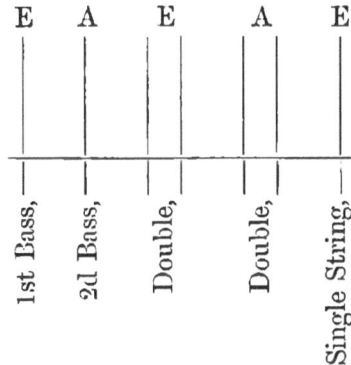

E	A	E	A	E
1st Bass,	2d Bass,	Double,	Double,	Single String,

and is capable of producing a most prodigious variety
of chords, owing to the manner of compounding the
open strings.

"Now, Sir, you may please let me hear from you
per the bearer ; and I am, Sir, most respectfully, your
most obedient humble servant,   WILL. SMITH."

XX. YOUNGER SONS.

BEFORE the acquisition of our Indian Empire, and
our numerous Colonial conquests, it was thought by
no means derogatory to the dignity of families that
younger sons should enter into trade, and even perform, in some instances, manual labour.

Sir Ludovic Gordon, the Premier Baronet of Scot
land, as grandson paternally of the Earl of Sutherland,
was a direct descendant of the Princess Margaret,[1]
daughter of King Robert the Bruce :—

"Thir Indentors, made at Edinburgh the ffour-
teenth day of August Jajvic thre scoir twell yeirs
(1672), in themsells proports, and beirs leill and south-
fast witnessing that it is appoynted, agreed, and
ffinallie ended betwix the pairties following—to wit,
Mr. Robert Blaikwood, merchand burges of Edinburgh,
on the ane pairt, and George Gordoun, sone laufull to
Sir Lodovick Gordoun of Gordounstoun, Knight Bar-
ronett, with the speciall advyse and consent of his said

---

[1] The Princess married William, fourth Earl of Sutherland.

father, and the said Sir Lodovick Gordoun for himselff, and takand the burthen in and upon him for the said George Gordoun, and as cautoner and suertie for him for fullfilling of his pairt of thir present indentors underwretten, on the other pairt; in maner, forme, and effect as efter followes : That is to say, the said George Gordoun, with advyce and consent forsaid, is become, and, be the tenor heirof, becomes bound preuteise and servand to the said Mr. Robert Blaikwood to his airt and trade of merchandizeing, and that for all the dayes, space, yeirs, and terms of ffyve yeirs nixt and immediatly following his entrie therto, which shall be, and, God willing, begin the day and date hereof; dureing the which space the said George Gordoun binds and obleisses him, be the faith and trueth of his bodie, to serve the said Mr. Robert Blaikwood, his master, leallie and truelie, night and day, holyday and workday, in all things godlie and honest : and shall not know nor heire of his said masters skaith dureing the space forsaid, but shall reveill the samen to him and remied it to his power; and shall not absent himselff from his said masters service, at noe tyme dureing the space contained in thir indentors, without the speciall lisence of his said master had and obtained to that effect ; and if he does in the contrar, he obleisses him to serve his said master tuo dayes, for ilk daye's absense, efter the expyreing of thir indentors ; and shall refund, content, and pay to his said

master tuo pennies for ilk pennies loss that his said
master beis damnified, in his default, dureing the space
forsaid : and if it shall happen the said George Gordoun (as God forbid) to comitt the filthie crymes of
fornicatione or adulterie at any tyme during the space
conteined in thir indentors, in that case he faithfullie
binds and obleisses him to serve the said Mr. Robert
Blaikwood, his master, thre yeares, efter the expyreing
of thir indentors, in the same estate as if he wer bound
prenteise as said is : and for the said George Gordoun
his lawfulie remaineing and fullfilling of the premisses,
the said Sir Lodovick Gordoun, be the tenor hereof,
becomes bound and obleissed as cautoner and suertie
for him.   Lykeas the said Mr. Robert Blaikwood faithfullie binds and obleisses him to ken, learne, teatch,
and instruct the said George Gordoun, his prenteise, in
all the poynts, pratiqes, and ingynes of his said airt and
trade of merchandizeing, and that alsweill without as
within the cuntrie ; and shall not hyd nor conceill no
poynt nor pratiqe thereof from him, but shall doe his
utter and exact diligencie to caus him conceave, learne,
and understand the samen, in so far as he is able or
can doe himselff; and shall furnish and sustain the
said George Gordoun, his prenteise, suffecentlie at bed
and boord dureing the space mentioned in thir indentors, according to the estate of siclyke ane prenteise ;
and also the said Mr. Robert Blaikwood binds and
obleisses him to send, or take with him, the said

George Gordoun, his prenteise, once to London and once to Holland befor the expyreing of thir indentors, and that upon the said Mr. Robert his own proper charges and expensses. For the whilks causses the said Sir Lodovick Gordoun has instantlie contented payed, and thankfullie delyvered, to the said Mr. Robert Blaikwood, in name of prenteise ffie with the said George Gordoun, ane certane soum of money, wherof the said Robert grants the recept and holds him weill satisfied, and, for him and his airs and successors, exoners and simplie discharges the saids Sir Lodovick and George Gordouns, their airs, executors, and all uther whom it effeirs, therof for ever, renuncand all exceptiones whatsomever in the contrar. And finallie, the said Mr. Robert Blaikwood binds and obliesses him to book the said George Gordoun his prenteise in the Gild Court books of Edinburgh, within fourtie dayes nixt efter the date of thir indentors, under the paines conteined in the act and ordor of the Counsill, of date the first daye of ffebruary 1656 yeirs. Consenting thir presents be insert and registrat in any register compitent, that letters of horning on sex dayes, and other executione neidfull in forme as effeirs, may pas therupon, and for that effect constituting   thir prors. In witnes wherof (wrettin be Thomas Pirrie, writter in Edinburgh,) both pairties have subscryved thir presents with their hands, day, month, place, yeare of God forsaid, befor thir witnesses, Mr. Robert Gordoun, brother-german to the said Sir Lodovick Gordoun, John Trotter, merchand burges of Edinburgh, and the said Thomas Pirrie.

R. BLACKWOOD.
GEORGE GORDON.

" Ro. Gordone, *witnes.*
To. Trotter, *wittnes.*
T. Pirrie, *witnes.*"

LODV: GORDON.

From his not having served the three additional years, we infer that it did not "happen the said George Gordoun to comitt the filthie crymes" mentioned in the "indentors."

" Be it keind to all men by these presents that wheras the within written Georg Gordon did truly and faithfully serve me the whole time of the within written indentors, and perform the haile oblessments therof; therforr wit me to haive exonared and discharged (lykas I be the tennor heirof exonors and discharges) him of the said indentors, and Sir Lodovick Gordon of Gordonstoun, his father and cautoner, for now and ever. In witnesse wherof I have wretten and subscryved this, at Edinburgh, this fourth of December Jajvic seventie eight yeares (1678).

" R. BLACKWOOD."

Guineas and Cadboll were two of the principal families of the Macleod clan. The Dumbreaks long possessed the estate of Orton on the banks of the Spey.

" To Mr. ARCHIBALD DUNBAR,

"of Thundertoun, at Duffus.

"INVERNES, 28th Nov. 1712.

" SIR,—The bearer, William M'Leod, a joiner to his imployment, burges and frieman heir, that lived at this place about a year and half, following his trade, that served his apprentesship at Edinburgh, and thrie yeares a journeyman at London; he is a brother of Donald M'Leod of Geanies, and coosein german of Catbolls, and, as I understand, is in tearmes of mariadge with our coosin Christian Dumbrek, and goes cast your lenth of purpose to have your consent and countenance, and proposes nothing else, as he tells me, but a good wyfe and friends by her. This is all I have to trouble you with, not doubting of your civilitie to him; and, with the tender of my own and spouse's humble duty to yourself and children, I remain, Sir, your affectionat cooseine and obleidged servant, JA. DUNBAR."

THE export and import trade of the North of Scotland, about two hundred years ago, was very considerable. An Elgin firm, consisting of Sir James Calder of Muirtown, William King of Newmiln, and others, carried on a most extensive business. So early as 1676, we find them exporting bear and malt to Bordeaux and Drontone, and from thence importing large quantities of wine and brandy—the postage connected with the outward and homeward voyage amounting to twenty-five shillings sterling. Good bills on Elgin and Inverness were, in 1692, remitted from Rotterdam, where "our country product, viz., best Aberdeins pladin, Elgin pladin, allmed lether, salmond, tallow, winter foxes, otters, old brass, and old copper," were generally in demand. To more fully elucidate the business transactions of the firm, we give copies of several of their papers.

Charter party, 1685 :–

" At Findhorn, the eighten day off February Jajvjc. and eightie fyve yeirs (1685). It is condescended

betxt the parties ffolouing, that is to say, be James
Calder of Muirtoun, and William King, marchants in
Elgin, on the one pairt, and James Young, master off
the Lodouick and William off ffindhorne, on the other
pairt—That is to say, the said James Young ffraughts
his shipp equalie betxt them, and oblidges him with al
conwenient diligence to receive aboard the said ship,
from them, her full loading off bear, within the harbor
off ffindhorn, wher she now lyes, and to transport and
delyver the samen at the port off Roterdam, wind and
weather serving (sea hazard onlie excepted), to them
or ther order, and to have his said shipp sufficientlie
furnished with able companie, and all other necessaries
for such shipp and voyadge : ffor the which cause the
saids James Calder and William King oblidges them
not onlie wholie to load the said shipp, but also to cause
pay the said master the soume off eighteen styviers,
Hollands mony, as ffraught ffor each boll that shall be
shipped at ffindhorn, and that within fourtie eight
hours imediatlie after livering the said loadine off bear
at Roterdam, with avarage and petie poilotage according to custome at sea, with thretie gilders in name off
Cap. Lacken ; and the said marchants to pay six punds
Scotts, as demurage, for ilk day the said shipp shall
happn to be detained, longer than the number of
days at both the saids ports, ffor loadning and livering ; and finalie, both parties oblidges them to perform
this present agreement, each one to other, under the

K

falyie of tuo hundredth punds Scots mony, to be payed be the partie falyier to the partie performer or willing to perform above performance of the premises ; and, for the more securitie, all parties consents to the re-grestration heiroff in the book of Concell and Session, or anie other Judge books competent within this kingdom, that letters and execucion may pass heirupon, in form as effirs, and to that effect constitutes

our prors.

In witnes wheroff, we have subscrived thir presents (writen be William Rhind, marchant in Elgin), day, yeir, and place above writen, beffor thir witness, William Calder, brother-german to the said James Calder, and James Fenton, Balzie in ffindhorne.

"J. YOUNG.
JAMES CALDER.
"William Calder, *witnes.*   W. KING.
Ja. Fenton, *witnes.*"

The date of the "accompt" is 1694 :--

"Accompt of all the beeff, tallow, and hydes bought be Sir James Calder of Muirtoune, William King, Provost of Elgin, Alexander Brodie of Tillieburies, and James Young, skipper in Elgin, from Baillie Calder in Weeck of Caithess, and others there, with the

ffraughts, custome, and all other expenses debursed
therupon, as follows :—

	libs.	sh.	d.

ffrom Robert Calder, Baillie in Weeck, and
his partners, conforme to contract, the
number of three hundred and twenty barrells of beeff, and fyve barrells of tongues,
at nineteen merks the barrell, . . . 4116 13 04
ffrom them, twenty-nine barrells of tallow,
weighing, nett, six thousand three hundred
and twentie two pound weight, . . 0885 01 04
ffrom them, ffyve hundered and thirtie ffyve
salt hydes, at three pounds twelve shillings
the peece, ... 1926 00 00
Bought on our accompt be Thomas Calder,
two hundred and nine salt hydes, which,
according to his particular accompt, extends
to the soume, ... 0779 12 00
Also bought be him, fourteen and a half barrells of tallow, weighing three thousand ane
hunder and twentie three pound nett, at
fourteen pounds ten shillings per cwt., as
per particular accompt, extends to . . 0452 16 10
To money deburst for ffraughts, salt to be
pickle, girds, custome, cocquet, and enterie-
money, as per particular accompt, the soume
of fyve hundered eighteen pound, fyfteen
shillings, ten pennies, 0518 15 10

Summa of the first pennie of the beeff, tallow,
and hydes, with the charges and deburse-
ments for, except the ffraught for the hydes
which are not as yet come over, extend to
the soume of . 8678 19 04"

An extensive order :—

"Commissione, from Sir James Calder of Muirtoune, William King of Newmilne, Provost of Elgine, Alexander Brodie of Tillieburies, and ane ffourth partner, to Alexr. Carstairs, merchant in Roterdame, and John and William Gordones, merchants in Camphire, for buying and sending home the goods[1] after following. Given at ffindhorne, the 24 ffebruary 1694 :—

1mo, Forty barrells soapp, whereof twenty in aughteendales, and twenty in ffirkins.

2do, 300 lb. small powder, in ten casks, beeing 30 lb. in each cask.

3io, Ane kinkine tarmaluk, for dying; lykewise, three casks of ombrdd mather, free of gust, about seven hundred weight the peece.

4to, Two barrells piliegrest; lykewise, four hogsheads alme; but care that none of it be dustie alme.

5to, Four barrells blew reasines; two hundered weight currens, in one or two casks, as you think fitt.

6to, Four ffirkins ffigs; two casks prunes. If the aforesd fruits be not speciall good, send none of them.

7mo, 400 lb. pannbrass, weell sorted, about 70 lb. weight in every matt.

8to, 1000 lb. good green ginger.

9o, 600 lbs. mellis suggar, 200 lbs. refinade, packt in two casks, with anize seeds, of which we desyre 600 lb., and what is not in amongst the suggar, lett be packt in the cask where the pepper is.

10o, 200 lb. gad steill; and the value of two hundred gilders best of fflott indigo, in two small casks.

[1] The gross value of the "goods" amounted to five thousand three hundred and thirty-four pounds, eight shillings, and eightpence sterling.

11o, 100 lbs. black piper, beeing packt up in ane bagg; 6 lb. mace, in three small baggs; 6 lb. cannell, in three matts.

12o, 002 lb. cloves; 2 lb. nutmuggs. Pack the black piper, mace, cloves, nuttmugs, and cannell in ane cask, with some suggar and anise seeds.

100 lb. rice, such as uses to come to this countrey, packt in ane cask.

A hundered thousand countrey needles, of the greatest sort, about fourteen styvers the thousand.

Three peece muslen, wherof one fyne stript about thirty six gilders the peece; one peece at thirty; another at twenty-eight.

50 lb. weight camels' hair, wherof 30 lb. black, 15 lb. white, and 5 lb. gold colour.

Four peeces mowrning creapp, about four styvers the Dutch elne.

Five dozen hatts of the newest fashione, and of severall sizes, all black; the one half about three gilders the peece, and the other half at three gilders three styvers; all packt in ane tuht cask.

ffour alms white Renish wine, not exceeding seventeen dollars per alme; and lett it be of the last yeares vintage.

Six hogsheadds good clear hard Seck, of ane good bodie, in strong casks.

Six casks tobacco, that is good and fresh for this countrey's use, in the largest cask yee can; have none of them under nine hundred weight.

ffour barrells single pypes.

Mynd the ffrench wynes, according to our letter.

Mark all the casks and matts thus, WK, numbred that we may know, be the number, what goods is in each cask. Wee doe earnestlie intreat you send us good casks, that they may be off use to us afterwards."

Printed bill of lading, 1694. It is embellished by a shield, with armorial bearings, below which notice is given that such forms were "Sold at Rotterdam by the Widdow of Mathijs Wagens, dwelling upon the Blaeck by the Fischmarket:"—

"Shipped, by the grace of God, in good order and wel conditioned, by [William King, Sir James Calder, and Partners[1]], in and upon the good ship called the [Ludovick and William of ffindhorne], whereof is master, under God, for this present voyage, [James Young], and now riding at ankor in the [river of ffindhorne], and, by God's grace, bound for [the harbour of Camphere in Zealland], to say [the number of three hundred and nyneteen barrels of beeff, ffyve barrells of tongues, and fourtie three and a half barrells tallow], being marked and numbred as in the margent, and are to be delivred in the like good order and well conditioned, at the aforesaid port of [Camphere in Zealland], the danger of the seas only excepted, unto [the said Sir James Calder and William King], or to [thir] assignes, he or they paying fraight for the said goods, [according to the charter partie], with primage and avarage accustomed. In witnesse whereof, the master or purser of the said ship hath affirmed to three bils of lading, all of this tenor and date, the one of which three bils being accomplished,

---

[1] The words within brackets were written.

the other two to stand void. And so God send the
good shipp to her desired port in safety, Amen.
Dated in [ffindhorne, the 20 day of February 1694
yeares]."

The Custom-dues on wine and salt :—

" I, William King, Provist of Elging, grant me be
thir presents to be justlie resting and owing to Sir
Archbald Muire of Thorntoun, Sir John Shaw of Grin-
ock, and John Howstone, younger of that Ilke, principal tacksmen of his Majesties Customes and foraigne
excise, the soum of two thousand one hundred and
sixtie eight punds Scots monie, and that for the excise
of five hundred and sixtie boals bay salt, Lithgow
meassur, and twentie nine tuns clarat and white wine,
imported be me, and partiners, in the Prophat Jonas of
Lunden, Cristian Andersone, master, from St. Abastins,
conform to my two subscrived entries, for cargo and
portadge, att ffindhorn the seventeeth of June last,
which sowme of two thousand one hundred and sixtie
eight punds Scots fforsaid, I bind and obledge me, my
aires, exektors, and successors, to content, pay, and
deliver to the saids Sir Archbald Muire of Thorntoun,
Sir John Shaw of Grinok, and John Howston, younger
of that Ilke, their aires, exektors, or asigns, or to John
Crauford, the collecter att Invernes, precislic againe

the seventeen day of December nixt to come, anno
present, but longer delay, with the sowme of seven
hundred and twentie punds, monie forsaid, of liquidat
expenss in caise of failie, and annualrent after the said
tearm of payment during the nott payment therof;
and, for the more security, I consent to the registration
hierof in the books of Theassurie and Exchakquer, or
other books competent within this kingdom, to have
the strength of ane decreet of the Lords, or other
Judges thereoff, therto interpond, in form as affeirs,
and to that effect constetuts

my prors. In witness
wherof, I have subscrived thir presents at ffindhorn,
the fourth of Jully one thousand six hundred and
nintie five years, befor thir witnesses, John Badon,
indweller in ffindhorne, and Patrick Comrie, surveyor
of the precinct of Invernes, and wryter hierof,

" WM. KING.

" J. Badon, *witness.*
Patrick Comrie, *witness.*"

XXII. DRINKING-SONG.

WILLIAM SUTHERLAND, merchant in Elgin, well
known in the North, early in the eighteenth century,
under the cognomen "Bogsie," had his virtues suitably
immortalized by the comic muse. "Bogsie" and his
brother merchants were evidently men of classical
education.

"Viri Humani, Salsi, et Faceti Gulielmi Sutherland, Multarum Artium et Scientiarum, Doctoris
Doctissimi, Diploma :—

UBIQUE gentium et terrarum
    From Sutherland to Padanarum,
From those who have six months of day,
Ad caput usque bonæ Spei ;
And farther yet, si forte tendat,
Ne ignorantiam quis pretendat,
We Doctors of the merry meeting,
To all and sundry do send greeting :
Ut omnes habeant compertum,
Per hanc præsentem nostram chartam,
Gulielmum Sutherlandum Scotum,
At home per nomen Bogsie notum,
Who studied stoutly at our College,
And gave good specimens of knowledge.

In multis artibus versatum,
Nunc factum esse Doctoratum.
Quoth PRESES, strictum post examen,
Nunc esto Doctor, we said Amen.
So to you all hunc commendamus
Ut juvenem quem nos amamus,
Qui multas habet qualitates
To please all humours and ætates.
He vies, if sober, with Duns Scotus,
Sed multo magis, si sit potus,
In disputando just as keen as
Calvin, John Knox, or Tom Aquinas
In every question of theologie.
Versatus multum in trickologie,
Et in catalogis librorum
Frazer could never stand before him,
For he, by page and leaf, can quote,
More books than Solomon ev'r wrote.
A lover of the mathematicks
He is, but hates the hydrostaticks,
Because he thinks it a cold study,
To deal in water clear or mudy.
Doctissimus est medicinæ,
Almost a Borehave or Bellini.
He thinks the dyet of Cornaro
In meat and drink too scrimp and narrow,
And that the rules of Leonard Lessius
Are good for nothing but to stress us.
By solid arguments and keen,
He has confuted Dr. Cheyne,
And clearly proved by demonstration,
That claret is a good colation,
Sanis, ægris, always better
Than coffee or tea, milk or water;

That chearfull company cum risu,
Cum vino forti, suavi visu,
Gustatu dulci, still has been,
A cure for hyppo and the spleen ;
That hen and capon vervecina,
Beef, duck and pasties, cum ferina,
Are good stomathicks, and the best
Of cordials, probatum est.
He knows the symptoms of the phthisis,
Et per salivam sees diseases,
And can discover in urina,
Quando sit opus medicina.
A good French night-cap still has been,
He says, a proper anodyne,
Better than laudanum or poppy
Ut dormiamus like a toppy.
Affirmat lusum alearum
Medicamentum esse clarum,
Or else a touch at three hand Umber,
When toil or care our spirits cumber,
Which graft wings on our hours of leasure
And make them fly with ease and pleasure.
Aucupium et venationem,
Post longam nimis potationem,
He has discover'd to be good
Both for the stomach and the blood ;
As frequent exercise and travel
Are good against the gout and gravel.
He clearly proves the cause of death
Is nothing but the want of breath,
And that, indeed, is a disaster,
When 'tis occasion'd by a plaster
Of hemp and pitch laid closely on
Somewhat above the colar bone.

Well does he know the proper doses
Which will prevent the fall of noses ;
Ev'n keep them qui privantur illis,
Ægre utuntur perspicilis.
To this and ten times more his skill
Extends, when he would cure or kill.
Immensam cognitionem legum
Ne prorsus hic silentio tegam,
Cum sociis artis greese his fist,
Torquebit illas as you list.
If laws for bribes are made, its plain,
They may be bought and sold again.
Spectando aurum now we find,
That Madame Justice is stone-blind;
So deaf and dull on both her ears,
The clink of gold she only hears,
Nought else, but a loud party-shout,
Will make her start or look about.
His other talents to rehearse,
Brevissime in prose or verse ;
To tell how gracefully he dances,
And artfully contrives romances ;
How well he arches and shoots flying—
Let no man think that we mean lying ;
How well he fences, rides, and sings,
And does ten thousand other things ;
Allow a line, nay, but a comma,
To each turgerent hoc diploma.
Quare ut tandem concludamus,
Qui brevitatem approbamus,
For brevity is always good,
Providing we be understood,
In rerum omnium naturis,
Non minus quam scientia juris,

Et medicinæ Doctoratum
Bogsæum novimus versatum ;
Nor shall we here say more about him,
But you may dacker if you doubt him.
Addamus tamen hoc tantillum,
Duntaxat nostrum hoc sigillum,
Huic Testimonio appensum,
Ad confirmandum ejus sensum,
Junctis Chyrographis cunctorum,
Blyth, honest, hearty, sociorum,
Dabamus at a large punch bowel,
Within our proper common school,
The twenty-sixth day of November,
Ten years, the date we may remember,
After the Race of Sherrifmuir,[1]
Scots-men will count from a black hour.
Ab omni probo nunc signetur
Qui denegabit extrudetur.

" Formula Gradus dandi :—

EADEM nos authoritate
    Reges memoriæ beatæ,
Pontifices et Papæ læti,
Nam alii sunt a nobis spreti,
Quam quondam nobis indulserunt,
Qua privilegia semper erunt
Collegio nostro safe and sound
As long's the earth and cups go round,
Te Bogsæum hic creamus,
Statuimus et proclamamus,
Artium Magistrum et Doctorem,
Si libet etiam Proffessorem ;

---

[1] The battle of Sheriffmuir was fought November 12, 1715.

Tibique damus potestatem
Potandi ad hilaritatem,
Ludendi porro et jocandi,
Et mœstos vino medicandi,
Docendi vera, commentandi,
Ad risum etiam fabulandi.
In promotionis tuæ signum
Caput honore tanto dignum,
Hac Hederā condecoramus ;
Ut tibi felix sit, oramus ;
Præterea in manum damus
Hunc calicem ex quo potamus
Spumantem generoso vino,
Ut bibas more Palatino :
Sir, pull it off, and on your thumb,
Cernamus supernaculum
Ut specimen ingenii
Post studia decennii.

" When he is drinking the chorus sings—

En calicem spumantem,
Falerni epotantem
En calicem spumantem
     Io, io, io.

" After he has drunk and turned the glass on his thumb, they embrace him and sing again—

Laudamus hunc Doctorem,
En fidum compotorem
Laudamus hunc Doctorem,
     Io, io, io.

"A COMPTE The Toune of Elgin since the eight of Apryl 1689.   Resting to Kenneth Mackenzie.

" ELGIN, *ij. off Janyr.* 1693.

Imprimis, the said day with Sir Robert Gordon, the Provost, and Balie ffiefe, ane chopin of seck and ane gill of brandy, ...	01	00	0
The which day, with the Provest and Balies, when ingadgeing Mr. John Mackean to serve at the school of Elgin, ane pynt of seck and ane gill of brandy, ...	01	18	0
The which day, with Mr. John Mackean at subscryving of ther take with him, to serve as schoolmaster at the Gramer school, ane pynt of claret, ane gill of brandy, a pennie for pyps, and T., ...	01	03	0
The 18 day, at the Cross, at the proclaming of King William and Queen Mary, Kinge and Queen of Scotland, four pynts of wyn claret, .	04	00	0
To fourteen glasses broke ther, . .	04	04	0
To thirteen pynts of wyn in the house,	13	00	0
To sixteen pynts at the toune's bonfier,	16	00	0
To eight glasses broke ther, ...	02	08	0
To four quarts when returned back to the Cross,	08	00	0
The 26 day, with Major Grahame, ane quart of wyn,	02	00	0

160   SOCIAL LIFE IN FORMER DAYS.

To ane quart ale, and ane oat bose for his
horse, ... 00 03 8

To ane half-muchkin of cinamon watters, . . 01 00 0

The first of May, with Captain Clevland, ane
pynt of wyn, ... 01 00 0

The 4th of May, with the Quartermaster, at the
wreating of the billets for horse and foot when
the Generall cam—thrie pynts of bire, . 00 06 0

The 15th day of May, to six chopins of mumbire,
with the Provest, Balies, and Sir Robert Gordone, ... 01 16 0

The 2d of Julie, with Balie ffieff, Balie Ogillvie,
and Clarke Andersone, and one of the comand-
ers that came express from the parliament to
the Generall and Collonell Leslie, ane pynt of
seck, ... 01 16 0

The 19th of September, at the makeing of
Major Eneas M'Kay burgis, to thre pynts of
seck, ... 05 08 0

To almonds and reasins, of each a pound, . . 01 10 0

To orang and lemon piels and cordecitron, of
each half a pound, . . . 01 12 0

To ane pynt of claret for the servants, 01 00 0

To two unces of wax for the bills, . . . 00 06 8

The 20th of Sept., with the Magistratts and the
Shireff-Depute, when the oath of alegence was
tendered, three chopins of seck, . 02 14 0

To the Sherriffe-Clarke, an Rex dollar, . . 02 18 0

At the making of Grant's childring, with ther
attendants, burgissis, sextin pynts and ane
chopin of secke, ... 29 14 0

The last of September, with the Magistrats and
severalls of the Toune's deacons, after the
Toune's mustering, ten pynts and ane chopin
of secke, 18 00 0

The 2d of October, with Major Æneas, after the
Magistrats see his troupe mustered, ane chopin
of seck, ...   01 00 0
To ane chopin of brandy, with foure unces of
syrope of clovegillifloor,   .   .   03 00 0

     *   *   *   *

The 7th of Apryl 1690, with Captain Balfure and
Captain Polwarte, when ordering ane troope
to goe to the country, to make room for tuo
troopes of Major Æneases that ware comeing
from Invernes, half muchkin of brandy and
ane unce of suggar, ...   00 07 0
The 30 of Julie, with the Provest, Balie King,
Mr. Moncrieff, and Mr. Broune, seven much-
kins off allacants, two muchkins of secke,   .   05 08 0

              Inde, in all,   £268 17 0

" The undersubscribers, presentlie Magistrats off
the brugh off Elgin, having seen and considered the
whole articles of the within acompt, dew to Bailzie
M'Kenzie, finds the same advanced to our predecessors by the said Bailzie M'Kenzie, at ther reasonabill
and just desire, and therefor orders William Rose,
our present Theasurer, to pay the same (amounting
to tuo hundreth and sextie-eight punds, seventeen
shillings Scots), to the said Bailzie M'Kenzie, betwix
this and the terme off Lambes next to come.

                  " WM. KING, *Provest.*

                  ROB. INNES.

                  JAMES STEWART."

" ELGIN, ij *off January* 1693.

We do not know for what offence Mrs. Young was publicly flogged :—

" WILLIAM ROSE, Threasurer.

" Pay to the toun's officers, for attending the sklaetters in repareing of the church, and for chargeing the toun's people to red the run of Tayock, and for guairding the Marshall at the whiping of John Young's woeman, fiftie-sax shillings Scots money.   As also giwe the Marshall twentie shillings Scots money, besyds what ye have advanced for tows to him for whiping Jon Young's woeman.   And theis are your warrand, given at Elgin 5 July 1693.

" Jo. RUSSELL.
ROB. INNES."

" Unto the Right Honourable the Provest, Baillies, and Councill of the Burgh of Elgin, the Petition of George Hay, Drummer in the said Burgh :

" *Humblie Sheweth,*

" That whereas your Honors' petitioner is stressed, and daily threatened to prison by certain, his creditors, ffor severall debts restand be me to them, such as housemealls and duties, &c. ; and nottour it is to your Honors that there is certain fees resting to me be your Honors, as serving the toune of Elgin in the station of a drummer for thir severall terms bypast,

and that your petitioner has noe otherway of living
nor defraying of debts but with the saids fees ; therefore, may it please your Honors to take some method
for ordring of my payment of a pairt of the saids
fees, ffor defraying of the saids housemealls, that your
Honors' petitioner may escape the danger of imprisonment and incarceration, wherewith I am daily threatened ; that your Honors' petitioner may be the more
encouraged to doe you service in tymes coming ; as
also, to order payment for reparation of the drum-
heads, broken on ffryday's night, by the rable of the
said burgh of Elgin, as is manifestly known to your
Honors. And your Honors' petitioner shall ever pray
for the weelfare and happines of your Honors in all
tym heiraftr.

"30 *Octr.* 1693.—The Counsell appoynts the supli-
cant to compt with the theserer, before Baillie Russell,
and to make report, the next counsell day.

"*Elgin, ij Dec.* 1693.—Baillie Russell reported, that
after compting with the supplicant, there is found
resting to him, preceding Mertinmas last, 1693, the
soum of fourtie-tuo pounds, eight shilling, four pennies,
which the theserer is appoynted to pay to him, and, in
tym coming, is appoynted pay to him eight pounds at
each quarteris end.
" ROBERT ANDERSON,
" *Clk. at Comand of the Counsell.*"

Services rewarded :—

"WILLIAM ROSSE, Threasurer.

"Pay the thretic shilling, ten pennies, that was
spent with the good-fellows that helped me, last night,
to aprehend men for our parte of the malitia that is
to be levied, and place it to Toune's accompt.   Given
under my hand, at Elgin, 26th ffebyr, 1694.

"Jo. RUSSELL."

"Unto The Right Honourable, Provest, Bailies, and
    Counsellers of the Brugh of Elgin, the Supplica-
    catione of Robert Kear, Alex. Young, Robert
    Spense, and James Nuckell, your Honors' Offi-
    cers:

    "*Humblie Showeth,*

    "That what fies your Honors ordaines for us we
ar not payed of it, nor have we nothing to live by ;
for we are ordered by your Honors to have our fies,
and we have gotten non of them, since Mertinmas was
a year ; and your honors knowes what truble we ar at
when sogers come to toune, for we are struckin and
beaten be ther officers, and are lyk almost to put us
to death, because we will not obey them how soon they
call to get them horse ; and the poor ones crayes out
aganes us lykwas, as we could helpe them.   Yet, not-

withstanding, we are geting nothing of our fies, nor of our stateter meals, nor so much as to buy shoues to our feet. So may it please your Honors to consider our steat and condisione, and to order to your poor suplicants that which is use and wount to them who shall alwayes pray for your Honors. Expecting your Honors' favourable answer.

"26 *Merch* 1649.—The Counsell orders the theserer to give the suplicants tuentie shillings, each one, with fourtein shillings Scots to the Marshall, extending in all to four punds, fourteen shillings Scots. Subscryved be order and at comand of the Counsell, be

"ROBERT ANDERSON, *Clk.*"

A musical treat :—

" WILLIAM ROSE, Dean of Gild of Elgin.

" SIR,—Give Alexr. Glass half ane crowne, for playing to the Magistrates in Measter Panton's companie the other night ; and this shall be your warrand. Elgin, 22d of Novr. 1694.

" JAMES STEWART."

Lossiemouth was purchased by the Town of Elgin, in the year 1698, from Brodie of Brodie.

"To the Right Honourable the Provost, Bailies, and Towne Council of Elgin, the Memorial and Representation of John Sinclair, Merchant there :

"*Humbly Sheweth,*

"That I was employed by the Towne Council to journey throw the Kingdom of Scotland, and collect what money could be hade, from parishes and privat persons, for the use of the harbour of Lossie, which task, tho' very toilsom and fatiguing, als well as prejudicial to my business and affaires at home, I undertook and performed ; but, to my great grief and surprize, I mett with worse treatment at my returne (by the malicious insinuations of designing invidious neighbours, who accused me as guilty of concealments in the money received), than I did in all my journey, and how farr their accusations were made good your Honors best know, who have given sentence against them on that head.

" The accompts, charge and discharge of all the money received and given out, having been given in to the Councill, and Comittee haveing perused the same, their report was given in and approved ; but since it hath pleased your Honors to make a review of the

said accompts, I humbly begg leave, for my own
defence and vindication, to justifie my conduct in
severall of the contraverted articles ; hopeing your
justice will agree therto, when I give reasonable evidence therfor.

"The first article contraverted, being the manten-
ance of the horse and servant at Elgin, it is answered
that the raesone of my stay at Elgin for some time
after the Council's Act, was not only the long time
which the writting of the letters took up, but also
ane excessive storme which for many weeks lay at
that time, and the horse, being bought immediatly
upon the Councils Act, behooved to be maintained
and to have a servant to take care of him, since it
is not to be supposed I could waite on him my selfe.

"To the nixt article of the boot of the horse ex-
changed, it is answered that the exchanging of the
horse was meer necessity and not choise, for, by sickness, he was turned so low he would not serve my
turne, wherby I behooved to have another. The
articles of the saddle, comb, brush, and clockbag,
these were, all, things which could not be wanted to
a journeying man, and are readie to be given in to
the Town's use, since they were bought and used for
their service.

"As to the servant's wages and cloathes, I answer
there was a necessity for mee to have a servant to
runn with me in such ane indirect journey, and I

could not but give servant-fees and cloathes, so that
I am perswaded upon second thoughts that article
will be found als resonable as any in all my accompt.

"As to the writting and number of the letters so
much quarrelled, I answer that that method was
judged be the, then, Magistrates to be the most proper way to address noblemen and gentlemen, and I
humbly conceive that the Magistrates signing these
letters, does sufficiently vindicate mee from any fault
in that point; and that I paid the whole money
charged, is clear by Alexr. Christie's recept; and since
I could not carry the whole number of letters my
selfe, was oblidged to send part therof be Alexander
Bawer, to Edinburgh, before mee.

"My charges at Banff was no wayes unnecessary,
being occasioned through the waiting on the Magistrates there, and staying for Mr. James Urquhart, who
was out of town.

"To the three quarreled articles of my stay at
Aberdeen, Glasgow, and Edinburgh, I answer as follows, viz. :—when I came to Aberdeen I made application to the Provost, who promised to aquaint the
Councill of my busines, first Councill day, but, before
that hapned, the oath of abjuration being enacted by
the Parliament did stumble severall of the members,
so that for severall weeks there was no meeting of
Councill, which forced mee to a tedious attendance
there; and when the Councill mett I could procure

nothing from their publick, but tooke another method
of accosting particular persons by the means of my
friends, and soliciting the Deacons, which consumed
a great deal of time ; and tho the event did not anser
expectation, it was not for want of dilligence and
aplication on my parte.

" My stay and time at Glasgow was occasioned by
the diversity of persons in publick trust, to whom I
behooved necessarly to address myselfe—namely, first,
to the Provost, who advised me to speak to each
Baillie and Councellor, which I accordingly did, and
my busines was not determined the first Council-day ;
nixt, I was advised by the Dean of Gild, in my application to the merchants house, to speak severally to
the members before they mett, which I did ; and,
lastlie, was advised by the Deacon Conviner to speak
to the Deacons old and new, who took very much time
to consult with their severall trades. So all this being
but preparative to the receiving of money, was the
most prudent and profitable way I could take, which
made the receiving of the money take up but litle
time afterwards.

" My stay at Edinburgh was occasioned by these
causes : first, it was three weeks' time before the
Council's order could be procured on the Chamber-
lan ; and, nixt, it was many dayes after, e're he payed
the money. I was at much paines, not only with the
Dean of Faculty and advocats, but with the trades,

as Mr. Couper and Deacon Anderson know very well;
and I left no stone unturned to come speed there, and,
I believe, Mr. Couper's letter, written to the Councill,
doeth sufficiently justifie my management while at
Edinburgh.

"It would be tedious to putt into writt the causes
of my stay at Montrose, Aberbrothock, and Dundee,
but I am ready to satisfie the Council by word of
mouth.

"My returne to Aberdeen was no wayes unnecessary; for, first, I could not cross the Cairn, for snow;
and, nixt, I received money from the Old Town Colledge and from my Lord Daskford, in my return that
way; as also, returned ane letter, from the Magistrates
of Banff, containing ane assignment to a collection
of theirs here; and some others subscreived my book,
which is yett to be seen.

"In generall, I answer, to the haill other articles, that
my charges were no wayes extrawagant, and are what,
I belive, few privat men could trawell cheaper; and if
it be considered what circles and turns I was obliged
to make in such a journey,—sometimes stopt by bad
weather, other times by sickness, and very often by
disappointments, and the confusion occasioned by the
Invasion, it will not be wondred the affair took up
so much time.

"And wheras the report of the Committee doeth
allow mee no charges, where I stayed at ane gentle-

man's house all night, I answer it is only stated for the
expense of that day, and that, whither I lived gratis at
night or not, I behooved to have something all day."

Mr. Robertson gave in his petition about the year
1715, we think :—

"To the Honourable the Provost, Bailies, and Councell
of Elgine, the Petition of Mr Wiliam Robertson,
Master of the Grammar School of Elgine :

" *Humbly Sheweth,*
" That I have been two severall presbytry dayes
conveined before the presbytry of Elgine, to subscribe
the Confession of Faith ; and, although at the first
presbytry, they allowed me a time to advise thereanent, yet, at the last presbytry, when I offered to
give in, in write, some scruples I had against severall
articles of the said Confession, which I could not comply with in point of conscience (and so till they should
satisfe me thereanent, I could not subscribe the said
Confession of Faith as the confession of my faith,
unless I had acted the part of a very great hypocrite),
they would not hear any of my scruples, nor enter
upon giving me satisfaction thernent, but would proceed as far as they could to depose me from being
schoolmaster. And seeing the presbytry of Elgine
are dealing more rigorously with me than with any of

my predecessors, schoolmasters here (neither of whom
ever subscribed the said Confession of Faith), and
that, I am informed, they are to use the utmost of
their power and law to get me deposed from being
schoolmaster of Elgin, therefore, and for preventing
of the Honourable the Magistrats and Councel of
Elgine their being at pains and expenses, in main-
taining and defending me in the possession of the
school of Elgin and benefices thereof, I do by these,
(with all deference and love to the Honourable Burgh,
and hail members thereof, and with regret that I
should have been placed amongst so good and worthie
a society, and yet oblidged to leave them when, in
conscience, I cannot comply with that which I think
not just) willingly and freely, from this date forward, renounce all interest and right I have or had, as
being schoolmaster of Elgin, to and in favours of the
Magistrats and Councell of Elgine and their successors
in office.

"May it therefore please your Honors to accept
of this my renounciation, and provide for
yourselves such a qualified schoolmaster as
may please the Burgh, and presbytry, of
Elgin ; and I ever am,
       "Right Honourable,
   "Your most obedient humble servant,
           "WM. ROBERTSON."

Free trade not approved of by the Elgin authorities :—

" To ARCHIBALD DUNBAR of Newton, Esq.

" ELGIN, 20*th* *March* 1738.

" SIR,—There is a complaint given in to us, by our
ffiscall and taxman of our pettie Customs, against the
fishers in Burghsea, Cousea, and Stotfield, for their
selling of fish without bringing the same to the fish
mercate of Elgin and making offer of them to the
Guildry ; and, as our predecessors in office have been,
time out of mind, by virtue of charters ffrom the
Crown, in use and wont to judge in such complaints,
either at Burghsea, Cousea, or Stotfield, so we have
wrote you this, to acquaint you that wee are to judge
in this complaint upon Wednesday next, the twenty-
second current, and to hear partys therupon at Burgsea,
when and where you will be very wellcome to see your
people gett justice.   We are, Sir, your most humble
servants, the Provost and Baillies of Elgin,

" JA : INNES.
JAMES STEPHEN.
WILL. ANDERSON.
GEORGE WILSON, Senior.
GEORGE WILSON, Junior."

Preventive measures :—

"To Sir Alex. Dunbar, Baronett, Duffus.

"Elgin, *7th January* 1783.

"Sir,—At the desire of the Magistrates, Council, and Incorporations of Elgin, and by their authority, I use the freedome of applying to you for your farms,[1] for the support of the inhabitants of Elgin, as there is appearance of scarcity in the country, and they wish to secure some supplys, and guard against any want. They therefore request, that you will say, nearly, what quantity of meal, bear, or oats you can spare them ; and the lowest price ; and your payments shall be good   I have the honour to be, for the magistrates of Elgin, Sir, your most obedient and most humble servant,   Geo. Brown, *Provost.*"

[1] The word "farms" often meant the grain paid as rent to the proprietor of an estate.

XXIV. INCORPORATED TRADES OF ELGIN.

THE tradesmen, or crafts, in Elgin, were long kept in a kind of serfdom by the Magistrates of the town. About the year 1675, however, they placed the regulation of their affairs in the hands of " Deacons" chosen by themselves :—

" For their much honored and very loving neighbours,
      The PROVOST and BAILZIES off INVERNESS.

                                    " ELGIN, 25th October 1675.

"MUCH HONORED AND LOVEING NIGHBOURS,—-Yours we received, dated the twentie-third of October instant, whairin you desyre the double of ane condiscendance, past betwixt the Counsell and the crafts of the said burgh, anent deaconrie ; as also, ane double of ane late condiscendance, and the back bond from them to the Counsell, upon their deportment to the Magistrates and Counsell. As for anser theirto, you shall know their was never any generall, or particular, condiscendance, betwixt us and them, that might doe prejudice to magistracie or gildrie in any burgh, far less to us. Only, in respect of the multiplicitie of craftsmen, inhabiting within this burgh, which are our

greatest numbers (we haveing no great trade of mer-
chandising be sea or land), we passied to lett them
have some order amongst themselves for regulating
of their crafts; who hitherto have carried so civillie,
that in all their just interests they have not been
troublesome to us, which is the only true accompt we
can give to you, much honored.

"Your loveing freinds and neighbours to serve yow,

"THE PROVOST AND BAILZIES OF ELGIN.

"Subscryved be our Clerk of Court at our command
(the Provest being unweill).

"JO. CHALMERS, *Clk.*"

"MUCH HONORED,—I am ordered to show you that
any articles of agriement that first was made with the
crafts, was shortlie therafter declared null, be reason
of some miscariages of theirs, and no agrement past
since that tyme.   JO. CHALMERS, *Clk.*"

Probably on account of the "miscariages," the crafts
were prevented from holding meetings where the Provost and Bailies had jurisdiction. The old kirk at the
Greyfriars, still a beautiful ruin, seems not to have
been repaired. It was converted into a mausoleum by
William King of Newmiln, who purchased the property
from the heirs of John Patersone, Bishop of Ross.

"Att Elgin the twentie-two day of ffebruary sixteen hundered and seventie-six yeares, in presence of
James Chalmer, younger, Deacon Conveener of the
Crafts of the said burgh, Gavin Watsone, deacon of
the glovers, Walter Smith, of the hamermen, Alexander Winchester, of the talzors, Thomas Geddes, of
the square wrights, John Purse, of the wyvers, and
Leonard Peddie, deacon of the shoomakers of the said
burgh.

" The said day the Deacon Conveener and deacons
of the crafts, above named, having obteined for themselves, ther respective crafts, and their successors,
ffrom the Right Reverend ffather in God, John, be
the mercie of the same, Lord Bishop of Rosse, heretable proprietar of that mannor-place, with the per-
tinents therof, lyand on the south syde of the burgh
of Elgin, comonlie called the Grayffriars, the libertie,
use, and attolerance of the old Kirk, pertining to
the said mannor, called the Grayfriar Kirk; with
power to the said crafts to build and repair the
same, or anie part therof, as they shall find niedfull,
and to make use of the same for their counsell and
meeting place, to all intents and purposes relating to
civill affaires onlie, as the attollerance granted be the
said reverend father to the said crafts, of the date the
fortenth day of ffebruary instant, in itselfe at more
length beares. And becaus the said Reverend ffather
has, out of his Lordship's meere kyndnes, favor, and

M

guidwill, granted the forsaid attollerance to the forsaid
crafts, therfore they obleise them, and ther sucessors,
to remove from, and leave void and red, the forsaid
kirk, called the Grayfricr Kirk, in alse guid case as
the same is at present, and that at any tyme or terme
it shall please the said reverend father, or his Lordship's aires, assinees, and sucessors, to require them to
that effect, upon ffourtie dayes premonitione.

" Extract out of the book of the crafts and ordi-
nances of the Deacon Conveener of the Crafts of
the burgh of Elgin.   .

" JA. CHALMER, *Conveener*.

JO. MUIRSONE, *Clk. to the Crafts of Elgin.*"

XXV. AN INVERNESS BAILIE'S ADVICE
AND ASSISTANCE.

CAUTION on the delicate subject of a projected matrimonial alliance :—

" For his Worthie, Estemed, Good ffrind,
" JAMES DUNBAR, Merchand inn Inverness.

" ROSEHALL, *this 7th of January* 1676.

"BAILIE JAMES,—Knowing ye are my frind, and presuming upon experince of former curtisis, I mak bold with yow to requist this favor off yow, in behallff of a frind of myn, that ye wold tak your owen secret and prudentiall way, to be trewly informd how James Robertson was lefft be his umqll (late) father ; what his father was ; whither what he had was his owen pur- chas, or lefft him by his parants ; iff he was in burding when he deied, aither by his owen contracting or cationre for frinds ; how he lefft his wyff and childring provoyded ; who exersd the ofcce off exccutor, and how it is dischargd ; how this yowng man hath de- mend himselff since his father's deth ; what childring ther is besyds himsellff ; what he was realy lefft to be his father, and how he hath improven it since his deth :

what his mother lyff-rents, and iff shee be secard and
satisfyd therin, and of the points off movabls; what
her nem is, and who's dochter; iff he hath beine in
sute of aney other befor, and what terms was offred or
desird; what his father, and also him scllff, folowd in
ordinary imployment and treding; what thos tenne-
ments ar that he hath, and how they ar imployd; what
ther rent may be worth besyd what is his mother's lyff-
rent; what is reported he hath besyds, and off his owen
purchas, and how he is to bestow it or lay it forth.
Bailie, its likly ye know much of this yer sellff, but
what ye know not, I pray you, in as grytt secresie as
can be, inform yer sellff, and be at pains to give me
ane particular acompt. I doe not quistion but the
young man mit be ingeneus to satisfye me him sellff,
and I could trust his owen word; but not thinking it
fitt to intertine him with interagats, and heaving the
happenes of yor good acquantance, resolvid, for my
owen and others, hir frinds, satisfaction, to lay the
truble heroff upon you; knowing, as ye are wise, will
wisly goe about it. Be intreted, lett no bodey know
off it; butt when ye heave perusd the leter burn it.
The young woman he seeks for is Lilias, my wyff's
sister's dochter, that is with, dear Bailie, yor afecteonat
reall frind,   WILL. BAILIE.

"Pray let not the berer know his erand to you, and
dispatch him so sune as posible. If ye wold favor me

with what ye know of his natural inclinations, his
Cristian way, and converse, ye wold grytly oblidg me,
for if that be good, some want as to the other wold be
the easir past."

Answer to the above :—

"INVERNES, 26th January 1676.

" SIR,—Yors I receaved, and has considered the contents therof. For answer, I cannot in ane short tyme
give yow so particullar and exack acompt of that gentleman as you desyre, onlie of what I know, I shall, as
followes :—1st, His father dyed one of the bailles of
this brugh, ane gentleman of good credit and respect,
and most of what he haid was his owin purchass, as I
am informed. 2d, As to his burdin when he dyed, I
heard litle or nothing of it, of his owin contracting ;
and as cationer for his freinds, I know no freind heir
he would engaidge for, but such as were in good conditione, so that he nor his could suffer no loss therby.
3d, As to the provisione of his wyf and children, and
how they were left, of that I cannot give ane accompt,
but, as I am informed, ther was no provisione to the
children but what James pleases ; and as to his wyfe,
she is infeft but in one tenement of land.   4thlie,
Know that James did enter det, and how it is discharged I know not. 5thlie, As to his cariadge since
his father's death, I know nothing, nor heard, but that
he has demend himself Christianlie and soberlie, and

is of ane frugall and vertous dispositione. 6thlie, As
to the children, they are two boys besyds him, but no
daughters. 7thlie, As to his mother's name, it is
Margrat Patirsone, daughter to ane toune's man
heir, whom I did not know. 8thlie, As to his being
in suite of ane other befor, that I heard nothing of.
9thlie, as to what was his father's, and his owin, ordi-
nare imployment, his father was ane merchent, and
therafter turned ane labourer, wictuall buyer, and
keeped ane malt kilne, which imployment his sone
followeth, being the onlie best with uss in this place.
10thlie, as to these tenements he hath, I cannot give
ane particular accompt what they are worth or what
rent they pay, but sure I am they are considerable,
and he improvs them to the best. 11thlie, As to what
he has besyds, as to that I cannot give ane accompt,
only that he is in credit and folows his imployment.
This is the greatest accompt I can give at the time ;
only that, in my judgement, ane gentlewoman may
like weill to be his wyfe, haveing the blissing of God.
I add no forder, but that I am, &c.,

"JAMES DUNBAR."

We trust that the " Captin" sent a handsome
" tokin" to his sister :---

"INVERNESS, 28 June 1678.

" Memorandum.—William Ross, burges and drumer

in Inverness, as ffollowes to James Dunbar, elder, merchant ther :—

Item, pleases God to send you to London, ye wil be pleased
to buy, for my use,—
Item, two poynts stoups of the best tin.
Item, two chapin stoups of the best—conform.
Item, two quarter muchkin stoups—conform.
Item, three hansum candlsticks of brese.
Item, two peires drum cords, conform to the sample heer
inclosed.

" And be pleased to receave three pair white plaids,
and sell the same to the best vantage. And if yee
meet Captin James Dunbar, my good brother, be
pleased to present my respects, and my wyfs respects
to him ; and if yee meet Captin James Dunbar, if he
send a tokin to his sister, I recomend it to yor self ;
and if ther be any superplus in the pryce of the plaids,
buy a pettiecoat to my wyf, and what shall be dew by
me to you, efter compt, it shall be payit—thankfullie
payit be yor lowing freind to serve you, to my power,

" W. R."

The reverend author's book has not come down to
posterity :—

" For JAMES DUNBAR, Baily of Inverness and
Laird of Dalcross—These :
" INVERNES, 17th October 1695.
" COUSIN,——Lest you should pretend ignorance
(which your words did insinuate last night) of my

errand to London, I thought fit to acquaint you that my business there, at this time, is a design I have to offer my book to be printed, since I cannot get it done here, the poverty of our nation not allowing our printers to expend money and be out of it for a considerable time, though the prospect were never so great, and that they should have it again with centuple profit. I dare not, I will not urge you to do anything against the grain ; but once for all, I think it would be worth your while to right me so far at least, at this juncture, as to advance my money a forthnight before the time, which was so often kept from me fortnights after the term. Remember, cousin, it is God's business that I am about, and your errand may come His way yet. Truly, if you laid out the whole sum necesarry, you are far more beholding to Him. As for me, whatever you do, I hope His will shall be mine. It may be, if I should go up in this ship, I may come back again, *re infecta*, and so blemish my repute, and wound my purse. As for this last, look to Psal. xxxvii. v. 3,[1] which is the charter that God has given me in (I had almost said miraculously) a great strait. And as for the first, the old saying will salve all. *In magnis voluisse sat est.*

" Your affectionate cousin and humble servant,

" ROBERT DUNBAR."

---

[1] " Trust in the Lord, and do good ; so shalt thou dwell in the land, and verily thou shalt be fed."

XXVI. MERCHANTS' LETTERS.

A LONDON built carriage arrives, in January 1717, at Findhorn.

" To the Much Honoured
  " THE LAIRD OF THUNDERTOUN,
    " att Duffes. Per Exspress.

" ffORRES, Jan. 4th, 1717.

"MUCH HONOURED SIR,—The shipe I expected from London arrived at ffindhorn yesterday morne-ing. At night, I went down and found your chercoat placed on the decke, soe that noe work can be don either in 'livering or loading, untill she be teaken away ; for that cawse, would intreat yow will send horses, to-morow, for cearyeing it off. If your con-veneancie could allow, its proper yow be their your self. I understand the chereoat is very fine. If you will come to ffindhorn, to-morow, aquent me, and I will meake it my bussness to wait of you.

"I am, with my most dewtyfull respects, Sir, your most oblidged servant,

" WILL. DAWSON."

" To the LAIRD OF THUNDERTOUN,
                " at Duffus.

                        " EDINBURGH, *December* 27*th*, 1719.

" DEAR SIR,— Your's of the 17th curent I recved
by the bearer, with a bill of forty pounds sterling on
Sir Thomas Calder, which he sayes he will pay. I
had likeways your's in course, by post, with bill of
fifty pounds sterling on Mr. Arbuthnott, which is
paid. Shall wait your orders for both. Noe word
of the Shereff as yet. Shall wait on him when he
comes. Receive the scarlet cloath and gold lace.
There is noe scarlet stockings with a gold-coloured
gushett, to be had at this place ; nor noe scarlet stock-
ing that is fine, to be had here, either with or without
a coloured gushett ; for what wee have here is not
above six shillings from London, which cannot be fine,
for scarlet. I had the offer of two or three pair with
white gushett, but they were small sised, and you
desire them large, so did not send them, both for the
sise and gushett. Sir Thomas Calder sent a sadle for
you, with his own things, more than six weeks ago.
Nellie is very weill, and both she and Jaessie has
their humble service to ladie and selfe ; and many
happie new years to ladie, selfe, and familie, is the
constant wish of both, and of your most humble
servant,   THO. GORDON."

" Inclosed is a letter from Bailie Gordon, with a

bill of a hunder pound sterling, on Sir Robert Gordon, from his brother Lewis, which is sent for acceptance.

"I have given the bearer eightein pence, so count accordinglie.

"I have sent a pair of stockings at venture. If does not please, may dispose of them to a mistress."

" The Much Honoured
     " Mr. ARCHIBALD DUNBAR,
          " off Thundertoun.

          " ffORTROSE, 26th Septr. 1723, N.S.

"SIR,—In obedience to your desyre, doe send you one hogshead claret, and one half hogshead whyte wine ; two els cambrick ; six barrels containing five bolls Spanish salt; with two loafes of fine sugar, weighing eleven pounds one ounce, and two loafes course, weighing thirteen pounds seven ounces ; there is neither brandy or iren to be hade in this place. Inclosed you have the skyper's receipt for the goods.

"Sir Kenneth Mackenzie off Cromerty is here, and desyres you may send him over your servant with the horse, you promised him, and by the same servant he will send you his horse. I received, in pairt payment off the above goods, three pound fifteen shillings in cash, with Inchcoulter's bill for seven pound seven shillings sterling. Iff in anything I can serve you, freely remind me. My wife and I makes offer off our most humble duty to yourself and good lady, and I most respectfully am, Sir, your most obedient and very much obliged humble servant,

" WILLIAM TOLMIE.

" *P.S.*—The bearer desyred one hundred weight of sugar, but not knowing whether it was fine or course you wanted, made me send you two loafes of each kynd.

" Sir William is, this night, here, and is to be, to-morrow, at Kessock, upon a tryst. I cannot miss to tell you that he is alarmed with a ffoolish information off a landing in the Highlands. This story proceeds from Culkairn, who went with it to Inverness, and theirfrom forwarded ane express about it to London. I hear Sir William's tryst, to-morrow, is in order to take affidavits upon the contrary, the story being actually falss, for we are ashured that there is no such thing."

Mrs. Fraser was in an "interesting situation;" hence the fear "that she would liver her loading."

" ARCHIBALD DUNBAR of Duffus, Esq.,
     " To the care of William Belcher,
          " at Elgin.
                    "INVERNESS, 21st Aug. 1741.

" SIR,—I sent last night, aboard Alexander Prott's boat, twelve ston butter, contained in your own cask and an anker of my wife's. She choosed it, and is

the best cam to our fair, but the dearest ever bought
at a Martimas market. It cost seven merks the ston,
all owing to some Murray lairds' servants sent here,
who stood at no price ; and the extravagance of it
made my wife and me not buy any for your mother,
as you can supply her till next mercat, when, I am
persuaded, it will be much cheaper, as the most of
the commissions from the east, if not all, are answered.
The fellow refused to bring your timber with him,
after sending it to the shore, so must wait the first
occasion of a boat. Mr. Inglish is to send your goods
with other peoples by a boat, this night or to-morrow.
My wife desires that your lady cause repack the butter
in a closs cask, with a rum head, with an almed skin
'twixt the head and cask, and take out a ston at once,
to prevent often opening or winding it. I expected,
that night she came from the mercat, that she would
liver her loading. She joins me in offering our best
respects to you and your lady, and I am your most
obedient servant, WILLM. FRASER.

" *P.S.*—I received seven pounds by the post, and I
shall send you, by next or following post, accompt of
what was given out, and either remitt you, or retain,
the balance for buying the remainder of the butter at
next mercat. The boatman by whom you wrote would
neither wait butter or timber."

" To Archibald Dunbar,
" of Newton, Esq., at Duffus.

" findhorne, 16th January 1741.

" Honored Sir,—I was obliged to come here, this day, and be here, the morrow, all day, setling accompts of consequence. However, as I promised in my last, I now run you this express, showing I am still satisfied to give you eight pound Scots per boll of your bear, and eight pounds for the boll of your victuall oats, to the extent of ffour hundered bolls of each, all good, and sufficient well dight, wholesome victuall, deliverable to me on the shoar of ffindhorne, any time 'twixt the date hereof and fifteenth Aprile next, wind and weather serving; tho' I will take it sooner if the winde permit. And I hereby oblige myself to pay you the one half the value at Whitesunday next, the other half at Martimas thereafter; and to give you a hogshead claret, the first I bring home, at prime cost and charges. Your answer will determine me, and this shall be binding on me as if on stampt, I say, as if on stampt paper. If you think this not so full, make out a copy, and I shall write over same and return it you, Munday next, since I must be at Blackstob, then and Tuesday, at a roup, and to take possession of Baker's land and mill by instrument. Believe me, for certain, that grain is falen, and dayly falling in England, and if you don't see the mercat fall, after this month and next, I will

perrill my car.   I make offer of my compliments to
Mrs. Dunbar and self, and am, honored Sir, your
most obedient humble servant,

"JOHN FRIGGE.

"Send a servant to my house, on Munday, for a
peck aples, fflanders, for Mrs. Dunbar."

.

XXVII. RECEIPTS AND ACCOUNTS.

THESE merchant tailors speak as if their firm were older than the globe which we inhabit :—

" Bee it knowne unto all men by theis presents that wee, Henry Ashhurst and Nicholas Gregson of London, citizens and merchant taylors, do by theis presents, remise, and release and discharge Alexander Dunbar of, and from, all bills, bonds, reckinings, accompts, and demands, whatsoever, from the begining of the world to the day of the date of theis presents. In witnesse whereof, we, the said Henry Ashhurst and Nicholas Gregson, have hereunto, interchangably, put our hands and seales, this twentith day of July 1662, and of Rex Carolus Secundus, decimo quarto. Sealed and delivered in the presence of

" H. ASHHURST.

NI. GREGSON.

" Rich. Salvonsvall.

Hen. Ashhurst, junior."

Printed schedule filled in by Mr. Dumbrake, whose treasure may have been in heaven :—

"Received from *Alexr. Dumbrake, in ffochabers, no wife, no stock, no trade,* in *Bellie* parish in *Banff*-shire, the sum of *six shilling Scott,* being the pole-money as *he* has classed *him*-self, as witness my hand at *ffochabers,* the *fifteenth* day of *December* 1694.

" THO : TURNBULL."

A yearly pensioner :—

" I, Mr. Hew Dalrymple of North Berwick, advocat, grant me, be thir presents, to have received from William Innes, writer in Edinburgh, in name and behalf of Sir Robert Gordon of Gordonstoun, ten guineas in gold, and that as a year's pension, due by him to me, as his advocat from the first day of January instant, to the first of January nixt, 1698 ; and therefor I, be thir presents, discharge the saids William Innes, Sir Robert Gordon, and all others whom it effeirs, of the said year's pension, for now and ever. In witnes wherof I have subscrived thir presents (writen be John Crawford, my servitor), with my hand, at Edinburgh, the twentieth eight day of January jayvic, nynty seven years (1697), before these witness, Thomas Ingles, also my servitor, and the said John Crawfurd.

" HEW DALRYMPLE.

" Tho. Inglis, *witnes.*
Jo. Crawfurd, *witnes.*

" Wee, John Crawfurd and Thomas Ingles, servitors
to Mr. Hew Dalrymple of North Berwick, advocat,
grant us to have received from William Innes, writer
in Edinburgh, six rix dollars, in name and behalf of
Sir Robert Gordon of Gordonstoun, and that as an
allowance granted by him to us yearly, from the first
of January instant, to the first of January nixt to
com, as attending and managing his affairs under the
said Mr. Hew, our master ; and therefor wee, be thir
presents, discharge the saids William Innes, Sir Robert
Gordon, and all others whom it effeirs, of the samen,
for now and ever. In witnes wherof we have subscryved thir presents (writen be the said John Crawfurd), with our hands, at Edinburgh, the twentieth eight
day of January jayvic, nynty seven years (1697).

" Tho. Inglis."

" Jo. CRAWFURD.

General assortment :—

" The Laird of Thunderton, his account to William
Dawson, Forres :—

1709.	Then delivered you when in company			
Oct. 12.	with Myrland, ane loafe double re- fined shougar, weighteing five pound four ounce, at eighteen pence per pound, is	£0	7	10
1710.				
Aprill 11.	To ane pound of green tea, is	1	5	0
	To ane fine silk napkine, is	0	5	6

1712.

July 16. Then sent two oacken plankes, at five
 shillings per piece, . . . £0 10 0
 At the same time, four and a half
 pound wheat soape, at sixteen pence
 per pound, is 0 6 0

Aug. 17. Then sent you ane pound coffie bens,
 is 0 7 6

1714. Ane quare fine writing paper, . . 0 0 10

May 18. To ane English Cheasser cheess,
 weighteing twenty five and three
 quarter pounds, at five pence per
 pound, is 0 10 8
 At the same time, ane ancor brandy, . 3 10 0
 To four botls fair drops, 0 4 0"

Items from an Elgin tailor's account (the money
is Scots) :—

" Accompt—The much Hon. the Laird of Thundertoun to William Blennshell.

Janoary 1719.   lb. sh. d.
To making an scarlet clok to yer Laidy, . . 01 10 0
To making an stiched night-goun to hir Leship, 01 00 0
To turning goun and coat of silk stuff to hir, . 01 16 0
To covering of ane furred cloak to hir, . . 00 16 0
To silk to the two cloks and two gouns and coat, 01 08 0
To five els riben to the foot of the above coat, 00 15 0
To making over again ane caligo goun and coat
 to Mrs. Betie, ... 01 04 0
To making over again goun and coat to Mrs.
 Rebeca,   01 10 0

	lb.	sh.	d.
To thred to Mrs. Bettie's, and silk to Mrs. Rebeka's goun and coat,	00	18	0

March 1719.

To making an pair stiched stees to Mrs. Bettie,	12	00	0
To making an pair stiched stees to Mrs. Rebeca,	12	00	0
To making an pair stiched stees to Mrs. Nell,	10	00	0
To making an mid coat to yer Laidy, with gold leace,	00	12	0

May 1719.

To making an blak and whyt night-goun to yer Laidy,	00	18	0

Agust 1719.

To widning of an mid coat to yer Laidy, .	00	08	0
To ten ells wad to hir clok and night-goun,	03	00	0
To turning of an big coat to yer self,	02	08	0
To an ell bukrum and three unces hare, .	01	12	0
To the working of the buttons, . . .	00	17	6
To the altering of the sleves of Mrs. Bettie's and Mrs. Rebeca's blak and whyt gound, and silk to do it, ...	00	18	0
To making an scarlet west to yer self, with silk and mul, ...	00	12	0
To the widening of an scarlet coat to yer Laidy,	00	06	0
To the turning of an silk goun and coat to Mrs. Bettie, .	01	10	0

Janury 1720.

To dying of threttie els of sairg red, with thrie pair stokins, ther being ninetcen pund weight of it, and wefing and pressing,	18	00	0
To muilds and stey teps, . . .	00	08	0
To an pair lether breches to Thomas Shaw,	01	04	0 "

Shoemaker's account :—

" Accompt—Mr. Archbald Dunbar of Thundertun to James Craigo.

1717. ffeb. Ane pair of boots, your honor,	. £01	00	00
ditto, Ane pair of strong shoes,	. . 00	05	06
1718. Jan. Ane pair of strong, or pair of Mara-ken, shoes with tops,	. . 00	10	00
ffeb. Ane pair of seamed Maraken shoes, your Lady,	 00	03	00
Mar. Ane pair of slipers with heils,	. 00	05	00
Aug. Ane pair of button boots, your honor,	 00	16	00
ditto, Ane pair of calf leather shoes with tops,	00	05	00
	£03	04	06

" *Edinburgh, 4th August* 1718.—Receeved the above contents, and all precidings, per me,

" JAMES CRAIGO."

Saddler's account :—

" LAIRD OF THUNDERTON, *Debter*,

To PATRICK CHRICHTON.

	£	s.	d.
1731.			
Sept. 4. Nine ounces of silk freinge,	. . . 1	7	0
Lyning for a houzen and bags, and making them,	 0	14	0
Six and a half yeards of white silk wating,	0	1	1
Pistol shanks,	. 0	1	6

A king's hunting saddle, with large stir-
rups and leathers, girth and curple, . £1 16 0
A pellem bridle, . . . 0 4 6
A pair of houlsters and belte, . . . 0 5 0
A suitt of neats leather covers for the
houzen and bags, 0 16 0
A silver-buttond whip, . . 0 5 6

Sum, . £5 10 7

"*Edinburgh, 7th Sept.* 1731.—Receved the contents, and all precedings, by me,

"PAT. CHRICHTON."

We are forcibly reminded of the judicial wig :—

" MR. DUMBAR, *Debter*,
                    To FRANCIS JEFFREY, Wigmaker.

	£	sh.	d.
Janry. 12th, 1753. To a fair cutt wig, . .	0	14	0
To shaving and dressing, .	0	6	0
To cutting and dressing Mrs.			
Dumbar's hair, . . .	0	3	0
	£1	3	0

"*Edinburgh, March* 18th, 1758.--Received payment of the above, and discharges the same, and all
preceedings, by   FRANCIS JEFFREY."

A Jack-of-all-trades :—

The enterprising Mr. Grant rented a billiard-table,
" with king and port, ten play clubs, a long club and
half long club, two big bals, and eight alagaire bals,"
which had been procured, in 1732, from Edinburgh, at
a cost of eighteen guineas.   No doubt the Elgin gentlemen often resorted to the " Garden Chamber," where
the table was set up :—

		£	s.	d.
" To thirteen months of the billiard table,	.	£13	0	0
A quarter's sheaving,	. £5	5	0	
For apprehending Wm. Jack,	. 3	0	0	
For executing summonds,	. 0	16	0	
For swan's skin,	. 0	8	0	
For a letter,	. 0	4	0	
For oil,	. 0	5	0	
		9	18	0
		£3	2	0

" *Duffus, the 2d March* 1743.—Reseved by me,
John Grant, wigmaker in Elgin, full and complete
payment from Archibald Dunbar of Newtoun, of all
sheaving preceding the date heirof ; I having paid for
the billiard table—all except three pounds two shillings Scots, as above.   JOHN GRANT."

XXVIII. POETIC EFFUSIONS, AND BEGGING-LETTERS.

WITH some hesitation we give the verses and letters contained in this division. They are, however, traits of old social life.

The happy event to which Mr. Whytte tuned his lyre took place in 1703 :—

" Epithalamium on the nuptials of the much honored Archibald Dunbar of Thundertoune, and the pious, vertuous, and comlie Mrs. Rebecca Adamsone, etc.

> Appollo come, and help me up the hill
> Of Helicon, that I may dip my quile
> Into its font, the fair Castalian streame ;
> That I may wreate upon this worthy theame,
> Upon the nuptials of them—good, gallant paire—
> Whose qualities are trulie fyne and rare ;
> For both are sprung from an old honour'd race,
> Which may be seen by symptoms in each face.
> He is a sparke—neate, comlie, lovelie, good ;
> In Albion ther's non of better blood ;
> Discreet and kynd, true, generous, and free,
> Prudent and wise, right humble altho' high :

His loyale spirit's endued with finest parts,
And he hath skill in science each, and arts.
Now for to speake the due praise of his ladie,
Her fame for good is broad and wyde alreadie :
Shee try'd before what was a maried lyffe,
And blameless liv'd while widow, maid, or wyfe :
Her lovlie face, and her sweet pleasantt eyes,
The best of men to love her might entice ;
Modest and meeke, frugale, wise, that is shee,
Of common vice being altogether free.
Now with what joy, what pleasure, and delight
May them, brisk paire, goe live both day and night
For briske Dunbare, the Laird of Thundertoune,
Is a brave sparke, of honour and renoune ;
He is a man of prudence, and greate sense,
And knows the right of due benevolence.
God grant them grow in grace, in peace and love,
With progenie to be blest from above.
                    " WILL. WHYTTE.

" SIR,—I am but latlie informed of your weding,
else I hade sent my complement before this tyme.
In the meantime mind the poet, and I shall be a good
serviter."

————

" The poet's address to his honble. and generous
Mæcenas, &c., anno 1722 :—

    Most worthy Sir, be pleased to excuse
    This bold address of my aspiring muse ;
    Which to your view ambitiously has sent
    Rude rhyme, for want of better compliment.

Did my hard ffates grant me the happiness,
Some fitter way your virtues to express,
Then, out of gratitude, I should allow
Whole Hecatombs, as to your merits due ;
But since my state a poet's case doth plead,
I hope you'll please to take the will for deed,
And drive from me the poet's plague away,
Hobgoblin-like, that haunts me night and day.
Lo ! at your gates I waiting here attend,
Till you to me some consolation send.
With hope and fear (like Mah'met in the air),
I'm toss'd 'twixt expectation and despair.
To kill or cure alike is in your pow'r ;
But, O ! your clement looks will ne'er devour
Your poetaster ; since a small relief
Will ease me of a multitude of grief ;
Which if you grant, I'll to the world proclaim
Your generous soul, and eternize your name.
Long may you live, and prosp'rous be your health,
Increasing still in honour, grace, and wealth !

   " Suppliciter posuit,

    " Humillimus tui cultor,

      " M. Jo. Colme."

We trust that " the good wife" was asked to give poor Croupie a Christmas-box :—

" ffor the much honered Mr. Archibald Dunbar
  " of Thundertoun : These ar—

    " Elgin, *the* 17*th day of December*, 1700 *year*.

" Much honored,—As it is my greatt duty to wrett to you and to shoe you that your nephew,

Archibald, is in verie good health, blessed be God ; and he is verie desiros to hear the like of you, my dear honerbl master ; and likewaise if ye knew the nakednesse that poor Croupie is in, your heart would be sorry for to see his nakednese ; but poor Croupie cannot help it, till it shall please the Lord to bring you weell hom, as I do wish from my heart ; or if it wer your honer's will to writ the good wife or to Mr. Reid they would not let me be naked, as I am ; and if your honer did nott help and send word to hyd my nakednese, poor Croupie will be in the dust ere ye com hom. And alwise, deer honrble master, I am still keeping the schooll, with Archibald, and, blessed be the Lord, he is lerning werie weell; and the master is werie weell content with him. No more at pres-ent, but untill death, I am, honered Sir, your humble, and poor, and obedient servant, Croupie, till death,

"A. CROUGHTLY."

Although pugnacious, the captive was honest. It was too bad not only to fine him a crown for the nose, but also to impose jailer's fees :—--

" To Sir ALEXANDER DUNBAR, at Duffes,

" ELGIN, TOLBOTH, *Maye* 18*th*, 1780.

" HONBLE. SIR,—I had the misforton of giving a chape to a man's nose in this pleace ; he has given me a right to a stout dryy roum, that one drop of reen hes not touched me thes tuo days. This day a Court was hold on me, and fined in five shelings, and jelor-fis, which I am not able to pay. Pray, Sir, be so good as to write any of your aquantanss to relive me, and your servant shall be for ever oblidged.

"I shall direckly com a longe with your servant, and worke til you be cleaired of what the damages is, Sir, GAVIN SKEOCH."

XXIX. INVENTORY OF HOUSEHOLD FURNITURE.

IF this "Inventar" may be taken as a correct index of their comforts and conveniences, the Morayshire gentry had no cause of complaint.

"Inventar of plenishing in Thunderton's lodging in Duffus, May 25, 1708 :—

"Strypt Room.

"Camlet hangings and curtains, feather bed and bolster, two pillows, five pair blankets, and an Inglish blanket, a green and white cover, a blew and white chamber-pot, a blue and white bason, a black jopand table and two looking glasses, a jopand tee table with a tee-pot and plate and nine cups and nine dyshes and a tee silver spoon, two glass sconces, two little bowles with a leam stoap and a pewter head, eight black ken chairs with eight silk cushens conform, an easie chair with a big cushen, a jopand cabinet with a walnut tree stand, a grate, shuffle, tonges, and brush ; in the closet, three piece of paper hangings, a chamber box with a pewter pan therein, and a brush for cloaths.

" *Closet next the Strypt Room.*

" Four dishes, two assiets, six broth plates, and twelve flesh plates, a quart flagon, and a pynt flagon, a pewter porenger, and a pewter flacket, a white iron jaculate pot, and a skellet pann, twenty-one timber plates, a winter for warming plates at the fire, two highland plaids, and a sewed blanket, a bolster, and four pillows, a chamber box, a sack with wool, and a white iron driping pann.

" *In the Fire Closet.*

" A standing bed with green cloath curtains and slips of silk sewens thereon, a feather bed, bolster, and two pillows, two pair blankets, and a single blanket, a leam chamber pot, and one timber chair.

" *In the next Closet.*

" A standing bed with green hangings, feather bed, bolster, and three pair of blankets.

" *In the Green Room.*

" A sute of stamped green cloath hangings, and a stamped stuff green bed, two feather beds and a bolster, a couple of pillows, three pair blankets, and a single blanket, and an Inglish blanket, five winscot chairs, a chist of olive-wood drawers, a table, and two stands, and a looking-glass, a pewter chamber pot, a chamber box and pewter pan therein.

" In the Garret.

" Two tyks of beds, and two bolsters, and a tyk of a bolster, two feather stands, with a large basket and a deal of feathers, and a frying pann.

" In the farest Closet.

" Seventeen drinking glasses, with a glass tumbler and two decanters, a oil cruet, and a vinegar cruet, a urinel glass, a large blew and white posset pot, a white leam posset pot, a blew and white bowl, a dozen of blew and white leam plates, three milk dishes, a blew and white leam porenger, and a white leam porenger, four jelly pots, and a little butter dish, a crying chair, and a silk craddle.

" In the Moyhair Room.

" A sute of stamped cloath hangings, and a moyhair bed with feather bed, bolster, and two pillows, six pair blankets, and an Inglish blanket, and a twilt, a leam chamber pot, five moyhair chairs, two looking glasses, a cabinet, a table, two stands, a table cloak, and window hangings, a chamber box with a pewter pann, a leam bason, with a grate and tongs and a brush; in the closet two carpets, a piece of Arres, three pieces lyn'd strypt hangings, three wawed strypt curtains, two piece gilded leather, three trunks, and a craddle, a chamber box and a pewter pann, thirty-three pound of heckled lint, a ston of vax, and a firkin of sop, and a brush for cloaths, two pair blankets, and a single blanket.

" In the Dyning-Room.

" A sute of gilded hangings, two folding tables, eighteen low backed ken chairs, a grate, a fender, a brass tongs, shuffle, brush, and timber brush, and a poring iron, and a glass kes.

" In my Lady's Room.

"Gilded hangings, standing bed, and box-bed, stamped drogged hangings, feather bed, bolster, and two pillows, a pallise, five pair of blankets and a single one, and a twilt, and two pewter chamber pots, six chairs, table, and looking-glass, a little folding table, and a chist of drawers, tonges, shuffle, porrin-iron, and a brush, two window curtains of linen ; in the Laird's closet two trunks, two chists, and a citrena cabinet, a table, and a looking-glass, the dow holes, two carpet chairs, and a chamber box with a pewter pan, and a little bell, and a brush for cloath.

" My Lady's Closet.

" A cabinet, three presses, three kists, and a spicerie box, a dozen leam white plates, a blew and white leam plate, a little blew butter plate, a white leam porenger, and three gelly pots, two leam dishes, and two big

timber capes, four tin cougs, a new pewter basson,
a pynt, chopen, and mutchken stoups, two copper
tankers, two pewter salts, a pewter mustard box,
a white iron peper and suggar box, two white iron
graters, a pot for starch, and a pewter spoon, thirteen
candlesticks, five pair snuffers and snuf dishes conform, a brass morter and pistol, a lanthern, a timber
box, a dozen knives and a dozen forks, and a carpet
chair, two milk cougs, a milk cirn, and kirn staff, a
symilk, and creamen dish, and a chesswel, a neprie
basket, and two new pewter chamber pots.

" In the Nursrie.

"A large neprie press, wherein there is six pair
Scots holland sheits, two pair of fyn linen sheits,
ten pair of courser linen sheits, eight pair of straken
sheits, twelve holland pillowbers and two little
holland pillowbers, twenty-three linen pillowbers
and five little ones, six linen top sheits, one dozen
of fyn Dutch damaz, and two tabel cloaths, two
dozen and eight of the rose knot, and two table
cloaths, one dozen and four of the levender knot,
and one table cloath, two dozen and eleven of the
dice about, and three table cloaths, two dozen and
five of the wals of troy, and two table cloaths, two
dozen and two new rose and dice about, and four
table cloaths, two dozen and one of burdseye, and
nine of several knots odd, three fyn towels, and five

of the walls of troy, four of dice about, three rose
and dice about, three old ones, and two coarse dornick
towels.

" There is of sheits, coarse and fyn, twenty-six pair,
there is of pillowbers, little and mikle, coarse and fyn,
fourty and two, there is of neprie coarse and fyn,
fifteen dozen, odd ones, four, there is of the hand
towels, twenty in all, and twenty coarse haggabag
servits, three pair fyn blankets and three pair coarse
blankets ; all the above-written is in the press.

" Three close beds, and a folding bed.

" In Collin's bed,—a feather bed, bolster, and two
pair of blankets.

" In Beatie's bed,—a feather bed, bolster, two pillows, and four pair blankets.

" In Rebecka's bed,—a feather bed, bolster, and
three pair blankets and a single blanket.

" In Nellie's bed,—a feather bed, bolster, and three
pair of blankets.

" A hand candle chist, two chairs for the children,
three little stools, two coarse leam chamber pots, a
pair of tongs, a large fire shuffle, and a pair of bellows,
a folding table, a milke stoup, a two-lugged coug,
three mikle capes, and six little capes, two pewter
bassons, a pair of collop tongs, and a collop brander,
two little wheels, and a check reel, two little pans,
a timber ball and brods, a dry rubber, and a wet
rubber, and a brush, a craddle and a chaff bed and

pillow therein, and a single blanket, a salt box, a meal box, and a hanging candlestick, and a goosing blanket.

"In Jannet's bed,—a bolster, two pair blankets, and a covering.

"*In the Stable.*

"In John Lamb's bed,—a feather bed, bolster, and three pair blankets, and a covering.

"In William Winchester's bed,—a chaff bed, and feather bolster, and three pair of blankets.

"In Frank's bed,—two pair of blankets.

"1709, to be added, four pair linen sheits, and two pair twidlen shiets, four course harn shiets, and three table-cloaths.

"*In the Parlour.*

"Three tables, and five backed chairs.

"*A Note of Plate.*

"Three silver salvers, four salts, a large tanker, a big spoon, and thirteen littler spoons, two jugs, a suggar box, a mustard box, a peper box, and two little spoons.

"*In the Kitchey.*

"A hanging candlestick, six dishes, and two ashets, eighteen pewter plates, twenty-one timber trenchers, two timber stoups, and a drinking cap, a mustard dish and a bullet; a sowen kirn, and a sowen sive, five timber plates and a laddle, a watter stoup, three cies, five pots, and three broads, three panns, and a kettle pann, a driping pann, and a frying pann, two branders, a flesh hook, and flaming spoon, one of pair pot bowls, a cockering iron, five smoothing irons and their stand, a toasting iron, four spits, and a girdle, a chofen dish, a pair of raxes, seven iron scewers, a crook, and a pair tongs.

" The Browhouse.

" A lead, and fatt, and taptree, and masken shield, a baken table, with a pill, colraik, and maiden.

" The Goolhouse.

" Five puncheons, and a waterstand, a quicknen bot, eight gallon trees, a four gallon barrel, a twenty pynt barrel, a ten pynt barrel, a timber tinvel, and white iron tinvel, and twenty pynts barely. A dozen of new pewter trenchers more, fifteen timber trenchers to the kitchey.

" Made new—four pair of course linen sheits, and six pair of fyn linen shicts, and nine fyn linen pillow-bers, two pair of twidlen sheits, and two pair of harn sheits, and four single harn shiets, three new dornick table-cloths, thirty new dornick servitors, and two new washing cloaths.

" *An Account of Bottles in the Salt Cellar.*

" *June the first*, 1708.

" Of sack, five dozen and one, .	5	1
Of brandie, three dozen and three,	3	3
Of vinegar and aquavitie, seven, .	0	7
Of strong ale, four dozen and four,	4	4
Of other ale, nine dozen, . .	9	0
In the ale cellar, fifteen dozen and ten,	15	10
In the hamper, five dozen empty, .	5	0
In the wine cellar, nine with Inglish ale,	0	9
White wine, ten,	0	10
Of brandy, three, . .	0	3
With brandy and surop, two,	0	2
With claret, fifteen,	1	3
With mum, fifteen, .	1	3
Throw the house, nineteen,	1	7
There is in all, forty-nine dozen and two,	49	2
And of mutchken bottles, twenty-five,	2	1

" Received ten dozen and one of chopen bottles, full of claret. More received—eleven dozen and one of pynt bottles, whereof there was six broke in the home-coming. 1709, June the 4th, received from Elgin, forty-three chopen bottles of claret."

XXX. PARLIAMENTARY EXPENSES, AND POLITICS.

MEMBERS of the Scottish Parliament had stated allowances for their services, etc. ; and heritors, wad-setters, life-renters, and other local parties, were assessed for the payment of these allowances. This system continued for a few years after the Union, as appears by the claim for expenses, made, in 1715, by a Scotch member of the British Parliament.

" The Laird of M'Intosh, his depursements for the shyre of Inverness, at the Parliament in anno 1681 :—

	£	s.	d.
Item, for fifty-two sitting dayes in Parliament, and sixteen dayes comeing and goeing, at five pounds Scotts per day, is . . .	340	00	00
Item, more for ane consultation with the Lord Advocat, ...	036	05	00
Item, more to Mr. David Thores and his servants,	021	15	00
Item, more given in with the comission to the Clerk-Register, ...	013	06	08
Item, more for the testificat of the dyetts of the Parliament sitting, ...	014	10	00
Item, more to Mr. Thomas Gordon for keeping the Counsell in mynd from dissjoyning of the shyre of Invernes with that of Ross in the excyse,	008	14	00
	434	10	08

"The Laird of M'Intosh, his expenss for his foot mantle[1] and furniture therof, and other expenss for the shyre of Inverness, at the Parliament in anno 1685 :—

	£	s.	d.
Item, for ten ells fyn black velvat, at sixteen pound the ell, is,	160	00	00
Item, for five and three quarters ells broad black kyligo,	005	15	00
Item, for silk, and workeing the knapes and frenzies,	026	00	00
Item, to David Denoon for makeing the footmantle and mounteing the same	024	00	00
Item, for his part given in to the Clerk-Register with the comission,	020	00	00
Item, for fifty-five sitting dayes in Parliament, and sixteen dayes comeing and goeing, at five pounds Scotts per day, is	355	00	00
Item, for the testificat of the dyetts of the Parliament sitting	013	06	08
	604	01	08
It is to be remembred that the Laird of M'Intosh, when the Parliament first sat, after calleing the rolls of Parliament, did protest for the shyre's precedencie, and depursed ane gaunie, as other shyres did, being	013	06	08
Sumed	617	08	04
The sowme of all is	1051	19	00

L. MACKINTOSHE
of Torcastell."

---

[1] Worn at the processions when Parliament was opened, prorogued, or dissolved, by the Royal Commissioner.

Two letters from the Laird of Brodie to the Sheriff-Depute of Moray.   " The President " was Duncan Forbes of Culloden :—

" To WILLIAM KING of Newmiln, Esq.,
    " at his house in Elgin. Post paid.
                          " BRODIE HOUSE, 11*th July* 1747.

"DEAR SIR,—As the writes for electing members of Parliament came to the hands of the Shirriff of Nairn on Thursday se'night, and were published on Friday thereafter, the second instant, I am surprised that I have not heard of your having sent a precept to the town of Forress before now ; which is the occasion of this trouble, to begg to know the meaning of it.

" I would also be glad to know what day you intend to appoint the election for this county, that I may regulate my measures accordingly.

" My kind compliments to your lady and ffamily, and believe me, dear Sir, yours most faithfully,

                          " ALEXR. BRODIE.

" *P.S.*—Excuse a borrowed hand, because I have been obliged to take a little blood this morning for a bad cough.   It would be agreeable to the President, McLeod, and me, &c., if you could, *as it were by accident*, appoint the day of election in Murray the same with Inverness, to disappoint the idle scheme of Major Grant for that county ; and if you agree to this, let me know, and before Friday next I will acquaint

you of the day intended for Inverness, which I know
will be delayed, on account of the President's coming
north, to the last day, which I think must be the last
day of this month, or the first of August."

***

" DEAR SIR,—My express from McLeod is not yet
returned, but, last night, Sir Ludovic and Major Grant
came here from Inverness, and told me that Colonel
John Stuart had appointed the 4th of August next
for the day of election of that county ; and that
McLeod and Major Grant had agreed that, as the
Frasers had the casting of the ballance, they did not
see it necessary to be jockying one another, nor put-
ting one another to expence, but to submit to the
Duke of Argyll's determination, who should have the
Frasers, and in case the Duke gave it for McLeod,
Major Grant would vote for McLeod.

" This has the air of truth, but in those times 1
don't choose to be an absolute believer untill I hear
both sides, and therefore I beg of you not to fix the
day untill you hear from me, to-morrow or Thursday,
since, after that, you will have time enough to pub-
lish it, on Friday, at the Market Cross.

" Sir Ludovic is to wait of you this day. He asked
me what day was most convenient for me, when I
told him that Tuesday the 28th of this month would

suit me best. He then pressed hard for Tuesday next, which I told him was not in your power, nor any day before Thursday se'night, the 23d; and that, as I was to be drunk at Inverness on Wednesday, the 22d, I could not be at Elgin the 23d, nor, conveniently, even the 24th; so that, unless it was absolutely necessary, I could agree to no day sooner than Tuesday, the 28th.

Kind compliments to your lady, and believe me, dear William, yours faithfully,

"ALEXR. BRODIE."

———

At the election for the county of Moray, in 1741, the Honourable Colonel Stuart of Pittendreich had been defeated by Mr. Grant, younger of Grant; but some years afterwards, on the instigation of his brother, James, seventh Earl of Moray, the gallant officer resolved to again contest the county. The correspondence on this subject between Lord Moray and one of his friends is interesting :—

" To ARCHIBALD DUNBAR, Esq. of Duffus.
" near Elgin. by Edinburgh.

" LONDON, *April 3d,* 1758.
" MY DEAR ARCHIE,—After you have read this epistle, I think I hear you saying to yourself, hum! the Earl is determined not to let me remain long in his debt, if I asked a triffling favour of him, he comes

upon me with a much heavier demand. The former proofs I have had of your friendship make me flatter myself that this application will not meet with a negative. My brother, the Laird of Pittendrich, will make his personal address to you, how soon he can get leave of absence from Ireland, to beg the favour of your vote and interest to represent the shire of Elgin and Forres in Parliament, the first vacancy there happens. As the interest of my family in that country, that I have the honour to carry the title of, has so long lain asleep, I shall at least have the satisfaction, upon this occasion, of knowing who are its friends and who not. Those who contribute towards the reviving of it will lay me under the deepest ties of gratitude, which no distance of time nor place will ever be able to eradicate out of the breast of, my dear Sir, your most devoted and obedient humble servant,   MORAY."

———

"DUFFUS, *April* 14*th*, 1758.

" MY DEAR LORD,—By last post I am honoured with your's of the third current, the first paragraph wherof I read and consider in a jocular manner, such as, I am sure, you only intended it. The second part, concerning the Laird of Pittendrich, I take to be a more serious matter; and since your Lordship seems to propose it as such, I shall consider it in that man-

ner, and treat it accordingly ; and in the first place,
as I hope your Lordship will indulge me the liberty
of conversing with you in the stile of a real friend, so
you may easily believe it would give me double pain
to see you and your freinds balked and disapointed
now again, as formerly your brother was. You have
no doubt weighed and considered, that though at last
tryal you had a competent number of friends of one
sort or other, yet considerable alterations have happened here since that time. Some on both sides are
gone, particularly of your own freinds, partly represented by minors, and partly by others, whom you
would need to be sure of, at least, for or against you ;
and to the list of our roll have been added a number
of new ones since that time, part wherof are abroad,
and part at home ; and such as are abroad and in
your opposition, I wish they may remain where they
are. And if you are seriously determined to push and
try this affair, I humbly conceive that if you have
already declared it, you have rather been too early, as
it must incite your adversary to muster up and secure
not only his old friends and allies, but also raise a
number of new troops, which otherwise, and without
seeing you as a commander-in-chief, he possibly would
not have done, at least not in such numbers as now
he may do ; though, at sametime, you can do as he
does, if you see cause. And if you are unalterably
determined on a tryal, and have not already declared

it, I think you should not neglect, but write to every
gentleman whom you have reason to think is or ought
to be your friend; among which number, if Sir William Dunbar is one, he should be written to, to cor-
respond with his cousin the Laird of Grange (lately
married to Mr. Campbell of Delnies's daughter, and
neice to Leathen), that Grange and his brother-in-law
may keep themselves steady, free, and independent,
till Sir William sees them ; and that as those Dunbars
are but very few now in number, your Lordship would
be glad to see them unite, that they may bear their
own proper weight in any society, whether they should
be for or against your Lordship's interest.

" It is possible your Lordship has made ane acquisition of new freinds, able and willing to serve and
gratifie your Lordship and themselves ; and if you are
pleased, so am I.   For my own share, your Lordship,
I believe, knows I have not the abilities of a politician ;
God Almighty has denied me the talents necessary for
those ends, and I don't repine ; but if your Lordship
is pleased to honour me with your foundation, plan of
operations, and hopes of success, I surely will not hurt
your interest in thought, word, or deed, and beg you
will believe that true regard wherewith I have the
honour to be, my Lord, &c.,

" ARCHD. DUNBAR."

" My dear Archie,—Yours of the 14th of April, in answer to mine of the 3rd, is now lying before me, and the oftener I read it over the more am I convinced of your friendship. I have the satisfaction to find that my ideas and yours hit in more particulars than one ; for by Sir William Dunbar's return to mine, he tells me that he was to send a copy of it to you, Grange, and Kilravock. Every word in your letter is most certainly true. Many changes have happened since the last tryal, and that will ever be the case in so long a tract of time. It is a common maxim amongst all good Generals to take the field as earlie as one can. That at least prevents your being told ' I am engaged. Had you spoke sooner it might have been otherwise.' Nay, sometimes one is told ' As you did not bestir yourself sooner, I thought you did not intend to do it at all, and therefore, &c., &c., &c.' In such a case as this, it is impossible to say how things will turn out, untill application is made, and, even then, it is difficult to do more than guess, because of the dubiety of the answers ; when people avowedly take a side, it is easie to tell how the bowls will roll. If auxiliary troops of Cossacks and Callmoucks are brought into the play, Pandours and Croats will be found to encounter them. The frequent protestations of regard and friendship I have had from the gentlemen, in the

low country, induce me to put them to the touchstone
of sincerity, and, as I mentioned to you before, I will
have, at least, the satisfaction upon this occasion to
know who are my friends from those who only profess
themselves to be so. Those who are really sincere
will use their best endeavours to bring all they can
along with them. I have got no return from Kirktown, Bishopmill, nor Linkwood. I wrote to Pit-
gaveny, but I wish my letter has not miscarryed, as I
directed it to Elgin instead of Portsoy. Lord Braco
pretends to be angry at my giving the preference to
your recommendation for Speymouth. I wrote him,
for answer, that your letter was dated the 12th of
December and his the 27th said month, though this
was only seeking a hair to make a tether of. *Tempora
mutantur* indeed! I hope when Pittendrich gets into
Murray land, his friends will be so kind as to declare
openly, and then we shall know upon what ground we
tredd. Untill they do that, we must live upon hopes.
You will easily guess that your neighbour, Sir Robert,
is plumb with me; and Sir Alexander Grant; and I
am in great hopes of having the Baron likewise. You
will be better able to form a judgment of those in
your neighbourhood than I can possibly do at present,
until I hear from them. As everybody is put upon
his guard, it now lyes in the breast of every gentleman to take what side he pleases. I hope to see
you soon. I am, what I ever have been, and that

is, my dear Archie, your most faithful friend and servant,

"MORAY."

The unexpected death of Lord Moray's brother, Colonel Stuart, blasted the political prospects :—

"DARNAWAY, *Oct.* 22, 1760.

"MY DEAR ARCHIE,—I am truly sorry that you have any complaints, and particularly at this season of the year, because there is no chance of a thorough relief until the mild weather sets in. For some time past, neither my body nor mind is so well as I am very sure you wish them. This stroke is the heaviest my family have felt these twenty years ; but from these dispensations of providence, tho' our duty call upon us to bear them with patience, our nature almost prompts us to revolt. God's will be done. Amen.

"I never doubted of application being made to you from Castle Grant, because I was informed by a friend of mine he was wrote to. My thoughts have been so unsettled since the fatal blow, that I have not been able to think upon any one plan in life. I leave the answer to your own honest friendly heart ; at the same time I could wish that none of my friends were hasty in giving a flat promise.

"All happiness attend you and yours. That you

have the warmest good wishes of all in this family
I can assure you of, and that no man can be with
more truth and sincerity, my dear Archie, your most
devoted humble servant, than   MORAY."

James, second Earl of Fife (an Irish Peer), for
some time represented the county of Moray in Parliament, but, being created a British Peer, he had to
relinquish his seat in the House of Commons. Several
of the real freeholders had entered into an "association" to annul the "paper votes" by which his Lordship had carried his election :—

"To Sir ALEXANDER DUNBAR, Duffus, Elgin.

"DUFF HOUSE, *July 12th*, 1790.

"DEAR SIR,—As a neighbour, I hope the late member for the county of Elgin has done away his offences
by retiring, and I hope the next will be more able, 1
am sure he cannot be more zealous, in serving the
country than I was. I waited on you to assure you
that I bore no ill-will, and that I only wished my
neighbour's spare money might be laid out in planting
and cultivating Duffus ; and even if you came not to
see me, I shall make personal enquirys after Lady
Dunbar and you ; remaining, with much regard, dear
Sir, your most obedient humble servant,

" FIFE."

P

The Baronet's reply :—

"DUFFUS, 14*th* *July* 1790.

"MY LORD,—Being an associator so long, I was surprised to receive your condescending letter of the 12th.

"Your Lordship will know that at the earliest period of my political race, I was, in a manner, pre-engaged by General Grant's procuring a commission for my brother ; and since that time I have been fighting with your Lordship, and vindicating my right as a ffreeholder, although, on all occasions, I always declared you were the most proper person to represent the county. Your Lordship's letter being calculated to exact something explicite from me, I go on to tell you that my interferance for General Grant cost me two hundred pounds sterling ; and my expence as an associator stood three hundred pounds more.

" I declare to your Lordship that I never received a single favour from Grant or Gordon, and that I was also tricked out of my reimbursement of the three hundred, foresaid, by the finesse, chicane, or, if you please, the address of your agent.

" In this situation I presently stand ; but your Lordship may be assured that I consider myself creditor to you in the article of ffriendship, and you may depend on an application from me in these presents. I know well that the foregoing declaration is forward, and perhaps imprudent, nay impudent ; but then your Lordship will consider that I have not seen the world for twenty years past, and that your letter encourages me to hope for extraordinary indulgence and favour, since I verily believe none of the Association can produce any testimonial of forgiveness or friendship, from your own hand. I forbear saying even a word of our present member, whom I have seen only once, about two years ago. But I observe to you, under silence, that our votes were no more significant in his case than in your Lordship's. I allwise expect and desire a competition, without which the member cannot know ffrends from ffoes.

" With your Lordship's permission, my two young lads shall wait on you when att Innes, or even at Duff-house. I despair of ever being from home, and I relinquish all ambition, save that of being considered as an honest person, under a quick sense of your Lordship's notice. My Lord, since I have not frequently an opportunity of addressing you, let me say, in a word, that Robert Guthrie, Cullen-born and young, is lately married to a cousin of mine. She is main ugly, but of great ingenuity, and very low in circumstances. He has only a smattering of the writer business, but dresses in taste, writes a noble hand, and figures well. Let me beseech your Lordship to think of these, when all your other petitioners are served, and let me, then.

have it to say that I was instrumental in procuring bread for one single ffamily. Since it was his Majesty's pleasure, and perhaps your own desire, to be created an English Peer, be it mine that you sitt as high in another kingdom, wherein there is neither death, nor marriage, nor change. I have the honour to be, &c.,   ALEX. DUNBAR."

The Peers of Scotland resent interference in their elections :—

" UPHALL, WEST LOTHIAN, January 1770.

" Lord Buchan presents his compliments to the Earl of Erroll, and is sorry he is obliged to acquaint his Lordship that, as the Duke of Grafton had the *audacity*, without the participation of his royall master, to interfeer in his Lordship's election, by writing a letter to the Peers of Scotland (among whom Lord Buchan had not the honour to be one), he cannot give Lord Erroll his vote ; though he is very indifferent about the choice of the Peer, whether now or at any other time."

In the contested election for the county of Aberdeen, in 1786, the Lairds of Skene and Pitfour were the rival candidates. The contest was really a trial of strength between the Gordons and the Earl of Fife ; his Lordship's party succeeded, by a very small majority, in placing Skene at the head of the poll. "Peer of Irish creation" was Lord Fife ; "Lord of the Protestant mob" was Lord George Gordon.

"I sing the election of Skene and Pitfour—
My song shall be sweet though my subject be sour ;
I'll tell you what Barons and beauties were there,
And tell you their characters all to a hair.
　　　　Derry down, etc.

There was a rich Peer of Irish creation—
A Commoner here, though a Lord of the Nation ;
And, because he could vote without favour or fear,
They voted this noble Lord into the chair.

And there was a Lord who had lately succeeded
To a troop of new friends, which he very much needed ;
But, this Lord being old, said not much pro or con,
Yet he still shook his head as the voting went on.

There, too, was the Lord of the Protestant mob,
Who came driving like Jehu to help at the job ;
And yet, after all, no assistance could grant,
For no oath he would take but the Old Covenant !

And there were some Knights of fame and renown,
With Generals and Colonels, all mustered in town ;
For, tho' a red-coat be forbid at elections,
There are colours besides that will suit all complexions.

A Colonel was there from the banks of the Shannon
He'd been better at home, looking after his cannon ;
For five hundred miles he travell'd in vain,
And had nothing to do but to ride back again.

And there was an Englishman married, in haste,
To an heiress that suited him just to his taste;
Yet his right of attendance in Court was not clear,
So they sent him to fiddle and dance, for a year!

And there were the Gordons, of every degree,
As stately and gentle as Gordons should be;
But, how many were true or false to their chief,
Perhaps I could tell, but you won't give belief.

And there were the Duffs, all ranged on one side,
Still true to the Red Cows, whate'er might betide;
Their chief, they were sure, would always prevail,
For ten of majority never can fail.

A Gordon there came some folks to reprove,
For he, now and then, pray'd to a Being above;
But, because he was thought to depend on his Grace,
They found he had pray'd in an unentered place!

A Duff, too, was there, but I cannot well tell
If ever he thought of a heaven or hell;
For, fearing his vote might be cast on that score,
He swore he pray'd none, for a twelvemonth and
        more!

And there were some parsons, of piety rare,
Who, with reverence, bow'd to the preses's chair;
But O what an honour they are to the cloth,
When, with fervent devotion, they take the trust oath!

And there were some gentlemen of the long robe—
With wigs of all sizes, curl'd, long-tail'd, and bob,—
The carcage had smelt, tho' cold was the weather,
And, therefore, the vultures were gathered together!

And there was some bundles of parchments and writes—
Had the boys but got them, what store of fine kites—
Such as made for the cause, were rub'd up and sustained,
And the rest, they as wisely sent home to be cleaned.

And there was prodigious huzzaings, without;
The walls of the Court-House re-echoed the shout;
While the members, within, had their hopes and their fears,
When they saw how a noble Lord prick'd up his ears!

But to know all was there, your patience would fail,—
Of Misses and Masters, tag-rag and bob-tail,
Who had all come to town with the pious intent
To keep the feast-day on the first day of Lent!

And a joyful day it was, to be sure;
The victuals were good, and the claret was pure;
While the rabble roar'd out, such roaring was never,
With Skene and Lord George, beer and porter for ever!"

XXXI. ECCLESIASTICAL.

MANY an old woman in Scotland has been heard to say that she cared little for the *sense*, provided she got "the *sough* (sound) of the word."

The parishioners of Creich may have been of a different opinion :—

"At DORNACH, *the* 31 *of August* 1623.

"Whilk day Mr. Alexander Duff, present titular of the Kirk of Creich, finding himsclff altogether unfitt to serve at the said kirk, becaus of his want of the Yrisch (Gaelic) toung, and the whole peopill having no other language, friclic dimittes and overgoes all richt and tittell that he has of the said kirk. Lykeas thir present Synod, in respect of his non-residence at the said kirk, and want of the Yrisch language to serve the same, removes and transportes him from the said kirk and cure thairof. And this present Synod, having a cair for the said Mr. Alexander that he be not altogither castin louse, ordaines that he shall imploy his talent at the Kirk of Kilmalie, at the whilk there is some that has the Scotische language, until the said Mr. Alexander be elswhair planted

at ane uther kirk whair he may fitly serve. And for
the mor corroboratione of the said act, and his consent thairto, he has subscryvit the same.

" Extract out of the book of our Synod, the fyfteinth
day of November 1623.

(Signed) " MR. ALEXR. CUMING,
" Cleark to the Synod."

———

Mr. Stuart had not so tender a conscience as the
minister of Creich. He was just the man to prosper
in those (1688-89) revolutionary times.

" Advice—Comissarie Stuart of Morray to Comissarie Patersone in Rosse :—

> " What ! are you madd ? do you intend to go
> And begg e're you subscrive a lyn or two,
> And swear as many ? you ar void of sense
> If you have such a squimish conscience.
> But I have sworn already, you may say,
> To be a member of another way.
> What then ? and so have many more you see,
> Men both of eminent and low degree :
> Think you yourself more wise than those men are ?
> I'm sure that you ar not so rich, by farr.
> Consider, friend, if you forbear to swear,
> You lose a place of many pounds by year ;
> Consider you have neither lands nor rent,
> And what you do enjoy may soon be spent.
> Likewise you have a numerous family,

Who, if you do not swear, must beggars be;
This is an argument which has prevail'd
With many men, when other topiks fail'd.
But they who, in the art of oaths, have better skill,
Have, for a purge, prescrived this following pill:
Take of new coyn'd distinctions ane ounce,
A pound of the nyce quiddities of dounce,
Three scruples of The Grievance of the Nation,
Two drams of Protestant Equivocation:
Of all, well mixd, compose two pills or one,
And guild them over with Religion;
And this will purge a scrouplous conscience,
As I have found it by experience.
It purg'd me so that I can now digest
The Declaration, Covenant, and Test.
I, when it served to advance my gain,
Jure Divino Bishops did maintain,
Treated Jack Presbiter in ridicule,
Call'd him tub-preacher, puritan, and fool;
And, for to evidence I was no Whigg,
I wh——, and drank, and danc'd the other jigg;
But then I learn'd for to change my coat,
And tune my fiddle to another nott;
Cry'd up the right of Popish princes, and
Stood strictly to ther absolute command.
But, with the tymes, now I am chang'd again,
And learn'd to chant it in another strain.
The Pope I call Beast in the Revelatione;
A Popish prince The Greevance of the Nation;
Bishops I call Supporters of the Wh——,
And helped for to turn them out of door.
My only cry is now—The Cause, The Cause,
Our sweet Religion, Libertys, and Laws;
And, that I may pass for a perfect sanct,

I cry, alace! the broken Covenant.
I never stick at Scripture or tradition;
I'm for religion of the last edition.
I never examine if it be the best,
If that it may advance my interest
I never scruple on't. Let others stray
In the strait passage of the thorny way,
I wil not on my libertys incroach,
ffor I intend to go to heaven in coach.
Let him be worried on a dish of broath,
Who hath not conscience to digest an oath.
I've sworn already, God be praised, The Test,
The New Assurance, also, and the rest
Of those sweet oaths of which our land hath plenty :
And, e're I lose my place, I'll yet swear twenty.
I'll scrue my conscience to receive all oaths---
Change my religion as I do my cloathes ;
In fyne, ere I should forfeit my estate
I'd swear allegence to Mahomet !"

Spiritual destitution :

" for WILLIAM KING off Newmiln,
" for the presnt at Edinburgh.

" ELGIN, 21 *November* 1689.

" MUCH HONORED,—Our church being now vaccand, throu laying asyd of the Bishop and minister, we intreat, while ye are at Edinburgh, that ye inform your selfe how others in our circumstances are caricng in such caises, and how wee sall behave in order to the planting of the churches ; for it is somwhat dificult for us to get ministers to come and preach to us ;

wherfor wee would the sooner know what to doe in
the matter, and expects your anser and advyce theranent; which will verie much obleidge, Sir, your
humble servants,

"THE PROVEST AND BAILLIES OF ELGIN,

"Subscryving be our Clerk, at our comand,

"ROBERT ANDERSON, *Clerk*.

"It is fitt ye supplicat the counsell to get order
and warrand to us to choise our owin ministers, for
we cannot continow at this rate without preaching."

Five years later than the above :---

" ffor the Much Honored WILLIAM KING,

"of Newmiln, Provost of Elgine,

" ffor present at Edinburgh,

" To the care of John Anderson, wreater ther.

"ELGINE, 14 *December* 1694.

"MUCH HONORED,—As to our procedure in order
to the calling a minister, wee mett with the Land-
ward Heretors, Town Counsell, and Elders, and, at
our first meeting, wee sent thrie of our number to
speak with Mr. fforbes theranent, and to take pains
upon him for that effect.   But Mr. fforbes refused
and declyned to be our minister, and told, positively,
that he would not accept of our call ; whereupon wee
keept a second meeting, and wee lited severall ministers, and then (by plurality of voices) we concluded

to call Mr. Thomsone (who was supplying our vaicencie when ye went south), and Mr. James Oseburne (who was one of the members of the Committee that sat here in summer last), and we oppointed Loggie, Baillie Innes, and Clerk Munro to go to the presbetrie of fforres, to accquaint them therewith, and to take their advyce, in order to the forming and prosecuting of there call ; but, when they had spoke with the presbetrie therof, they got no satisfactory anser, but only the presbetry insinuate to them, first, that before we had votted for to call any minister, we ought to have had one of the presbetry present at our meeting ; and, second, we could not expect to get Mr. Oseburne, because he is already called to Aberdeene, nor Mr. Thomson, becaus he is tender and valletudinary, and so not fitt for such a charge ; and, upon these grounds, were not free to give us any farder advyce anent prosecutione of the said call. Whereupon wee called another meeting, this day, for advysing what methods to take with the presbetry, and anent the forsaid call, or any other ; but neither heritor nor elder keeped the samen, but, allenarly, the Baillies and one or tuo of the Counsell ; and, therefore, wee intreate ye may considder therof, and send us your advyse theranent, ffor wee stand in great need of it. As for this year's vaiceand stipend, wee are plagued with Mr. Turnbull (who has already sold all the tynd sheawes), to give him up the decreets of locality, and rentall of the tynd

bolls; and he has charged us with horning for that
effect. Your bedfellow and her young sone (who is
baptized Alexander) are both in health. So, wishing
you good health and ane safe journey home, wee continue, much honoured, your most oblcidged servants,

"THE MAGISTRATES OF ELGIN.

"Subscrived at their command by

"GEO. CHALMER, *Clerk.*

"All your family and friends are weill; and our
inhabitants have all payed their pollmoney, and what
farder occurrs we shall give you accompt."

James Gadderer, Bishop of Aberdeen, a prelate pos-
sessing great influence, drew up, and introduced into
the Service of the Scotch Episcopal Church, that form
of "The Communion Office" which has been objected
to by many members of the Church of England.

A burning heart, with the sacred monogram I.H.S.,
pierced by a cross, and having, on the surrounding
ribbon, "*Amor meus Crucifixus*,"[1] is the beautiful
device on the Bishop's seal :—

"To WILLIAM KING of Newmill, Esquire.

"At Elgin.

"FOCHABERS, *August 4th*, 1726.

"DEAR WORTHY SIR,—Tho' I have not much spare
time, and am ready to leave this place on my way

[1] My love crucified.

homeward, yet I cannot proceed without making some acknowledgement of your civilities, first and last. For you, Sir, and my other friends at Elgin have distinguished yourselves in your friendship and respect for me: all I shall say is, that if it was as much in my power as it is in my inclination, my returns should keep pace with the obligations you lay upon me. You, Sir, have very much refreshed my spirit, by agreeing to my advice as to your future conduct with respect to my worthy brother, Mr. Gordon, your pastor, who is well qualified to direct and assist you in your most important concerns. Your example will much strengthen his hands in the work of the holy ministry, as being the most considerable in his congregation for parts, influence, and fortune, which I hope you are so good as to employ for God's glory and the service of his Church. As we are united in principle, so ought we to be in affection and charity, that with one mind, and one heart and mouth, we may glorify God, and be glorified together.

"I took notice to you of the incompetency of the salary of your minister, and I cannot but recommend to you and to the other worthy managers, to take it into your serious consideration; and I doubt not but you will easily find ways and means, without being too burdensome to any, to raise it to a comfortable maintenance for him, by letting the seats of the meeting-house at reasonable rates, and a voluntary stenting of yourselves, according to your respective abilities and good inclinations ; and to set apart the weekly collections for the relief of the poor, who, I am sorry to hear it, have of late years been very much neglected.

"I beg you will make my respectful service acceptable to your worthy relatione, and to my other friends with you. I heartily pray for you all, recommending you to the protection, favour, and blessings of Almighty God, and I am, with a particular regard, dear Sir, your most affectionate humble servant,

"JA. GADDERAR,
" *Bishop of Aberdeen.*

"*P.S.*— I assure you, Sir, it was not Mr. Gordon, but one of yourselves, that prompted me in what I write in relation to him.　Adieu."

Baptismal regeneration :—

" Magdalen, naturall daughter to James King and Janet Cumming, was, as born within the visible Church (without regard to the said parents), the 4th of September jajvijst and thirty-two years (1732), baptized by me,　ALEXR. YOUNGSON, *Minister.*"

A vacancy having occurred in the Kirk of Duffus, June 1736, a dispute arose between Sir Robert Gordon of Gordonston (acting for the Duke of Gordon then a minor) and Archibald Dunbar of Newton, as to the right of patronage. The claim of each party was laid before the Synod of Moray, who decided in favour of Mr. Dunbar; a decision which, on appeal to the General Assembly, was confirmed. The correspondence on this subject embraces letters from the celebrated Simon, Lord Lovat, and there is one, of particular interest, from Ludovic Brodie, W.S., who describes how the clergy were feasted by the rival claimants.

Henrietta, Duchess of Gordon, to Mr. Dunbar, who eventually presented the Rev. John Bower :—

" GORDON CASTLE, *June* 27, 1736.

" SIR,—I understand the minister of Duffus dyed, Saturday last, and am informed there is one, Mr. William Collie, presently helper to Mr. Hugh Anderson, minister at Drainie, ane honest sensible man, and weel known to the circumstances of the parish of Duffus, who, it is thought, would be a very fit successor to the deceased. If you have no particular objection against him, I shall desire the favour of your interest in his behalf. My son's ffactor, Doctor Stuart, will meet and commune with you upon this matter, and concurr with you in such joint measures as will be most expedient for this end and the good of the parish. Wee are, Sir, your assured friend to serve you,　　　　　　　　　　　　　　H. GORDON."

Q

Reply to the Duchess of Gordon's letter :–

" MAY IT PLEASE YOUR GRACE,—I had the honour
of your Grace's letter, of the twenty-seventh June, in
favours of Mr. William Collie, with whom I have but
very little acquaintance ; but, having occasion to see
him at the burial of my deceast freind and minister
of this parish, he told me with a great deal of honesty
and sincerity (which I am not to doubt of), that he
never expected to be a successor to the defunct, he
never thought, he never heard, nor did he know,
directly or indirectly, any manner of application made
or to be made for him in that matter by any person
whatsoever.

" It is yet too early to think of any successor, as the
defunct's relict has a legal title to the current half-
year's stipend of cropt 1736.   And, as my nighbour,
Sir Robert Gordon, is but unkind to me, in regard he
has been pleased, for some years past, to cast those
lands into ley, out of which his share and proportion
of this stipend always was and ought to be paid, and
to the teinds of which lands I, as patron, have undoubted right, (and as I am, therby, deprived of this
benefit, the whole, to a trifle, of this stipend falls upon
me, which, as it is no less, by decreet of modification,
than one hundred and twenty-eight bolls bear, three
hundred and fifty merks of money, with sixty merks
for communion elements yearly, is a very heavie burden

upon me), if I should find out some freind of my own
sufficiently qualified for this charge, and acceptable to
others as well as to me, I am hopeful your Grace
would neither think it offensive nor unreasonable that
I should give any interest I have, in favours of such
a man, though, I assure your Grace, I would neither
present nor recommend my brother to the parish,
unless he was indued with all the qualifications necessary for a minister thereof.—I remain, &c.

" ARCHD. DUNBAR."

Lord Lovat's letters are written on gilt-edged paper,
and enclosed in envelopes :—

" To the Honourable ARCHIBALD DUNBAR, Esqr.,
      " At his house at Duffus.
                        " BEAUFORT, 26th March 1737.

" DEAR SIR,—I had the honour of your letter by
your express, late Thursday night, but, as I have been
out of order since the beginning of this month, and
that yesterday was my post day, it was impossible for
me to answer your letter till this day.

" I am exceeding glad to know that you and your
lady are well, and having enquired at the bearer if
you had children, he tells me that you have a son,
which gives me great pleasure, and I wish you and
your lady much joy of him, and that you may have
many more, for they will be the nearest relatives I
have of any Dunbars in the world, except your father's

children ; and my relation to you is not at a distance,
as you are pleased to call it, it is very near, and I
have not such a near relation betwixt Spey and Ness ;
and you may assure yourself that I will always behave
to you and yours as a relation ought to do ; and I beg
leave to assure you and your lady of my most affectionat regards, and my Lady Lovat's, and my young
ones, your little cousins.

" I am very sorry that you are oppressed, but I am
surprised at nothing of that kind that comes from that
airt. You may freely depend upon all the assistance
in my power, and I believe I have as much to say
with the ministers of that Synod as any one man that
you can write to. I have three particular friends,
beyond Elgin, that I hope will be useful to you, and
that I will strongly solicite for that purpose ; that is
old Mr. Gilchrist, and young Mr. Gilchrist, and Mr.
Sim of Mortlach, who are three pretty fellows, and
they have a great deall to say in the presbyterys that
they are in. I shall send my letters to you, to be
delivered to them when you think it proper ; and as to
the presbyterys of Inverness and Abernethy of Strathspey, I shall have as much to say there as most men,
and I shall solicite them all, and send them a copy of
your letter, which describes the affair better than I
could tell it ; in short, I shall leave no stone unturned,
in my power, to serve you. My cousin, young Achnagern, is with me here ; and Mr. Rose, the minister

of Nairn, was born in Achnagern's land, and has a
dependence upon him, and I have begged of my cousin
to solicite him strongly in your favours, which I hope
will have a good effect; and I make no doubt but you
will carry your affair at the synod.   I am sure I shall
use all my endeavours for that effect, more than if it
was for a settlement in the parish that I live in.   You
may expect letters from me for the two Mr. Gilchrists
and Mr. Sim in eight or ten days, and I will send an
express with letters to all my friends of the presbytery
of Inverness and Strathspey, and send a copy of your
letter in every one of my own letters, since it is the
best account I can give of the matter.   I am sorry
that our cousin, Bailie Robertson, is so much concerned about his late loss that he is not in condition
to go about for you; however, I think you should write
to him, for you know he is an active pretty fellow.

" I beg you give my most humble duty to your
honest father and his family; and I am, with a very
sincere esteem and respect, dear Sir, your most affectionate cousin, most obedient and most humble servant,   LOVAT.

" I will write to my friend Dalrachanie, and to my
other allys in Strathspey, to ride about for you, on
my account, among all the ministers in that country,
and I will write, myself, to every one of them that I
am acquainted with."

" Beaufort, *9th Aprile* 1737.

" Dear Cousin,—This moment I got your express from Inverness, and I wish you had done me the honour to come out this morning, that we might concert matters about your minister, since I have now the matter at heart as much as you have, in order to serve you. I beg you may do me the honour to come out, to-morrow morning, with my cousin, Bailie Robertson, and dine with me. I offer my dear Tom my most sincere respects. I am heartily sorry for his loss,[1] and if I had been in condition to go abroad, I would have gone to her burial, without a call. I have been writing, these three days past, to severall ministers about your affair ; and if it could do you service, I would write to all the ministers in Scotland, that I am acquainted with. I have written the inclosed two lines to Mr. M'Bean, and other two lines to my cousin, Mr. Fraser. I cannot attack Mr. Baillie of Inverness, because I am informed that he is, already, on the other side of the question ; in short, if you will be so good as to come here, we shall concert what is to be done, so far as I have interest ; for you may assure yourself that I am, without reserve, with a sincere esteem and respect, my dear cousin, your most obedient and most humble servant, Lovat."

[1] Thomas Robertson, bailie of Inverness, was a member of the Inshes family ; he had lost his wife.

"BEAUFORT, *Aprile 9th*, 1737.

"DEAR SIR,—I did expect to have had the honour to see you in this house, when you was at Inverness, and I was a little surprised when I did not see you nor hear from you, after I sent you my letters for Mr. H. M'Bean and Mr. Fraser, but I suppose you have gone away in a great hurry. I beg leave to assure you, and your lady and young son, of my most affectionate respects, and my Lady Lovat's, and my young ones, your cousins. I have sent you, enclosed, three letters for three as pretty fellows, in my opinion, as is of the clergy, and they are my three intimate friends, and I am very sure they will serve me in any affair that is not against their conscience. You will be so kind as to send them the letters, or deliver them out of your own hand, with a copie of your case. I find your adverse party have been very busy making great interest against you everywhere, but I believe that the final decision must be by the General Assembly, where I will use my utmost endeavours to do you all the service in my power. I have written to all the ministers of my acquaintance in the presbytery of Inverness, and in the neighbouring presbyterys of Strathspey and Badenoch, and sent them a copie of your first letter to me. You may assure yourself of any service in my power, for I am, with unalterable esteem and respect, dear Sir, your most affectionate cousin, and most obedient humble servant,

"LOVAT."

"DEAR SIR,—I had the honour of your letter, with
the state of your case as to the settlement of your
minister. I do assure you that, in all my life, I never
took so much pains in any ecclesiastick affair, and
if Mr. Bowar was my brother I would do no more
for him. I wrote to every minister, of my acquaintance, betwixt this and Keith. I had favourable answers
from most of them, and I had a letter last night from
my good friend Dalrachanie, who is to be at Forres as
a ruling elder ; he gives me good encouragement from
the ministers of Strathspey, and, as he is married to
my Lord Elches's sister, I am sure you will find him
very assisting. I have beged of Mr. Thompson, who
delivers you this letter, to let you know the dispositions of all the ministers of his particular acquaintance ; he has promised me to be for your man if it is
not directly against his conscience. I do not doubt
but you will carry your affair at the synod. I wish
you good success at the General Assembly. I have
some leading men of the Church, that are in the first
posts in the nation, who, I think, are the prettiest men
in the Church, who are my very good friends ; and
when you think it necessary that I should write to
them, I shall do it in the strongest terms that I can
think of to serve you.

"I offer you, and your lady and son, my most affectionate respects and my Lady Lovat's ; and I am, with

a very particular esteem, and a very sincere regard and attachment, my dear Sir, your most affectionate cousin, and most obedient humble servant,

"LOVAT."

Mr. Brodie's report :—

" ARCHIBALD DUNBAR, Esq. of Newton, Elgin.

"EDINBURGH, 20 *May* 1737.

" SIR,—-The appeal about the settlement of the parish of Duffus was, yesterday, determined, after a very long and full hearing which lasted from near twelve till five o'cloak at night, in favours of Mr. Bower. The votes were, for affirming the sentence of the synod, a hundred and twenty-two ; not affirming, about thirty-two ; nonliquots, about twenty ; and, for all this plurallity upon your side, there was never a call wherein greater pains was taken than Sir Robert used against you. His Lady went to the west country ; but he himself stayed in town, went and visited the Commissioner, made himself apparently very great with him, and addresst all the members personally, whether acquainted with them or not, with the greatest earnestness. He was, since the Assembly sat down, always in the forenoons travelling amongst them ; and I believe his great assurance did him no service in the cause.

" Mr. Geddes left Lord Elchies at Aberdeen, and

came up here himself, and did all was possible for
Mr. Bower. Your friend, Mrs. Peggy Dunbar, her
sister, and Mr. Baillie, were very active for you,
especially Mrs. Dunbar, who went through all her
acquaintances, members of the Assembly, and engaged
a multitude of ladys in your favours, to whom she
destributed above a hundred cases, and was as anxious
and carefull about this matter as she could have been
in any of the greatest importance. She had a multitude of ministers every day at tea with her, particularly Mr. Gordon of Alloa, who, notwithstanding the
letter sent him, and all she could say, was strongly
your opposite. Sir Robert kept open table at Mrs.
Herdman's for the clergy always, at dinner ; and they
were bidden resort there, for breakfast, and call for
what they pleased, on his account. We, on the other
hand, invited and intertained as many ministers as
we could find, for three or four successive nights, at
supper in a tavern, which comes to no small expens ;
but since so much hath been wared on this cause, and
now that it was to receive a final decision, I thought
it was a pity to lose for this. Mr. Bower's personal
acquaintance got him almost all the members for Fife,
and some for Perth. I wrote to Provost Hay of
Aberdeen, who got us Professor Lumsden who spoke
strenuously, Provost Stewart (a ruling elder), and Mr.
Hay, minister at Crimon. Lord Lyon wrote to the
Commissioner, to Mr. Gordon of Alves, to Mr. Win-

chester, &c. Mr. Winchester was of good service to
your cause. I also spoke to Mr. Gordon very roundly ;
but he was immovable, and, with Squair, were constant attendants of Sir Robert's, and strong sollicitors
among the ministers. The express came very timeously here, on Wednesday night, with the certificate
and ministers' declaration about your being qualified,
which was the strongest argument they had against
you. Wee concealed the certificate of declaration till
the cause was pled, and Sir Robert's lawyers having
spoke a great deal upon it. In answering their debate,
Mr. Ffraser's certificate was produced, and read in
open Assembly. In the reply for Sir Robert, his
lawyers pled everything that was derogatory to Mr.
Ffraser's character, and produced not only a certificate
from Burdsyards,[1] absolutely bearing that you had
never been qualified by him or his substitutes ; they
also produced a complaint of Thomas Watson's before
the session against James Fraser, with two wrong extracts of the fiars and the Lords' proceedings ther-

---

[1] The original certificate from Robert Urquhart of Burdsyards, Sheriff-
Depute of the shire of Elgin and Forres, is among these papers. It
" certifies and declares that Archibald Dunbar, younger of Newton,
never did quality " to Government, before him or his substitute, since his
accession to his estates ; yet it is certified by the two ministers of Elgin
(Rev. Lachlan Shaw and Rev. Mr. Irvine), that they had read in the
Sheriff-Court book that Mr. Dunbar had so qualified himself before the
said Robert Urquhart, and that they had seen his signature to the cus-
tomary oaths, on a parchment in the hands of the Sheriff-Clerk ; and that
he had truly subscribed the same.

upon, which they had sent an express for to the house
where Mr. Watson was, that he might order his servant to deliver them. The lawyer for you, to disprove
these, insisted that the clerk was the proper officer
in law, and produced the certificate by the Ministers,
Provost, and Baillie of Elgin, which being read in
open Assemblie, did fully convince the members that
the certificate produced by Burdsyards was false. Sir
Robert had for lawyers, Mr. Archibald Murray, Mr.
Michael Menzies, and Mr. Charles Gordon. I had
imployed only, for you, Mr. Patrick Haldane ; and
could get no other fit lawyer in town to add to him.
I gave him, for drawing the case, and, at another time,
for making remarks on this case, and for his attendance in the Assembly, six guineas. I must say he did
acquit himself very handsomely and to advantage.
Mr. Gordon of Alves was the first of the clergy that
spoke against you, very warmly, for upwards of an
hour, and took great offence at a passage, of the remarks, reflecting upon him and the Committee for
Moderation, as partial for refusing sixteen to sign by
proxy at the Moderation without any just cause.   He
said all he could in his defence, as if he had been
preaching, and sweat heartily at it; but his vindication
of himself, and all he could say, had no influence.
Then Mr. Squair spoke, but I never heard him speak
so ill; what he said was perplexed and confused,
scarcely intelligible.   Next to him Mr. Miln and Mr.

Syme of Mortlich. Mr. Miln spoke long; but Mr. Syme spoke, though to very good purpose, but short, because at this time the Assembly were wearied and anxious to have the cause determined. The Synod of Murray being put out, except the Laird of Grant and Duff of Crombie, who, being absent from the division, were allowed to stay in, there was then a great contest about the state of the vote. It carryed 'Affirm the sentence of the Synod of Murray or Not?' Grant voted 'Proceed;' Mr. Crombie 'Affirm.' Sir Robert, while the Synod of Murray and the parties were out, intertained with a glass of wine some of his opposites, such as Mr. Haldon, Mr. Syme, &c., in a tavern; but when partys were called in, to hear the sentence intimat to them, Sir Robert, being informed that he had lost the cause by so great a majority, did not return to the Assembly to hear the interloquiter published, and, I believe, will not be at the Commissioner's levee this day, as he usually was before.

"This is a long narrative of the proceedings; much more might be said upon it, but I shall send you doubles of the prints, on both sides; and for further information I remitt you to the ministers when they come home. It was moved in Assembly to write a letter of apology to the Duchess of Gordon (who had wrote a great many letters to several of the members of the Assembly), in name of the Assembly, and was agreed to; but whether upon second thought they will

write this letter or not, I know not ; the thing is of
no great importance to you. I am, Sir, your most
humble servant,　　　　　　　　　　　Lud. Brodie.

" *P.S.*—You should return letters of thanks to Mrs.
Dunbar and Mr. Baillie, and separately acknowledge
the favours ; also to Lord Lyon and Mr. Winchester,
&c. I shall send you an extract of the Assembly's
sentence, by next ; and, instead of the ten pounds you
designed, you must remit at least twenty pounds, per
first."

Sir Robert Gordon never forgave Mr. Bower his
success :---

" To Mr. Archibald Dunbar, younger
　　" of Newton, att Duffus.

　　　　　　　" Manse of Duffus, 1*st* *Septr.* 1740.

" Sir,—You may remember I waited off you, a day
or two after Sir Robert had been here, and shewed
you the paper he had write anent what his tennants
were resting, and told you he threatned me by calling
me, several times, a Lyar, and that his doer att Edinburgh had said I was a Fool in taking out a caption
against him, at random, as he accounted it. I was
then, you may remember, very uneasie with the remainder of the cholliak, I had been under att Rothes,
and not able to endure either his threats or long com-

pany ; and, to be free of him, I wrote a sort of letter
to him, wherein I declared, that though I had caused
Evan Macbain, messenger, intimate to him the caption
I had against him and the rest of the heritors for my
stipends that were unpayed, yet I designed not to
execute that caption against him or the other heritors,
till the Lords should give sentence anent a locality.
This was the contents of the letter he gott, as, when it
is seen, it will show. I shall be heartily sorrow if it
any wise prejudge you ; I can assure I never designed
it, nor, by no threats, would have been driven to it, if
I had thought so.—I am with all regard, Sir, your
most obliged humble servant,

"Jo : Bower."

On the death of Mr. Bower, in 1748, several candidates applied for the kirk. One offered to marry "any
particular friend or relation ;" another promised "to
demit" when required by the patron :—

" To Archibald Dunbar of Newton, Esq.,
        " at Duffus.

"Manse of Duffus, *March* 8, 1748.

" Sir,—It is very reasonabel that you should please
your self, as well as the parish of Duffus, in the choice
of a minister, so I am sensibel that applications have
been and are making to you, as patron, by several

candidates to fill that vacant church ; and, if ye will
be pleased to prefer me, by granting a presentation in
my favours, so as I may be settled before Michaelmas
next, which will entitle me to that half-year's stipend
next after expiration of the ann. at Whitsunday first,
then, and in that case, I shall hold this lasting favour
of your goodwilling, with more grateful acknowledgments than are usually paid, during all the days of my
life. And as ye may have necessary use for seques-
trating the first half-year's stipend, above-mentioned,
for any particular pious use or other just intention of
your own, I hereby promise and oblige myself, after
ingathering of the same, to grant you my bond for
the value, bearing interest and payable yearly, in such
manner, and for such use and behoof as you shall be
pleased to appoint, either for the encouragement of a
schoolmaster, or any other use, so as I shall be no
more than the debtor, borrower, and user of the said
principal sum, for payment of the ordinary legal
annual rent, till such time as I shall think myself in
condition, and judge it proper for me, to pay up the
same, so as that it may be lent out upon interest to
any other person for the uses you may intend. And
if ye shall judge it proper to bestow any particular
friend or relation of yours upon me as my wife, I also
hereby promise not only to keep my affections free,
but also, with God's assistance, to accept of her, pre-
ferably to any other person whatever, as my future

spouse ; and for this effect I also hereby promise to take and re-enter (at least) the twenty pound sterling class in the Widow's funds, as the same is established by Act of Parliament ; and I shall always consider that, along with your relation, you have also given me one thousand pounds Scots yearly to maintain her. These concessions and promises as they are cheerfully and voluntarily made, with a sincere and faithful intention of being performed, so I leave them with what else you judge proper to be added, to your serious perusal and consideration ; and, in the meantime, I beg they may be secreted from the world.—I am, Sir, your very humble servant, A. B."

Extract from a letter from Brodie of Brodie. "Spynie" was grandfather of Elisabeth, last Duchess of Gordon :–

"LONDON, *Aprile 9th.*

"I hear Mr. Bower is past recovery ; so, if he dies, I recomend James Brodie to you, as a man cut out to your own mind—a good preacher, and a modest, civil, obliging, obedient fellow, with whom you can be quite easy ; nay, you cannot find such a man for your purpose in the island. Nay, further, Spynie and I can become bound he shall demit whenever you are tired of him.

R

" Accept of all our kind compliments to you, Nellie, and the bairns ; and believe me, yours faithfully,

" ALEXR. BRODIE.

" The doing of this would have no other bad conse-quence than piquing the Laird of Gordonstown."

Two certificates addressed to the patron, in favour of the Rev. Alexander Murray, the successful candi-date.   Mr. Godsman was a Roman Catholic priest.

" ACHANASY, *June 5th*, 1748.

" SIR,—Being told that Mr. Alexander Murray, some time ago helper in the parish of Keith, is by his enemies accused of having informed against the poor gentlemen in distress after the battle of Cul-loden, I, who lived in the same parish, and was in distress, do certify that he was so averse from such ways of doing that, as far as it consisted with his own safety, he was willing to aid or assist them; so that he is aspersed most maliciously, and without any grounds, by his enemies ; and you may have this for a certain truth.   I am, Sir, your most humble servant,

" ALEXANDER GODSMAN."

" KEITH, *June 7th*, 1748.

" SIR,—Though we have not the honour of your acquaintance, yet justice to Mr. Murray's injured character, who, we hear, is represented to you as an ill-natured man and a notorious informer against those in distress after the battle of Culloden (and especially against us and Mr. Simpson, who is at present out of the country), hath obliged us to trouble you with this, assuring that although we had the misfortune to fall into the hands of the King's forces, or at least to suffer by them, and altho' we are conscious to ourselves that if Mr. Murray had been such a man as he is represented, he had cause of resentment, yet he was so far from informing, or taking the advantage of our distress, that, so far as his interest could goe, and safety permitt, he was usefull to us; and we can farther assure that Mr. Simpson looked upon him as the chief instrument of his liberation; and instead of being in any shape an ill-natured man, we always found him most agreeable, and, in every thing, to act suitable to his character. As we find his name hath been so unjustly traduced, we think it a piece of material justice, so far as we can, to vindicate him from these malicious and invidious aspersions; which we hope you will be so good as excuse from, Sir, your most obedient humble servants,

" WILL. PATERSON.

WILLIAM STODHART."

We have no means of knowing how Sir Robert
Gordon behaved to Mr. Murray, but the reverend
gentleman, in January 1751, thus informed the patron
of the Baronet's state of health : —

" There has been for some time past a good deal of
sickness amongst the country people here, and severals are daily dieing, so that we sometimes bury at
the rate of three a-day. Your friend Sir Robert, I
am told, was like to have gone to the Elisian fields,
but has so far recovered as to be able to thrash John
Gow's wife for traveling on his forbidden ground. I
am, dear Sir, your most obliged and humble servant,

" ALEXR. MURRAY."

XXXII. WITCHES.

As a belief in witchcraft long prevailed in Scotland, we are tempted to give some papers, showing how, in 1704-5, the Magistrates and the Minister of Pitten-weem disgraced themselves.

" Unto the Right Honourable the Lords of Her Majesties Privy Counsell,

" The Magistrats and Toun Counsell of Pittenweem, and Minister and Kirk Session theirof

" Humblie Sheweth,

" That wher their being att present a great many malifices committed upon the person of Patrick Mor-toun, son to Patrick Mortoun, smith in Pittenweem, by severall witches now in prison there, wherof the greatest part have already confessed to us their guilt in tormenting the said Patrick, and of their compact with the devill, and renounceing their baptism, wee humbly crave liberty to give your Lordships the fol-lowing representation of the matter of ffact, to the effect your Lordships may grant a commission, to

such as your Lordships shall think fitt, to take tryall
of the persons who have confessed, and others against
whom there are not only presumptions of guilt but
lykwise a clear probation readie to be adduced.

"The matter of fact, in short, is as follows :—In
the beginning of March last, the said Patrick Mortoune, about sixteen years of age, and free of any
knowen vice, being imployed by his ffather to make
some naills to a ship belonging to one of the merchants in Pittenweem, when he was working in his
ffather's smiddie, one Beatrix Laing, who is one of
these who have confessed, desired him to make some
naills ffor her, which he modestly refused, in regard
he had been already imployed to make the naills ffor
the ship, which were in haste, and could not abide
any delay.   Upon which answer Beatrix did shew a
great deall of discontent, and went away, threatning
to be revenged, which did somewhat ffrighten him,
because he knew she was under a bad ffame, and
reputed ffor a witch of a long time.   The next day,
when he was passing the door of her house, he
observed a timber vessell with some water and a fire
coall in it, att the door, which made him apprehend
that it was a charme layd ffor him, and the effects of
her threatning ; and immediately he was seased with
such a weakness in his limbs that he could hardly
stand or walk, and continued in a languishing condition till the first of May last ; and the phisitians were

imployed ffor his recovery, yet no means they could use had any effect, but still grew worse, having no appetite, and his bodie strongely emacerated.

" About the beginning of May his caice altered to the worse, by haveing such strange and unusuall fitts as did astonish all onlookers. His belly, att sometime, was distended to a great height; at other tymes his breast and his back were so distended, that the bones, both of his back and breast, did ryse to a prodigious height, and suddenly fell; and in the mean tyme his breathing was like to the blowing of a bellowes; att other times his bodie became rigide and inflexible, in so much that neither his armes nor legs could be bowed or moved by any strength, tho' frequently tryed; and all his senses benummed, and yet his pulse in good order. Att some tyme his head turned quite about, or to his shoulders, and no strength able to turne it back or repone it ; and was many tyme in griveous agonies, and sometimes in soonds; att other tymes his toungue drawen back in his throatt, especiallie when he wes telling who were his tormentors; and when either the magistrats or minister did bring in any of these women, whom he had discovered to be his tormentors, before they came within the door, he cryed out his tormentors were present, and named them; and tho' severalls present did cover his face, and caused severall women touch him (besides those he discovered to be his tormentors) by turnes, yet,

when these did touch him, upon whom he made no
complaint, no effect followed; but upon the approach
and touch of these whom he complained of, his
agonies increased, and cryed out his tormentors were
present.

"The poor man has bein in this condition since the
beginning of May last, and continues to be so, haveing very short intervalls; and his condition is much
about the same with that of Bargarran's daughter in
the west.

"Their are seven imprisoned, viz., Beatrix Laing,
lsobell Adam, Nicolas Lawson, and Jane Corseitt,
Thomas Brown, Margaret Wallace, and Margaret
Jack. The first ffour of these have confessed their
being guiltie of a compact with the devil, renunceing
their baptisme, and tormenting the said Patrick Mortoun, upon ane examination by us, the Magistrats and
Minister, in the Tolbuith of Pittenweem; and the
other three are not only loaded by presumptions but
fyled by the conplents, as not only guiltie of witchcraft but lykewayes of the malefecis upon the said
Patrick Mortoun.

"And seing there is here in the discoveries alreadie
made, as to ffour of the imprisoned, a plaine confession of there being guiltie of witchcraft and of the
malefeices above represented upon the said Patrick
Mortoun, and that *constat de corpore delicti;* and
lykewayes, that the rest are loaded with presump-

tious and delated by the conplents as guilty, with
themselfes, of witchcraft and tormenting of the said
Patrick ; as also, seing it would be a great deal of
expence to bring so many witnesses, as will be necessary to prove the different and distinct points that
falls under probation, ffor convicting of the fornamed
persons, and that the matter will be made more clear
than if the same were cognosied here before the Lord
of Justiciary,

    " May it therfor please your Lordships, in con-
    sideration of the premisses, to grant warrand
    and commission to such gentlemen or others,
    that live in and about the place, as your
    Lordships shall think fitt, to take cognition
    and tryall in this matter, and to determine
    therin by a Justiciary power from your
    Lordships, as has been frequently done in
    such cases, according to justice ; and your
    Lordships' servants will ever pray.

" *Beatrix Laing's Confession before the Magistrats
    and Minister of Pittenweem.*

        " 23 MAY 1704.

    " Wherin she acknowledges that she was angry at
Patrick Mortoune—the person who is tormented—
for refusing her nails, and that she designed to revenge it of him by useing the charm of the coall in
the water, and that the devill was with her, when she

used the charm, and appeired to her first in the lik-
ness of a dog, and then in the likeness of a boy, and
said to her that he would help her to destroy the lad ;
in order to which she made a pictur, to torment the
lad, of whyt wax, and that there was none with her
at the makeing of it but Nicolas Lawson, and that
she did putt pinns unto ; and did engadge with the
devill about twelve years since, and the caus that
moved her to engadge was that she should have success in her merchandise, and that he appeared to her
at that tyme in the likeness of a litle man, and the
first thing he desyred of her was to renunce her
baptisme, which accordingly she did ; and acknowledges that she got the devill's mark in her shoulder,
which was very painfull at the tyme.

" *The Confessione of Nicolas Lawson, aneother of the*
Witches.

   " She acknowledges that she was at the makeing of
the pictur, wherwith Patrick Mortoun was tormented,
and acknowledges that she put in only ane pin, and
there was about twelve pins in it, and that she did
renunce her baptism at her first meeting with the
devill, for which he promised her a good milk cow,
but he never gave it ; and likewayes, acknowledges
that the devill apperred to her since she came to
prisone, which was upon Saturday night, the twen-

tieth of May; and that it was a long time since she engadged in the devill's service; and that she was likewayes at the meeting with the devill in Alexander M'Grigory's house, and that ther wer present with her, Beatrix Laing, Janet Corfortt, Thomas Broun, and Isobell Adam, and some strangers, that she knew not; and that the same Thomas Broun did play to them on a pype.

" *The Confession of Isobell Adam, aneother of the Witches.*

" Confesses that about a fourtnight after Mertimess she came to Beatrix Laing's, and that she saw a litle black man with a hatt and black cloathes, sitting at the board end, and Beatrix said ' Heir is a gentleman that will fie yow, if you will not fie with me ;' upon which she engadged, and the devill kissed her, and told her that he knew she was discontent with her lot, and that in his service she should get riches as much as she could wish ; and that upon New Yeir day therafter, the devill appeired to her in Thomas Adam's house, and ther she renunced her baptisme voues ; and likewayes acknoledges that she was in M'Grigor's house with Beatrix Laing, Nicolas Lawson, Janet Corscitt, and Thomas Broun, upon a designe to strangle the said M'Grigor."

The unhappy fate of one of the reputed witches is thus described in a letter from a gentleman in Fife :—

"*Febr.* 5, 1705.

"SIR,—I doubt not of your being exceedingly surprized with this short and just account, I give you, of a most barbarous murder, committed in Pittenweem, the 30th of January last. One Peter Morton, a blacksmith in that town, after a long sickness, pretended that witches were tormenting him ; that he did see them, and know them ; and, from time to time, as he delated such and such women to be witches, they were, by order of the magistrates and minister of Pittenweem, apprehended as such, to a very considerable number, and put into prison. This man, by his odd postures and fits, which seemed to be very surprising at first, wrought himself into such a credit with the people of the place, that unless the Earl of Rothes, our Sheriff, had discovered his villany, and discouraged that practice, God knows how fatal it might have proved to many honest families of good credit and respect. Sir, however, at first many were deceived, yet now all men of sense are ashamed for giving any credit to such a person. But how hard it is to root out bad principles, once espoused by the rabble, and how dangerous a thing to be at their mercy, will appear by the tragical account, I give you, of one of these poor women, Janet Corphar.

" After she was committed prisoner to the tolbooth, upon a suspicion of her being a witch, she was well guarded with a number of men, who, by pinching her and pricking her with pins, keept her from sleep many days and nights, threatning her with present death, unless she would confess herself guilty of witchcraft ; which at last she did. This report spreading abroad, made people curious to converse with her upon the subject, who found themselves exceedingly disappointed. The Viscount of Primrose, being in Fife, occasionally inclined to satisfy his curiosity in this matter ; the Earl of Kellie, my Lord Lyon, the Laird of Scots Tarves, and the Laird of Randerston, were with his lordship in Pittenweem. Three of the number went to the tolbooth and discoursed her ; to whom she said, that all that she had confessed, either of herself, or her neighbours, were lies, and cried out ' God forgive the minister ;' and said he had beat her one day with his staff, when she was telling him the truth. They asked her how she came to say anything that was not true. She cried out ' Alas! alas! I behoved to say so, to please the minister and the bailies ;' and in the meantime she beged, for Christ's sake, not to tell that she had said so, else she would be murdered. Another time, when the Laird of Glenagies and Mr. Bruce of Kinross were telling her she needed not deny what they were asking her, for she had confessed as much as would infallibly burn her, she cried

out ' God forbid !'— and to one of the two, she said
that from which he might rationally conclude she
insinuat she had assurance, from the minister, her life
should not be taken.

" A little before harvest, Mr. Ker of Kippilaw, a
Writer to the Signet, being in Pittenweem, Mr. Robert
Cook, Advocate, went with him to prison to see this
poor woman. Mr. Cook, among other questions, asked
her if she had not renounced her baptism to the devil.
She answered she never renounced her baptism but to
the minister. These were her words ; what she meant
by them I know not. The minister having got account
of this from Mr. Cook, he sent for her, and in presence
of Mr. Cook and Mr. Ker in the church, he threatned
her very severely, and commanded the keeper to put
her in some prison, by her self under the steeple, lest
(as he said) she should pervert those who had confessed. The keeper put her into a prison in which
was a low window, out of which it was obvious that
anybody could make an escape, and accordingly she
made her escape that night.

" Next day, when they missed her, they made a
very slight search for her, and promised ten pound
Scots to any body that would bring her back.

" Mr. Gordon, minister of Leuchars, hearing she
was in his parish, eight miles distant from Pittenweem, caused apprehend her, and sent her prisoner
under custody of two men, on the 30th of January, to

Mr. Cowper, minister of Pittenweem, without giving
any notice to the magistrates of the place. When she
came to Mr. Cowper, she asked him if he had any
thing to say to her. He answered ' No.' She could
get lodging in no house but with one Nicolas Lawson,
one of the women that had been called witches. Some
say a bailie put her there.

" The rabble hearing she was in town, went to Mr.
Cowper, and asked him what they should do with her ?
He told them he was not concerned ; they might do
what they pleased with her. They took encouragement from this to fall upon the poor woman, those of
the minister's family going along with him, as I hear.
They fell upon the poor creature immediately, and
beat her unmercifully, tying her so hard with a rope
that she was almost strangled ; they dragged her
through the streets and alongst the shoar by the
heels. A bailie, hearing of a rabble near his stair,
came, which made them immediately disappear ; but
the magistrates, though met together, not taking care
to put her into close custody for her safety, the rabble
gathered again immediately, and streached a rope betwixt a ship and the shoar, to a great height, to which
they tyed her fast ; after which they swinged her to
and fro, from one side to another, in the meantime
throwing stones at her from all corners, until they
were weary ; then they loosed her, and with a mighty
swing threw her upon the hard stones, all about being

ready in the meantime to receive her with stones and staves, with which they beat her most cruelly. Two of her daughters came, upon their knees, begging to be allowed one word of their mother before she expired ; but that being refused, the rabble threatning to treat them in the same manner, they went off. The rabble never gave over till the poor wretch was dead ; and, to be sure she was so, they called a man with a horse and a sledge, and made him drive over her backward and forward several times. When they were sure she was killed outright, they dragged her miserable carcass to Nicolas Lawson's house, where they first found her ; laying on her belly a door of boards, and on it a great heap of stones.

" There was a motion made to treat Nicolas Lawson after the same manner immediately, but some of them, being wearied with three hours' sport, as they called it, said it would be better to delay her for another day's divertisement ; and so they all went off.

" It is said that Mr. Cowper, in a letter to Mr. Gordon, gave some rise to all this ; and Mr. Cowper, to vindicate himself, wrote to Mr. Gordon, whose return says if he were not going to Edinburgh, he would give him a double of his letter. It is strange he sent him not the principal. In the postscript he assures him he shall conceal it to meeting. .

" It is certain that Mr. Cowper, preaching, the Lord's day immediately after, in Pittenweem, took no notice of the murder, which at least makes him guilty of sinful silence. Neither did Mr. Gordon, in his letter to Mr. Cowper, make any regrate for it; and this some construe to be a justifying of a horrid wickedness, in both.

" We are perswaded the Government will examine this affair to the bottom, and lay little stress upon what the magistrates or minister of Pittenweem will say to smooth over the matter, seeing it is very well known that either of them could have quashed that rabble, and prevented that murder, if they had appeared zealous against it.

" I am sorry I have no better news to tell you. God deliver us from those principles that tend to such practices.—I am, Sir, your humble servant,

" ____ ____."

NOTE.—The petition from the magistrates and the minister of Pittenweem, and the confessions of Beatrix Laing, Nicholas Lawson, and Isobel Adam, are copied from an old manuscript. The letter from a gentleman in Fife is copied from a printed paper. Both documents are at Duffus House, Elgin.

XXXIII. FUNERALS AND FUNERAL LETTERS.

THE lady whose funeral charges follow, was the "Bettie" to whom Dr. Innes of Elgin prescribed the "gilded pills" (see page 20). She died in Edinburgh.

"*May 5th*, 1732.—Accompt of the funirall charges of Mrs. Elizabeth Dunbar, dispurst in the Grayfriers church yeard, be John Antonius, wright :—

	Sterling.		
	£	sh.	d.
For a warrand to break ground,	01	05	00
For the mort-cloath, .	01	01	06
For the truff, .	00	10	00
To the bell men, . .	00	04	00
To the grave men,	00	05	00
To the recorder, .	00	01	00
To the poors' box, ...	00	02	00
To the common poor at the lodging, . .	00	01	00
To the common poor and blew-gowns' boxes at Grayfriers, ...	00	01	00
To a hearse velvit pall, with six horses, . .⎫ Two mourning, and two other plain, coaches, ⎭	02	05	00
For a fine coffen, with fine polished iron work, and mourning cords, and least with white tackets, and kane within by way of sheer cloath, . . .	04	00	00
	£09	05	06"

Torches were used at the funerals of the Northern nobility and gentry.

"Account—The Earl of Sutherland to Archibald Dunbar of Newton :—

1733.

September. To forty-eight flambeaus, furnished at Elgin for his grandfather's funerals, weighing eighty-seven and a half pounds, and appreciat by Bailie Mackenzie, apothecary, and Ludowick Gordon, merchant in Elgin (as two men of skill), at three shillings per pound; which Mr. Macalister, by his letter (of date 17th January 1734), promises to pay quickly, and complains of the cost, else he had paid, before, that demand, £13, 2s. 6d.

To horse-hyre from Elgin to Burghead, where the boat lay, 1s.

"*N.B.*—These four dozen of flambeaus were in the house after Lady Thunderton's funerals, and though Mr. Dunbar has no knowledge of the price or value, yet he is apt to think the appretiators have valued them extravagantly, and therefor he submits this article to be reduced to reason."

In Morayshire no funeral took place without a hospitable supply of good cheer for those who attended, but the expense so incurred was trifling, compared with the present price of provisions. With strong old claret at fourteen pence per bottle, twelve

chickens for sixteen pence, and eggs at one penny
per dozen, there was a wide margin for a sum total
of twenty-one pounds, eight shillings, and tenpence
sterling, which was the whole expense (including
coffin, hearse, gratuity to the poor, expresses with
the burial letters, etc., etc.), of the funeral of which
two of the accounts are given.

"To Robert Innes, merchant in Elgin, for sundrys
furnished to the deceast Robert Dunbar of Newtowns
ffuneralls, viz. :—

1742.	£	sh.	d.
Sept. 26. To Zerrey wine, for two botles, the empty botles returned, .	0	2	4
To claret, for two botles, .	0	2	0
To do. more, for six botles do., .	0	6	0
To brandy, for six botles, .	0	6	0
27. To strong old claret, for one dozen, botles being returned, .	0	14	0
To two dozen, smaller old claret, botles being returned, .	1	04	0
28. To cash, for thirteen loads of peats to ffuneral house, .	0	04	4½
To four dozen more, smaller old claret, botles returned, .	2	08	0
To Zerrey, for one dozen, botles being returned, .	0	14	0
29. To new claret, for one dozen, .	0	12	0
To sugar, for four pounds, twelve ounces, at three pence half penny,	0	3	4
	£6	16	0½"

	sh.	d.
" Mrs. Nairn's account for bakeing and cooking,	9	0
Six pecks flower, used at Duffus and Elgin, .	8	0
Five dozen of ale, strong and small, .	5	0
A leg of beef, .	6	0
A side of mutton,	2	2
Six hens, . .	2	0
Twelve chickens,	1	4
Five dozen eggs, .	0	5
Five ducks, . .	2	6
Two tongues, ...	0	8
Pigeons, patridges, marrow tarts, and apples, and a hare, and cod, . .	5	0
Two turkeys, .	2	0
A hawm, . .	4	0
A half ston of butter, . .	3	0
Five pounds moulded candles, .	2	6
	£2 13	7"

The funeral of the Duchess of Buckingham is thus alluded to in a long letter, dated 9th April 1747, from Brodie of Brodie, then in London attending his Parliamentary duties :—

" The fracka of the Dutches of Buckingham's parade through the streets you will see in the prints.

" Yesterday was a very cold day, and she kept many thousands waiting the show, by which she killed more since her death, than she did while alive with all her charms. For the effigie of her, taken in wax work, and carried on the pall above the coffin,

was immently beautifull, according to her orders,
although that figure was taken while on her death-
bed.   At that time she sent to the Dutches of
Marlboro for a sight of the pall used at the Duke's
burial ; to which her Grace made answer that she
would not, since she believed she intended it as a
pattern for her own, and it did not become her Grace
to be buried with the same magnificence as the Duke
of Marlboro.   To which Dutches Buckingham returned, for answer, she only wanted to see it that hers
might not be of the same fashion with her father's
Page.   In short, the many idle, vain, ridiculous storys
we hear of her Grace, just now, would fill a quare of
paper."

———

The practice, now so common, of hiring experienced
waiters, to hand the wine, etc., is not of yesterday :—

" To the RELICT OF THE MINISTER
    " of Duffus.
        " ELGIN, 28th July 1736.
  " MRS.,—I wrote to you before, with John Forsyth,
to send me my wages for the attending your husband's funerals, and for receaving the wins, and
comming alongst with them to Duffus, which your
servant cann tell you ; and for serving that day till
after dinner.   I told you, in my last letter, what
was the ordinar I used to gett in Elgin ; and for my
comeing to Duffus, I did referr to your selfe.   If you

do not send me payment by the berar, I will cause
Deacon Blenshell pay me, whether he will or not,
because he imployed me for that purpose. I know
you do not understand the matter, utherwayes I
would been payed or this time. I expect your answer, by this berar, whither or not, in wreating ; and
I am, Mrs., your most humble servant, when called,

"JOHN HAY."

Funeral letters were, generally, written on foolscap
paper having a small edging of black, and sealed with
the family arms. The large size of the paper formed
a striking contrast to the brevity of the contents.

The Countess was wife of Alexander, fourth Earl
of Moray, and daughter of Sir William Balfour of
Pitcullo.

" For JAMES DUNBAR of Inchbrok.

" *From* CASTLESTEWART, *January 5th*, 1683.

‑ " SIR,—I doe intend the funerall of the Countess
of Morray, my mother, upon Wednesday the 17th of
January instant, to which I intreat your presence, be
eleven a clock, att Darnuay, from thence to her buriall
place in Dyke ; and this last Christian duty shall verrie
much obleidge, Sir, your assured to serve you,

" DOUNE."

Though much cast down by his wife's death, the Laird of Barmuckatie wished to have fashionable linens, holster-tops, and hose. He also determined that the invitations to the funeral should be sealed with his own coat-of-arms :—

" For Mr. ARCHIBALD DUNBAR of Thundertoun,
To the care of George Sutherland,
Master of the Royall Cofe-hous,
Edinburgh—Heast.
"INVERNESS, *December* 31, 1700.

" LOVING BROTHER,—On Sabothday's night last I cam here, which was the night after Barmukaty's lady expired, who, as I am informed, dyed weall and perfect. Ye know his present condition is such that he canot write to you by reason of his great affliction, onlie desires ye may reade, seall, and deliver the inclosed to his ffaither, and keepe him in mind of the contents thereof. Ye will write to Barmukaty by the first, and acquaint him of the fashion of linings proper to be worn, with the fashion of holster-topes and hous. Ye will likeways buy ane steell seall, for his use, and cause cut his name and airmes thereon, which ye will send, whousoon ready; and at meeting ye will be satisfied; therfor leat all be dispached to the caire of Mr. Blak, regent, or Mr. William Smith, who will fordward them here by our post. I expect to here from you myselfe with the occurranse; which is all, with our servise, and I ever am your affectioned brother,
" R. DUNBAR."

Robert Gibson of Linkwood, writer of the following letter, eventually "turned furious," and, for lack of a more suitable asylum, was confined in the jail of Elgin, where, "for preventing of harm to the neighbourhood," he remained, for many years, till his death :—

" ffor Mr. ARCHIBALD DUNBAR of Thundertoun.

"ELGIN, 23*d October* 1701.

" SIR,—Your sometyme landslord and my nybur has takin his eternall ffairweill of you, and is inttered this day betwixt two and thrie aclok. I hope ye will be so Creistianlie inclyned as to weip fourtie dayes weiping and walling ffor him, *because of his honestie.* All your uther ffreinds heir ar in good helth, for ought I knowe. I wishe you ane merrie Cusenmess.—I ame, Sir, your affectionat cusin,   ROBERT GIBSON."

We can, unfortunately, give no information about "the Laird" who borrowed the black suit :—

" ffor The LAIRD OF THUNDERTON.

" MUCH HONOURED,—The Laird is gone to my Lord Balantirs buriall, this morning, and your black cloaths ar on him as yet, but you will have them, to-morrows morning be seven a clock. This is all att the tyme, and I am, as becomes, much honoured, your most obedient and ever obliged servant,

" ALEXR. SPENS."

Thunderton House, in which Lord Huntly wished to entertain the company, attending the funeral of Alexander, second Duke of Gordon, was a noble-looking mansion, with a square tower and balcony. We much regret its demolition in modern times.[1]

" The Much Honoured
        " The Laird of Thundertoun.

                            " Gordon Castle, *Decr.* 9*th*, 1728.

" Sir,—I shall have occasion for a house in Elgin, to entertain the company at my father, the late Duke of Gordon's, buriall. As none in that toun is so fitt for me as yours, I expect, from the friendship which has been between this family and you, that you will allow me the use of it for some days, and that my friend the Lady Thundertoun will consent to take some trouble on this occasion. I offer her ladyship my kind service ; and I am, Sir, your humble servant,

                            " Huntly."

[1] It was, we believe, originally known as "The King's House." In 1601 it belonged to the three daughters of the deceased James Dunbar of Westfield (as heirs of their father, and of their great-grandfather, Sir Alexander Dunbar, Sheriff of Moray), and was designated "The Sheriff's House." We are unable to say when the Earl of Moray became possessor of the house, but he sold it in 1653 to Lord Duffus, who bound the Earl, however, to defend him against all claims from the heirs of John Dunbar of Westfield. About fifty years thereafter, it became the property of Archibald Dunbar of Thunderton, and, after nearly a century, it was sold, in 1800, by Sir Archibald Dunbar, to John Batchen, who took down the greater part of the house, and feued out its grounds,—now forming Batchen Street and adjacent lanes. See Vignette.

Mr. Cumming of Logie seems to have borne his loss with much resignation :—

" To The Laird of Newton, Younger,
    " At Duffus.
                    " Loggie, *January 18th*, 1734.

" Sir,—As it hath pleased God, in his wise providence, to remove my dear wife, I am determined to bury her, Tuesday next, since the body can keep no longer. I therefore intreat the honour of your presence here, by ten a'clock that day, which will very much obledge, Sir, your most humble servant,

" Alexr. Cumming."

The presence of Mr. Forbes under such circumstances was not desirable :—

" To Archibald Dunbar of Duffus, Esqr.,
    " Elgin.
                    " *Tuesday, 28th Sept.* 1742.

" My dear Sir,—I told you that I could not doe myself the honour to witness the interment of your worthy father. This is to tell you that I have been drinking, this whole day, with our Magistrats and Town Councill (God bless them), and am, just now, almost unfitt for your conversation ; and therefor choose to goe home rather than expose my self; which I hope you will approve off. I hope you will ever believe that I am, with the greatest faith and truth, my dear Sir, yours to serve you, Will. Forbes."

XXXIV. WILL OF THE DEAN OF
SALISBURY, 1618.

JOHN GORDON, Dean of Salisbury, was a son of Alexander, Bishop of Galloway, only brother of that Earl of Huntly who was slain at Corrichie. He died, 3d September 1619, in the seventy-fifth year of his age, and was buried at the place pointed out in his will.

His widow, Dame Geneviev Petaw (a French lady), died at Gordonston, 6th December 1643, in the eighty-third year of her age, and was buried at Kinnedder in the county of Moray.

Louise, only child of the Dean, married Sir Robert Gordon of Gordonston, second son of the Earl of Sutherland, on the 16th February 1613. Of this marriage there are numerous descendants.

" Anno Domini 1618, Die 16, Mense Septembris.

IN THE NAME OF GOD THE ETERNALL, CALLED IN THE HEBREW, JEHOVAH ELOHIM, one in substaunce or essence, and three in subsistence or persone, I, Jean Gordon, borne in Scotland, of the

House of Huntly, Doctor of Divinitie, and Deane of
the Cathedrall Church of Salisburie, being in health of
body and of minde, now of the age of seventy-four
years, beginning the ffirst of September last past,
prayes the said Eternall and Allmightie to direct my
minde by His Holy Spirit, that I may make this my
latter will and testament, in such a manner as shall be
agreeable and conforme to His Divine Majesties will.
Imprimis, I give thankes to the saide God, all power-
full and all bountifull, that He made me to bee in-
structed and taught, from my youth up, in scholes
and collidges, as well in Scotland as in ffraunce, in all
good discipline and liberall arts and sciences, and in
the knowledge of the Greeke and Hebrew languadges,
and other Orientalls ; and, by that meanes, called me
from the invocation and adoration of creatures in-
feriors to the saide Holy and Blessed Trinitie, practised
in the now Romaine Church, and other new erronious
doctrines of trans-substantiation and adoration of the
hostiamissalis exercised therein ; and hath called mee
to the reformed Church of England, Scotland, and
Ireland ; protesting by me, before the Eternall and
Allmightie God, and before the celestiall powers, arch-
angells, angels, cherubins and seraphines, and all other
His ministeriall spirites, that by the grace of God and
the assistaunce of His Holy Spirit, that I shall con-
stantly persevere and continue, unto the seperation of
my soule from my body, in the doctrine of salvation,

now preached in the said Church. I give also thankes
to the said Holy Trinitie, who, after I had bine gentleman of three Kinges chambers in ffrance, to wit,
Charles the Ninth, Hencry the Thirde and Fowerth, in
the flower of my adge, and there was assailed with
many corruptions, as well spirituall as temporall, and
many dangers of my life, that my said Lord and
Saviour did miraculusly preserve me and deliver me
from all the said daunger, and called me by King
James, my dread soveraigne's gratiosness, to this habi-
tation in Ingland, and to this holy ministerie, being
then fifty-eight yeares of adge ; and that from that
time the said most gratious God hath opened to me,
allthough unworthy, the intelligence, in such a measure as hath pleased His Godly Majestie, of His Holy
Scriptures, and of the high and deepe mysteries of life
eternall ; most humbly craving from His gratiousnesse
that He will be pleased to augment in me, His unworthy servant, the knowledge of the saide misteries ;
and, that I may leave to posteryty all the bookes that
I have written, both in Latine and also in Inglish, in
matters of religion, praying ernestly Sir Robert Gordon of Sudderland, my soone-in-lawe, that if God
shall call mee to His hevenly kingdome before I may
publishe the saide bookes, that he will be carefull of
them, that they that are in Inglishe be published in
Scotlande, and these which are in Latine, beyond the
seaes, so that the greate and long labors and paines,

that I, by the grace of God, have bestowed in compos-
ing the saide bookes, be not loosed. Now, because the
Apostell, Heb. ix. ver. 27, hath taught me and all
Christians that *Statutum est hominibus semel mori,
post autem hoc judicium,*—It is ordained to men once
to die, and that after that is judgment,—I believe con-
stantly and firmly in Christ's saying, in St. John's
Gospell, chap. v. ver. 24, *Qui verbum meum audit, et
credit ei qui misit me, habet vitam eternam, et in
judicium non venit,sed transiuit a morte in vitam;*—He
that heareth my word and beeleveeth in Him who hath
sent me, hath everlasting life, and shall not com into
condemnation, but is passed from death unto life;—and
therefore (seing that God hath given me an assured and
stedfast faith that the Eternall Father hath sent His
Eternall Sonne in this worlde, for to redeeme, from
Satan, hell, and condemnation, all faithfull beeleevers,
acording to His eternall forknowledge, purpose, election, predestination, effectuall vocation, and viuificant
justification and sanctification), that I, beeing of the
number of them, by His only grace and mercy, shall,
after the seperation of my soule from this corruptible
body, receive glorification, ffirst in my soule, and after-
ward in my body, when, at the time apointed in God's
eternall councell, the bodyes of all men shall be resuscitated and immortallised, and rejoyned with their
soules ; that as we beleeve in the Holy Trinity, and
are baptised and speritually regenerated by water

and the Holy Ghost, by the which we are made the
adopted sonnes of God, and allso our bodyes are nurr-
ished and fedd by participation and communion with
the spirituall fleshe and blood of Christ, the which is
in our bodyes a seede of imortalitie, by the which, as
Christ promised, our bodyes shall bee resuscitated to
injoy with our soules eternall life ; that as wee glorifie
and worshipp the Holy Trinitie in this worlde with our
bodyes and soules united in one person, called man,
that evin so we shall after this life and the resurrec-
tion, we beeing made perfet men, wee shall worshippe
and glorifie Him eternally in His triumphant Church,
with spirituall hymnes and songes, prayses and
thankesgiving, in the society of all His holy archangels
and angels ; and, seeing that sinne and death was
brought in this worlde by Satan, and by it death, and
that the Eternall Sonne of God did suffer death, in His
human nature, to deliver and save all faithfull beeleevers from eternall death, and not from the first and
corporall death, I confesse that all wee of this ellected
flocke must suffer the death of our bodyes, and therby
are partakers of the sufferinges of Christ ; and that
thearby wee, persevering to the end in true faith,
working by charitie, shall be pertakers of His glory ;
and I protest before His Divine Majestie that I have a
firme faith and hope, by His grace to attaine to that
selfsame glorification, beeing purged from all my
sinnes by the unspeakable suffraunces of my Lord,

my God, and Saviour, renouncing to all merites of myself, or any others, angels or men. Allso, because I am bound to be carfull of my wife and familie, and to dispose to their profitte the goodes, landes, and possessions which God hath liberally and miraculusly given me, I refer the dispositions of all that I have in ffraunce, to the donation which I have made heartofore to Geneviev Petaw, my loving wife, and to Sir Robert Gordon, and Lucie Gordon, my only childe, his wife; praying them all that they will end-vor themselfes to be righted against the wronges that I have suffered, by my absence from ffraunce, against all the lawes and customes of that kingdome. As for my goodes and moveables, and house situat in the Close of Sarum, my will is that they be sould, and that the one halfe of the money shall bee for the use of my wife her life during (the which shee shall leave after hir to my saide sonne and daughter), the which moietie, with the other that I give by this my will to them, shall be by them injoyed theire life-during, and then shall leave both the saide moities to the children gotten and to be begotten of them; and, to that effect, both the saide moities shall be employet in leases or other purchises, which my wife and they shall injoy (as said is) theire life-during, and shall leave the proprietie thereof to theire saide children : to the performaunce wheareof I charge them, in the name of God, as they shall awnsweare to God at the fearfull

T

day of judgment. My will allso is that the gould
and money that shall be found in my possession, or
shall bee due to mee by bandes or billes at the time of
my death, shall remaine to my saide wife only, whome
I do charge with the costes of my buriall (and not my
sonne and daughter), and with the doles that shee may
give to the poore at the time of my buriall ; willing
my body to be buried before my seate in the quier,
and I refer to my saide wife the forme and manner of
my saide buriall. To my loving wife allso I give the
some of forty poundes to bee laide in a stocke, and
that the use of the said stocke shall be kept for the
maintenaunce of poore boyes of the choristers, for the
space of three yeares, during the which they may be
provided other ways, and that after they goe from the
quier, (not comprehending in this guift those boyes
who have parents to meintaine them, to whome, at
theire going forth, shall be given, every one, forty
shillinges) ; and this stocke be put in Chamber of
the Cittie, which shall be bound to pay yearly the use
thereof to such one that shall be appointed by the
Deane and Chapter of Sarum, to whome he shall render accoumpte. I give allso to my servantes, men
and women, a yeare of theire wadges and hire, during
fower termes that shall fall out after my death. I
give to the library of the church the tomes of the
Annales of Barronius, togither with such bookes as I
have or shall have the day of my deaceas, to the use

of them that will studdie on them in the saide library.
I ordayne that the debtes which I may be owing, the
day of my death, in this kingdome of Ingland, bee
payed on my *annus post mortem*, and especially, if
God call mee before the hearnestes of my personadges,
that which shall be repaied to the baylife of them for
the termes of Christmas, the Annuntiation, and Mid-
somer, if they have paid them or any of them during
my life, and that the rest of the saide *annus post
mortem* remayne to my saide lovinge wife only, who
shall paye the saide debtes to the concurrens and
vallues of the said *annus*.   I doe make and ordayne
my saide loving deare wife to bee the whole execu-
trix of this my saide last will, referring all other
thinges to her conscience and discretion.   In witnesse
whearcof I have written with my owne hand, and
have subscrivit with my ordynary singe, this my will,
the day and year above-mentioned.

" J. GORDON."

XXXV. CATTLE-STEALING.

THE plains of Moray were subject to constant incursions by the Highlanders, who " lifted cattle," took whatever fell in their way, and returned to their hills with the booty. Cluny Macpherson thus writes to the Baronet of Gordonston :—

"CLUNY, 6 *Novr.* 1676.

" RYTT HONORIBLE,—I received ane lyne from you directed to Nuid[1] and me, showeing that you are informed the Claneranald are in some place in the Breay of Murray, which if they be, treuly it is unknowen to me; but it is wery probabile they may be their or els wheir at this tym. Therfor it is my advice to your honour, that you cawse your people of Dollase look well to their cattel, and let them waitch, every neight, souch of their beasts as ar not housed, aithervayes they may come to misse a pairt of them; for our contry watch is, ere now, dissolved for this year. Therfor let your people be cairfull, and your honour shall fynd that I shall doe them, on your accompt, all the good service that lyes in the power of, Ryt Honorible, yors asuiredly to serve you,   D. M'PHERSON.

[1] Macpherson of Nuid.

" SIR,—I received in September last your papers againest Drumond, sent to me by Connadge who is coosen germond to Drumond, and before the papers cam to my hands Drumond was putt on his gaird, and eafter sending of ane party horse, I could not get ane sheight of him, but, if I be ane leiveing man, I shall be about with him some one way or another."

———

Some of the Strathspey Highlanders had " lifted" cattle belonging to Sir Robert Gordon, who, in October 1691, sent a messenger to cite the Laird of Grant as answerable for his clan ; but it was a dangerous enterprise to enter the Strath on such an errand :—

" I, Hugh Thaine, messenger, heirby declaire that I am not at this tyme able to goe the length of Edinburgh, by reasone of sickness and unabilitie of body, haveing beine now sex or seven weeks wery unabell, by reasone of the hard usage I mett with in Strathspey, in the wood of Abernethie ; and therefor I doe heirby dyser, and give full power to, Sir Robert Gordone of Gordonstoun (who did imploy me about executing of Councell leters in that place) to suplicat the Lords of ther Majesties Privie Concill, or any other of ther Majesties Judges to whom it may belonge, that the saids Lords or Judges may, in ther prudence, apoynt some way for reddressing and punishing the abusses

comitted, against the law and government, upon my
persone and those in my company, which wer as
followith, viz. :—I (having upon the fyftinth of October last citted some wittneses, and upon the sextinth
therof citted the Laird of Grant, and upon the seven-
tinth therof, be eight houres in the morning, as I went
about three myles from Ballichastell towards Culnakyle,
both the Laird's houses, at a place called Craigemur,
at the wood of Abernethie) and three men, called Peter
Morison in Fochabrs, John McEdwart in Glenrinnes,
and Alexr. Bogtoun in Khieclehik, that were with me,
were seized upon be a pearty of armed men, who most
maisterfullie and violently struk me with ther gunnes,
gave me a stobbe with a durke in my shoulder, and a
stroak with my owen sword ; robbed me of my money,
my linnens, some cloathes, my sword and provision,
and of the principel Councell leters many coppies
therof, and uther papers ; then bound me and my
compeny, and allways threatned me with present
death for exceeuting the forsaid leters, and examined
me on oath whither any of those men did belonge to
Gordonstoun, that they might instantly kill him ; and
offred his liffe to any one of our company that wold
hange the rest of us ; therafter laid us down and
secured us with horse-roaps on the ground within the
wood, wher we leay in cold, hunger, and great miseris
for four dayes and three nights, threatned hourly
with present death. My conditione of healthe is welle

knowen to the minister and nighbours in the paroch wher I live, and may be atested be them if neid require. In testimony of the verity heircof, I have written and subscribed ther presents with my hand, at Fochabes, the fourt day of December jajvcj nynty one yeires (1691)."

A friendly message had more effect on Macdonald of Keppoch, than the legal summons had on the Laird of Grant :—

" ffor LODOVIC GORDONE,
　　" Brother to Sir Robert Gordone
　　　　" off Gordonstone — These :

　　　　　　　　　　" *the 8th August* 1693.
" SIR,— I receaved yours, but er it came to my hands I ordred the restorcing of your brother's goods, haveing gotten ane lyne from Alexr. Gordon off Cromdell, informeing that some off this cowntriemen had taken nintine heads of catles from Sir Robert Gordon ; soe that ye may send the owners off the said goods my lenth about the twentieth instant, that they may carry home their goods. I am very sorrie that any of my people should have medled with your brother's interest, and I resolve to punish them for it, besyds the restitutione of the goods ; and ye may assurr your selfe that no Gordon shall be wronged by any whom I can stope or lett, and, particullarlie, your brother is a

man whom I resolve to serve in any thing lyes in my power.--I am, Sir, your most humble servant,

"COLL. MACKDONALD."

Answer to the above :—

"SIR,—I receaved yours, and am very sensible ot your readinesse to doe a kindnesse to my brother or any of his concernes ; of which I was allwayes confident ; wherfor I have now, according to your appointment, sent some of the owners of the goods to know their beasts ; and I intreat you, Sir, that with the rest of your favours, you will be pleased to send a guaird back with this countrymen the length of the Braes of Badenoch, otherwayes they may come to loose their travell, and be necessitat to give you a new trouble, which I doubt not but you will prevent ; for all which trouble, I assure you, Gordonstoun will be your debtor, and also he who is still yours, &c.

"L. G."

XXXVI. JOHN, EARL OF SUTHERLAND:
HIS INFLUENCE AND POWER.

DEPUTATION of Lieutenancy :—

" I, John, Earl of Sutherland, Lord Strathnaver,
&c., Heretable Sheriff, Lord of Regality, and Crowner
of the County of Sutherland, Heretable Admiral of
the Countess of Sutherland and Caithness, Vice-
Admiral of the Stewartry of Orkney and Zetland,
Lord-Lieutenant of the Counties of Elgine, Nairn,
Inverness, Ross, Cromertie, Sutherland, and Caithness, and of the Stewartry of Orkney and Zetland,
President of the Court of Police in Scotland, Lieu-
tenant-General of his Majesty's Forces, and Knight
of the most antient and most noble Order of the
Thistle ; By these presents nominate, constitute, and
appoint Mr. Archibald Dunbar of Thunderton, to be
one of the Deputy-Lieutenants in and for the said
county of Elgine. To have and enjoy all powers,
authorities, and privileges, which by law do now,
or may hereafter appertain to the said office or trust
of Deputy-Lieutenant, and generally to execute and

perform all and every the matters and things, which
on the part of the Deputy-Lieutenants, respectively,
by law may or ought to be done, acted, executed,
and performed. And I do hereby recal and declare
null all deputations of any Deputy-Lieutenants of
the said county, granted by me preceding the date
hereof. In witness whereof, I have hereunto set my
hand and seal, at London, the sixteenth day of
ffebruary one thousand seven hundred and twenty-
two years, according to the Scots style, before these
witnesses, Alexander Gordon of Ardoch, Esq., and
Alexander Ross, Writer to the Signet, filler up of the
blanks.   SUTHERLAND.

   " All. Gordon, *witness.*
   Alexr. Ross, *witness.*"

———

The man whom the Earl delighted to honour in
1722, had, several years before, suffered most unjustly
at his Lordship's hands. The " obligement" was a
right to an estate in Sutherland. Dunbar of Thunderton died in 1773, but his heirs brought an action of
reduction.

   " ARCHIBALD DUNBAR of Newton, Esq.

                                " ELGIN, 24 *June* 1734.
   " DEAR SIR,— In answer to yours of the 12th in-
stant, know that I was not at Inverness when
Thunderton granted that obligement, whether to the

late Earle of Sutherland, or late Lord Strathnaver,
I know not; but it is certain that Thunderton was
incarcerate in the Tolbooth of Elgin, in the year
1715, by the Earle of Sutherland's order, and kept
in that prison for severall nights by a strong guard,
and ill used by them, untill Mr. Duncan fforbes, now
Lord Advocate, the late Sir Hary Inness, and some
other ffriends, mediate with the Earle of Sutherland
to liberate him upon a baill bond to present himself
to the Earle at Inverness (as I think) sometime in
the beginning of January 1716. His baill was for
five thousand pounds sterling, and the said Sir Hary
and William Duff of Dipple were cautioners. The
baill-bond was wrote by this Lord Advocate, and I
know not but that I am a signing witness.

"Thunderton, in implement of the said bond, did
present himself at Inverness to the Earle, and was of
new imprisoned; and, as the story goes, no release-
ment to be given untill he should grant that oblig-
ment, and threatened, if he did not, that he was
immediatlie to be carried prisoner for London, to
undergoe a tryall as a traytour. The proper persons
for proving the commission must be these treaters
betwixt the Earle and Thunderton, who, I suppose,
were my Lord Lovat, Sir Robert Gordon, my Lord
Advocate, John fforbes of Culloden, and, in particular,
the witnesses to be adduced for proving the tenor of
that obligement.

"George Innes of Dinkinty, William Dawson of Hempriggs, and James Charles, late Bailie of Elgin, were then the Earle of Sutherlands prisoners at Inverness with Thunderton, and, I presume, your friend Thomas Robertson, at Inverness, cannot be ignorant of the story.

"I was threatened by the Earle to be made prisoner also, but, by the mediation of friends, escaped that lurch. You may likeways (if there be occasion for it) cause summon my Lord Rae and Captain George Grant, who were then with the Earl at Inverness. There are several witnesses that could have been of use if on life, such as Mr. Baily, minister at Inverness, Baily Dunbar, etc. I am, Sir, your most humble servant,   JA. WISEMAN."

Simon, Lord Lovat, was requested to name a day for his examination :—

"To the Honourable
    "ARCHIBALD DUNBAR, Esqr.,
        "at his house at Duffus.

                "BEAUFFORT, 13th of Aprile 1735.

"DEAR SIR,—I had just now the honour of your letter of yesterday's date, and I would, with great pleasure, consent to any day you please for my examination if I were not oblidged to meet my Lord Munto, who has acquainted me that he is to come

north by the Kings road to Fortugustus, and from
that to Inverness, through my country of Strathcrrick,
by the road on the syde of Lochness ; and, as he is
my intimate ffriend, he has acquainted me to ffeed
himself and his horses in that country, so that, if I
be able to travel, I resolve to wait upon him at
Fortugustus, where he must be the 28th. Therefore,
if you think that my examination can be of use to
you, I beg you may order it so as to be here, either
the 24th, 25th, or 26th, in the morning, because after
that I cannot be master of my own diet till my Lord
Munto leaves this country.

"I believe Mr. Bailly, my Shirref-depute, will be
as good a judge as you can find for that purpose,
but as you know your own interest better than I can
do, you may choose for yourself ; and any man that
you will be pleased to bring with you shall be very
acceptable to me, for I am, with a very sincere esteem
and respect, dear Sir, your most affectionat cousin,
and most obedient, ffaithful, humble servant,

"LOVAT.

"*P.S.*—I am very sorry for the accident that
happened to the Dutchess of Gordon and to her
company. The poor young Lord's breaking his thigh
is very melancholy, for he may come to be lame all
his lifetime by it."

Extracts from Lord Lovat's examination, which took place at Castledowncy, 26th April 1735, by order of the Court of Session :—

" *Interrogator*.

" If your Lordship did not hear the Earl, in a great passion, swear or say that he would have Thundertoun hanged or putt to death, or that he would cause carry him prisoner, in irons on board the King's yatcht or ships of war (then attending the Earl), to London, in order to be tryed for his life, as being guilty of treason or some such crimes as the Earl alleged ; or if your Lordship did not hear the Earl threaten and menace him with bodily harm, ruine, and destruction, unless he would deliver up, and discharge, the oblidgment passing from or discharging the recognition of Skelbo, which the deceasd Lord Strathnaver gave Thunderton ; or what other matters did your Lordship hear the Earl threaten or say upon this subject, of or concerning Thundertoun ?

" *Depones*,

" He believes he might have heard the Earl say that he would cause hang or put Thundertoun to death, and carry him to London and try him for his life, as being a rebel and guilty of treason ; but depones that he did not hear the Earl threaten and

menace him with ruine and destruction upon account
of the write mentioned in the interrogators.

" *Interrogator.*

" Whether or not after the said Earl's menaces and
threatenings against Thundertoun, and the Earl's
message to him, ordering him to grant the said discharge of the said Lord Strathnaver's oblidgment
aforsaid (or an oblidgment to deliver up the same
to be cancelled), had been told and communicate to
Thundertoun as the only means to procure his safety
and liberation, and after your Lordship had used a
great many arguments with him to that purpose, was
not Thunderton at last, with great difficulty, prevailed upon to say that he would subscribe any
writing the Earl should demand of him for his liberation, rather than undergo the dangers and hardships
threatened to him ?

" *Depones,*

" He believes Bailie James Dunbar might have said
to him that Thundertoun said he had a great deal of
difficulty in granting the write demanded of him, but
that he would subscribe any write rather than be confined to the Castle of Inverness or such a bad prison
as it was ; and that this negotiation of my Lord
Lovat's was without the participation of the Earl of

Sutherland or the Lord Strathnaver, to the best of his memory.

" Interrogator.

" If, immediately after Thundertoun had subscribed the said writing or deed, which the Earl desired and insisted for, he, the said Thundertoun, was not released and sett at liberty, and allowed to return home by the Earl's order?

" Depones,

" Immediately after signing the said write Thundertoun was sett at liberty and allowed to go home ; and that the deponent did not see Thundertoun under any guaird or restraint at signing of the write. All of which is truth to the best of the deponent's memory, as he shall answer to God.

" Sic Scribr.

" LOVAT.
EVAN BAILLIE.
DONALD MACKQUEEN, *Clk.*"

THE city of Perth was in 1651 invested by Oliver
Cromwell, when, to avoid a general assault, the Governor, Lord Duffus, capitulated. In the following
year, the English made demands which the Magistrates considered unwarrantable, by the terms of
capitulation, and therefore his Lordship, the late
Governor, was applied to for the original deed.

" ffor our verie honoble Lord,
    " The LORD DUFFUS—Theis :

                " PERTH, *the last of Marche* 1652.

" MOST NOBLE LORD,—The Great and Eternal dis-
poser of al things, having so by providence ordered it,
that when this burghe was in great strait and eminent
inevitable ruine, your Lordship was honored (and to
the future and happie memorie of your honorable
familie be it recordit) by the Lord to be instrumental
in our delyverance, and of ane as honest as necesser
surrender of this place to the Inglishes, who ar now
urging and putting us to such ingagments upon oaths,

as in conscieuce or in resson we cannot undergoe, having such condition in the capitulation to be excemed of oath ; and being confident of your Lordship's dispositione to men straitted in this nature, besyd your never-to-be-forgottine cariage in honor and honestie, actit and concludit here for us, we haif sent this bearer, William Grant, merchand of this burghe, expresse to your Lordship, humblie to desyr your Lordship wold yit add this favour to former, as to send us that Principal Capitulatione, subscryved be Lord Oliver Cromwel, that our hard-to-puttings, and sad condition wherunder we ar now lying, may be the more constantlie and conditionallie resisted ; and, whenever your Lordship sal haif use to mak of the sam again, we doe ingadge upon our honor and credite to restore the samen, upon demand, to your Lordship. The tyme limited, be the Inglishe Commissioners, to this burghe for our positive anser to thair so hard proposals is so short, that we, with pardon, creave humblie your Lordship's tymous dispatche of the bearer, that naked men, wanting al means of schelter (as now our condition is), may have that support (all glorie to God and praise to the instruments) whiche we ar assured may be produced to us be that capitulation.   And, by your Lordship's condescendence to this, as God sal be honored, your supplicants preserved from perjurie and guilt, so your Lordship sal ever

obleidge, my Lord, your Lordship's most humble servants, the Magistrates of the toune of Perth.

"AN. GRANT, *Provost.*
JOHNE CONQUEROR, *Baillie.*
NA. BATESSON, *Baillie.*
HENRY GREY.
PA. ROSS."

Prices of provisions in Inverness when held by
Oliver Cromwell's troops :—

" By Collonell Thomas Fitch, Governor of Invernes,
with the aprobation of the Gentlemen of the
Countrey and the Provost and Baylifes of this
Brough, September the 15, anno 1654 :

" Whereas their hath bene diverse complaints made
to me by the souldery of the garrisson and the townes
people, of the increase of the prices .of all sortes of
provissions, conceivinge themselves verie much injured by the sellers therof ; and the countrey people,
on the other side, oftentimes complaines they have
not a price answerable to the worth of their provissions that they bring to the market.

" For the prevention, therfore, of fforther differences
in the like kind, the several prices of all sortes of provisions arc agreed upon by the countrey gentlemen
and baylifes of the brough, that soe the buyer and

seller may for the future avoid all differences of that
nature, by observinge the prices of all sorts of provisions as underwriten, viz. :—

	£	s.	d.
A good slaughtering cow, betwixt the first of August and the last of October, upon foote, is worth	01	06	08
The karkase of such a cow may be sold for	00	18	00
Muton upon foote, of the best sort, betwixt the last of May and the last of October, is worth	00	04	06
The karkase of such muton, dureinge that time,	00	03	04
The pound of such muton, dureing that time, .	00	00	01½
A beefe of the best sort, loaden upon foot, betwixt Janury and May, ...	02	10	00
The karkase of such a beefe, during that time, .	01	16	00
A pound of such beefe, during the said time, .	00	00	02
A veale of about 1 month or 6 weeks old, the karkase, ...	00	03	00
The countrey veales that comes to market, the best, ...	00	01	04
Henns, a peece, good, .	00	00	05
Caponns, a piece, good, . . .	00	00	06¼
Countrey market kids, beinge good,	00	01	06
Lambes of the best sort, .	00	01	06
Eggs, per dozen,	00	00	02
Geese, a peece,	00	01	02
Cockes, a peece,	00	00	05
Porke, per pound,	00	00	02
Bakon, per pound, . .	00	00	04
Read dried hearons, three for .	00	00	01
Milke, the Scotch pint, .	00	00	02
Beare, a Scotch pint, good,	00	00	01⅜
Ale, if good, a Scotch pint, . .	00	00	01⅞
Killinge fish, of the greatest, a peece,	00	00	06

The lesser sort of fish, . .	00 00 04
Haddock, ane dozen of the greatest sort, .	00 00 05
Salmond of the greatest sort, a peece,	00 01 08
The lesser sort of salmond, .	00 01 00
The girsle, a peece, .	00 00 06
The salmond, per pound, . . .	00 00 01
White bread, a loafe weighing $\frac{9}{16}$ of a pound, the bowle costing within twenty shillings sterling, ...	00 00 01
The loafe weighing 18 ounces, white bread,	00 00 02
The loafe weighinge $3\frac{6}{16}$ lb., ditto bread,	00 00 06
The loafe weighinge $6\frac{12}{16}$ lb., ditto bread, .	00 01 00
The loafe weighing $13\frac{1}{2}$ ounces, brown bread, .	00 00 01
The loafe of ditto bread, $5\frac{1}{16}$ lb.,	00 00 06
The loafe of ditto bread, $10\frac{2}{16}$ lb., . . .	00 01 00
The loafe of oaten bread, weighing 19 ounces, when it costs within ten markes Scotch the bowle, . . .	00 00 01
Salt hearons, barreld, four for .	00 00 01

" It is hearby further ordered and required that noe person or persons whatsoever, in or belonginge to this garrisson, presumes to buy or sele any of the before-said provissions before it come into the market place, under penaltie of confiscatinge the provissions soe bought or sold ; and that noe person or persons doe presume, after tenn dayes from the date hearof, to violate this proclimation in referrence to the prices of all sortes of provissions, under penaltie of incuringe forther and greater dammage upon themselves. Given under my hand, at Invernesse, the 15 day of September 1654.　　　　　　　　THOS. FITCH."

An episode in the Monmouth Rebellion, 1685.

" Order to the Master of Tarbot, Beaufort, and Gordonstoun :—

" His Excellence the Duke of Gordon, his Majesties Lieutenant in the North, having sent his orders to me, John, Lord Strathnaver (who am by him entrusted to bring up the northern forces toward Argyleshire), for commanding away, in haste, six hundred men out of the whole army, by way of detachment; and upon the deliberate advice of the whole officers conveened in a Councel of War (it being found impossible to perswade or command a Highland people not yet regulated, to do any service except under the command of their own cheiftains), it hath been concluded absolutly more conducible to the promoting of his Majesties service, and answerable to his Excellencie the Duke of Gordon's design, to send away rather particular bodies of men then a detached partie— Therefor, I hereby command the Master of Tarbot, with the men under his command, and Thomas Fraser of Beaufort, with such as are under his command, and Sir Robert Gordon of Gordonstoun, with the Frasers of Stratherrick, the Grants of Urquhart and Glen- moristoun, and the Duke of Gordon's men of the Castlelands of Invernesse, under the command of the said Sir Robert Gordon, to march with all expedition

forward, till they joyn his Excellence the Duke of
Gordon.

" Given at Drumnochter, the sixteenth of June javie
eightie-five.   STRATHNAVER."

" INTELLIGENCE.

" There most be ane Ajutant, whose duty is to
receave order from the Cheif-Comander, as to order
the ranking of the severall bodies of men in their
marching, and the drawing up of them at the halt,
and at ther quarters in the camp each night. This
Ajutant, for his help, most have ane Quarter-master
Generall, who goes before, each morning, after having
receaved orders from the Generall where to take up
the ground, which most have wood, grasse, and watter ; and the ground most be spacious, suitable to the
bodies to be encamped.

" There most be lykwise a Generall of Artillery, to
look after the marching of the bagage and amunition.
The bagage of the severall bodies most march in the
same ranks that ther severall bodies marches. There
most be a small guard at the head of each severall
bagage, by and outtour the van guard, and the guard,
and the guard of the amonition.

" There most be also good care taken for good
guids for the bagage for the Agitant, and for the van
of the armies.

" There most be likwise good care taken of there
nightly guards, that they be neither too strong, for
fear of too mouch fatigue, nor too little, for fear of
surprise.

" *Generall Rulles to be observed in the Camp and*
Marching.

" *Imprimus*, That no shouldier be seen out of his
rank, nor officer of his division, if not detached to a
particular command.

2*do*, That no man, under paine of death, fire without comand, nor be seen out of the camp after the
tap-too.

" That no man, under the said paine, disobey ther
severall officers, or rebell against them ; that no man,
under the paine of death, draw a sword, or quarrel in
the camp or march, but repaire to ther severall officers
to complaine of any injury.

" There most be a particular signe given be the
Generall when near the enimi, to be made knowen to
the Generall Major, who most comunicat the same to
the severall Majors, and they to the comissionat officers, and the sergants to the officers of the guard, who
most comunicat it to the centries when posted.

" There most be also a word every night given be
the Cheif Comander to the Generall Major, and he to
the severall Majors, who most mak it knowen to the
severall sergeants, to be maid knowen be them to ther
several officers.

" There most be good van and rerr guards of horse dragounes. The dragounes most be founed out of the heritors.

"That no man carry a staff but a comander, wherby the officers may be knowen ; that all officers may regulat any disorder, to be present when it falls out.

" The severall shouldiers of each company to be sworn to their collours."

Extract from a letter dated London, March 2d, 1686 :—

"The King has lately issued out a proclamation of generall pardon to all in the rebellion in the west with the late Duke Monmouth,[1] excepting a world of men and women, persons of quality, among others my good friend Esquire Charlton (I once told you of), the Earle of Maxwel, &c., so that the pardon reaches only to the meaner sort, such as labourers, workmen, &c. ; and they are not to have it either, unless within three months after the date of it, they come in and sue out their pardons. His Majestic also has written a letter to the two Archbishops—Metropolitans of England, Canterbury and York, to which are annexed some orders to be put in practise by the clergy, and a good order of observing strictly the Lord's day. Amongst

---

[1] He was executed in July 1685.

other things, his Majestie enjoyns a forbearance to
preach sublime and abstruse controversies upon all
inferiour contraversies, unless upon speciale ocasion ;
and that benefices, or livings, or (as with you) churches,
be not granted to any hereafter, but during the pleasure of the Bishop.   Again, he seems to enjoyn but
preaching once a-day, but in that he is not positive.
You have heard of the Earle of Morray to go down
your Comissioner ; but we hear your Parliament is
prorogued till May."

The gallant stand made by Alexander, first Duke
of Gordon, as Governor of Edinburgh Castle, in the
spring of 1689, is matter of history.   The fees of
commission paid by his Grace may therefore be interesting.

" Accompt of Duke Gordon's Commission as Captain to the Castle :—

Imprimis, given at the Chancelarie, .	66	13	04
Item, for registration and drink-money,	05	16	00
Item, for ribbons, six elns,	04	04	00
Item, to the purss, ...	26	13	04
Item, to the presenter of signatur's servant,	02	18	00
Item, to the usher and door-keiper in Exchequer,			
at revising, .	05	16	00
Item, for the declaration, .	05	16	00
Item, at the register of signaturs,	05	16	00

Item, for wax and drink-money at the Great
Seall,   .   .   11 12 00
                                                 _____
                                                 135 04 08
Item, for the secretarie's dues for his commission, seven pounds sterling, *inde*,   .   . 084 00 00
Item, for the secretarie's dues for his commission to be captain of the company, seven
pounds sterling, *inde*, ... 084 00 00
Item, to the clerks of the counsell and their
servants at the production of the commis-
sion to be read, and recording the same, . 029 00 00
                                               _____
                                               332 04   08

" *Edinburgh*, 15 *March* 1686.—Receaved by me,
Mr. John Nisbet, servitor to Mr. Thomas Gordon,
Writer to the Signet, in name of the said Mr. Thomas,
from Sir John Gordon,[1] Advocat, in name of his Grace
the Duke of Gordon, the abovewritten soume of thrie
hundreth threttie-two pounds, four shilling, eight
pennies, Scots; which is in sterling money twentie-
seven pound, thrittein shillings, eight pence, and three
farthings, and which soume I presentlie delyvered to
the said Mr. Thomas Gordon.   Jo : NISBET."

Alexander Dunbar of Barmuckatie, having got into
pecuniary difficulties at home, took service as a volunteer in the army serving in the Low Countries

---

[1] Sir John was a younger son of Sir Ludovic Gordon of Gordonston,
and a brother of the apprentice whose indentures are given at page 138.

under the great Duke of Marlborough, and was en-
rolled as " Alexander Dunbar, gentleman, in Major
John Brodie's company, in the Right Hon. the Marquis of Tullibardine's Regiment of ffoot." We give
extracts from his letters to his cousin, and also a letter
from Captain Brodie to the same gentleman, showing
the miserable pay of an officer :—

"*ffrom the* CITEADAILE *of* LIEGE, 18*th Decebr.,*
New Styll, 1705.

" I expect, when you see our cousen, Captain John
Dunbar, in my Lord Mordaine's regement, ye will give
him alse much monie as will make upp ffour hundred
merks, either in pistolls or Duradounes, ffor Duradounes or cross dollars are the best passeing monie in
this countrey, that pass in Scotland. Ye may send
me ane night goune by Captain Dunbar—I mean ane
Highland plaid—and let it be about twenty-four
shillings pryce, or therabouts, for that is ane thing
I cannot want either summer or winter."

" WERWICK CAMP, 8*th August, New Styll,* 1708.

" I have the honnor to be posted Ensigne[1] on Captain Young's company of the Marquise of Tullibardine's Regement."

———

[1] It was in consequence of this promotion that Captain Brodie wrote
the letter given at page 319.

" LILE, the 18th Decr., New Styll, 1708.

" Ye may be ashured I will see you this nixt year, iff I be spaired, in order to make recruits, so aquant me to whom I will wroit, in order they may be assiste-ing to me. In caice ther be any roges[1] a goeing either at Elgin, Invernes, Forres, or Narin, pray you aquant me particularly, and I shall wroit to you, so you require them for my use, and let them alwayes be keeped to about the first of January nixt. Give my humble duty to your lady, and in caice ye or she wants anything from Holland, let me be aquanted therof, and I shall doe my indeavour to bring it over, iff my trunk can hold it. Give my duty to Asleisk, now the Laird of Brodie ; to the Laird of Innes, and to Coxtoune, and Dunkentie; to Grainge, Milnetoune, Bishopmilne, and to all other freinds that ask for me ; and so all freinds heire are in health, and give their service to you all."

" GANT, 18th Nover. 1710.

" I am ordered for recreuiteing, and am this lenth on my journey, wherfor I expect ye will let me know iff ther be any dilligences against me, for to the tyme I hear from you I desyne to stay att the Abbay."[2]

---

[1] Able-bodied vagrants, etc.

[2] Probably Holyrood, where debtors were safe from arrest.

" Receive Factory, subscryved by me att Reims, in Champaine of ffrance, the twenty-seventh of October seventeen hundred and twelve years, befor these witnesses, Ensigne William Brodie of Sir James Wood's Regement, and James Brodie, lawfull sone to John Brodie of Windiehills, and gentileman carryeing airmes in the said regement."

" *Att* CHALON SUR SAUNE IN BURGONE, *Novr.* 19*th*, *N. Styll*, 1712.

" I am prisoner. Our coosen, Collonell Brodie, is gone to Brussells, for his health ; and Captain Brodie is att Dijon, within twelve hours of this place ; and his nephew, Earnsyde's sone John, dyed at Reims. Direct for me, A. Monsieur—Monsieur Dunbar, Lieutenant du Regement Chevalier Wood, Ecosses, —Prisonier du guerre—A. Chalon Sur Saune."

" BRUSSELLS, 4*th May, N. S.*, 1717.

" I am now putt to that extremity, that I am obleidged to sell my cloaths, and everything else I hade, to mantaine myself from starveing. I now, for the last tyme, let you know that our regement is broken, and that the States will give us no pensions, and wee are obleidged to goe for London to solicite for halfe pay. Pray be so kynd as to aquant Ensigne Dunbar, Boath's brother, of this newes."

" To Mr. ARCHIBALD DUNBAR of Thundertoun,
" att Edinburgh, Britain.

"CAMP ATT WERWICK, *the 8th August* 1708.

" SIR,—Your cussin, Barmukety,[1] is att last made
ane officer ; and a man that comes from carrying armes
to be ane officer, is one of the poorest creatures in the
world, if he have not some other ressource than the
pitifull pay of eight guilders a week, which our masters
generousely bestow upon ane Ensigne. You remember, when you and I were last together, you desyred
we should endeavour to purchase him a commission
att your expenss. Now that providence hath thrown
a small bitt of bread in his way, it were a reflection on
us who have interested ourselves for him, if he were
not drawn out of the difficultyes he lyes under ; in
order wherto I have advanced him money to equippe
him, and he hath given me a bill on you for twenty
pounds sterling, which I have indorssed to Mr. John
Lillie att the Hague. I doubt not your punctuall
payment, and if you find me capable to render you
service in any maner, you may very freely command,
Sir, your most humble servant,   AL. BRODIE."

---

[1] His daughters are mentioned at page 16, and the death of his wife
forms the subject of the letter given at page 280. He had begun life
with bright prospects, having inherited the estate of Barmuketie from
his maternal grand-uncle, under whose auspices, as Provost of Inverness,
the bridge over the Ness was, in 1681, commenced, and by whom the
stately old building, still known in the capital of the Highlands as
" Dunbar's Hospital," had been, in 1668, founded and endowed.

Letter from the Adjutant of a regiment quartered in Majorca.

" ARCHD. DUNBAR, Esqr. of Duffus, near Elgine,
         " by Edenburgh, North Bretain.

                     " PORTMAHON, *August 6th,* 1742.

" DEAR SIR,—This is the first time I have hade an opertunety of writting to you since my last, which I think was dated from Spithead, June 1st, which was the time we sait saile for this place, where we arived June 30th, having made the voayage in thirty days, which is something not common at this time of the year, when calmes are very frequent on the Spanish coast. I was in great hopes that we should have called at Gibralter, which would have been something to my advantage, as I had a little bussiness there ; but, to my great disapointment, the man-of-war who was our convoy, lay too untill such time as shee seed the regiment who are to relive the other regiment there, safe into the bay, and so proceeded imediatly on our voayage without coming to ancker.

" Although I have been about a month in this place, yet I can give you but very small account of it, as my time has hitherto been taken up with the affairs of the regiment. There are five different places in this island, where the King's troops are quartred, viz., St. Phillips, Mahon, Citydilla, Allyhore, and ffornellas Castel ; but in case of any invasion, St. Phillips is the only place of refuge to which all the regiments must retire, as being the only fortification upon this island, the others being small places without being capable of making much deffence.

" The island seems to be provided naturely with every necessary of life, and prety plenty ; but as a squaderon of ships of war has been in these seas for some years past, it occasions every thing to be dear.

" We have no particular newes here, further than what, I presume, you may have heard by this time by the news papers, viz., Admiral Mathews having burned five Spanish gallies in a French port, and afterwards had the modesty to demand the ruins of the five ships from the French governour. We have at this time five hundred men detatched from the several regiments upon this island, under the command of Admiral Mathews, which are now encamped and mainteaning a narrow pas near Villa Francia, in the teretorys of his Sardinian Majesty.

" We have had several Neapolitan prizes brought in to this place, within this few days, so that we now seem to be in earnest.

" The English fleet are now crouzing off the bay of Taloon, where the French and Spanish fleets lay.

" I have had the honour to dine several times with General Anstruther (since I have been here), who is Lieut.-Governour of the island, and who seems to be prety complacent to us strangers. I am sorry I was

not wise enough before I left England, to aply to
you for a recomendation to him, since probably you
might have had it in your pouer to have procured
me one.

" This letter comes to England by the transport
ship that brought me here ; but there is a paquet that
goes from this to Marsells, and through France to
England some times, and allthough it is not above
seventy leagues from this to Marsells, yet as they
oblige the packet to ride quarantan, it is some times
five moneths before we can have a site of a letter in
that manner, so that unless in cases of necessity it is
not worth while to write by the packet ; however, in
case there should be any necessity to write in that
manner, I will acquant you per next, in what manner
you are to answer per paquet.

" When you have an inclination to write to me, you
will direct to William Dunbar, Adjutant to Colonel
Graham's Regiment, to the care of William Adair,
Esqr., at his house in Pall Mall, London. Mr. Adair
is our Adjent.

" I had ane opertunuty of puting my wife ashore
at Gibralter, without goeing myselfe ; so that she is
now there.—I continew, dear brother, yours most
affectionatly, WILL. DUNBAR."

THE exactions laid on the town of Elgin by the
Earl of Sutherland and Lord Lovat, both then in the
Hanoverian interest, and the pillage made by their
Lordships' retainers and by the Rebels, amounted
to three thousand eight hundred and sixteen pounds,
thirteen shillings, and eight pence, Scots money. In
the list of their losses, a document too long for in-
sertion here, it appears that the town's-people were
deprived of "sixty-three guns, fourty-five muskets,
thirty-two small swords, twenty-one broad swords,
four Dane's axes, three carbines, two halberds," and
a great number of pistols.

The county gentlemen, also, even those in the Hanoverian interest, had to give up their horses and arms
for the use of Government.

" For the Honourable
        " THE LAIRD OF GRANGE.

                " GRAINGEHILL, *Febry. 5th*, 1716.

"DEAR SIR,—I receved your horse, sadle, bridle,
hulsters, pistolls, and broad sword. I truly know
not the value of those things, but I have sent you a

recept which you may fill up at your own pleasure, as
you think them worth. I would gladly imbrace any
oppertounitty of doing a greater faivor to the young
ladies of your familie, than not to allow them the use
of your own horse, and, if the truce is prolonged, he
shall be sent. I have two niegbours that are very
well provided in horses, but does not incline to give
them for the service of the Goverment ; but, I am
sure, if any of the ladys with you made but the lest
application to ether of them, they could not refuse
them a horse. I have taken a womitte this day, and
I am not wery well, otherwayes I had not made use
of ane other's hand. I am, most sincerely, Sir, your
most obliged servant,   ROB. DUNBAR.

"I have filled up the recept in the same terms other
gentlemen have gote ; if it does not please you, it
shall be altered.

" Pray cause Windiehills[1] have his horse early here
to-morrow, for I have had no account of the cessa-
tion's being prolongued."

" I, Robert Dunbar of Graingehill, Commander of
the Murray horse, be vertue of the authority and
commission given to me by the Right Honourable
John, Earl of Sutherland, Lord-Lieutenant of the six

----

[1] John Brodie of Windyhills, now Milton-Brodie.

northern counties, grants me to have receeved from
Lodvick Dunbar of Grainge, a horse, sadle, bridle,
hulster cases, a pair of pistols, and a broad sword,
for the use of the Goverment; which he declairs,
upon his word of honour, are all together worth the
sume of fiveteen pounds sterling, which is to be re-
payed to him by the Goverment, in the terms of the
Act of Parliament.   Subscribed by me, at Graingehill, the sixth day of February 1716.

" Rob. Dunbar."

_____

" Wee, John Grant, merchant in Elgin, James and
John Burgesses, and Alexander Forbes, gunsmiths
there, and John Anderson, armourer there, five persones appointed by the Deputy Lieutenants of the
shire of Murray, to receive and value the armes
within the said shire, pursuant of the late Act of
Parliament, made anent secureing the peace of the
Highlands of Scotland, doe hereby acknowledge and
declair that we received from Ludovick Dunbar of
Grange (who is ane faithfull subject to his Majesty
King George, his person, and government, and did
continue the same the time of the late rebellion), the
armes after specified, and did value the same upon
oath to the sums following ; viz., from the said
Ludovic Dunbar, twelve guns, estimat att twelve
punds Scots each ; in all, one hundred and fourty
four punds Scots.   Item, received from ditto, three

guns more, estimat at fourty-two punds. Item, received from ditto, three guns, estimat at twenty-three
punds Scots money. Item, received from ditto, three
guns more, estimat at twenty-three punds Scots
money. Item, received from ditto, four guns more,
estimat at twenty punds Scots money. Item, received from ditto, one pistole, estimat at six punds
Scots money; amounting in haill, the armes of this
recept, to the number of twenty-five guns, and one
pistole; and the values thereof, to two hundred and
fifty-eight punds Scots money; which armes we
lodged in the Tolbooth of Elgin for his Majesty's use.

"The above valuation is just and true, as we shall
answer to God; as witness our hands, at Elgin, the
last day of October Jayviic and sixteen (1716) years.

"ALEXANDER FORBES.
JOHN ANDERSON.
JO. GRANT.
JAMES BURGES.
JOHN BURGES."

"Wee, Alexander Dunbar of Bishipmln, Sheriff of
Murray, and David Dunbar of Dunphail, Deputy
Lieutenants of the shire of Elgin, be virtue of the
powers given us by the late Act of Parliament anent
secureing the peace of the Highlands of Scotland, doe
hereby require and command you, James Wiseman,

collector of the land tax for the shire of Elgin, upon
sight hereof, to pay out of the first and readiest of
the land tax, that now is or hereafter shall be in your
hand, to the above designed Ludovick Dunbar (whom
wee certifie to be a true and loyall subject to his
Majesty King George, his person, and government,
and continued loyall to his Majesty dureing the late
rebellion), the values of his armes, amounting to the
sum of two hundred and fifty-eight punds, Scots
money.   Given under our hands, at Elgin, the last
day of October one thousand seven hundred and
sixteen years.   ALEXR. DUNBAR.
                              DAVID DUNBAR."

Lord Lovat's letter was written in February 1716.
Notwithstanding the King's thanks and rewards, his
Lordship afterwards, in 1745-6, espoused the cause of
Prince Charles Edward, for which he was executed on
Tower-Hill :—

" The much honoured
        " The LAIRD OF THUNDERTOUN,
                    " At BRODIE, on heast, the 12th.
  "MY DEAR THUNDERTOUN,—I thought to have had
the pleasure of seeing you here, and at Duffus to pay
my duty to your worthy lady, whom I heartily salut.
I heer you and Mr. Wiseman have got a great many
horses of the Rebells, for almost nothing.   I intreat

you give me that mark of your ffriendship as to oblidge Mr. Wiseman to give me six of those horses at
fifty per cent. profit, which I ofer and will pay to your
cusing James Dunbar, or any other at Inverness. I
got the kindnest letter imaginable from Argyl. The
King both thanks me and rewards my services.

"I am, with love and respect, your own

"LOVAT."

Receipt by Major Fraser of Culduthel, on the back
of the above letter :—

"*Gatesyde, in ffebry.* 1716.—Receaved ffive horses,
which I am to deliver to my Lord Lovat.

"Receaved by me JAMES FFRASER."

General order :—

"Joseph Wightman, Esqr., Major-General commanding His Majiesties Forces in the North of Scotland etc. :

"Whereas I have been informed that several of the
Rebells' horses and armes are hidden in the town and
countrey of Elgen, and that several arms and horses
have been bought up contrary to law, this is to require
you to make such search for any such persons, horses,
and armes as are hidden, and give me constant ac-

counts of the same, at Inverness or elsewhere, in order to be disposed on for His Majesties service.—Given under my hand, att Elgen, the twenty-first day of Februay 1716. J. WIGHTMAN.

" To the Honorable LORD PROVOST OF ELGEN,
  his Bailiffs or under Magistrats."

William Dawson, afterwards Provost of Forres, had a narrow escape for his life :—

" To the much honoured the LAIRD OF THUNDERTOUN,
                " Provost of Elgine.
                        " FORRES, Febr. 17th, 1716.

" MUCH HONOURED SIR,—You will be surprised to here of my treatment at Inverness, all occasioned by your freind James Dunbar, whoe I most say is the most revengable man on the face of the earth. I gave baill for two thousand pounds sterling, yet this morneing ther cam thirty or forty of Fowls men whoe is cearyeinge me prisoner to Inverness this moment, upon a signed information James Dunbar heas procured from Shiper Hume, beareinge that I imported airms in his shipe, for the use of the Raibls ; yet I declair, upon all that is good, I never imported or exported any kind of goods in his shipe, nor did I ever import any airms, or any other, but what was for the use of Brodie and Culloden.

" Mr. Dunbar heas mead me odiouse to the Earle of

Sutherland, and to my Lord Lovat, by meakinge them
belive a thousand leise ; in short, he represents me to
be the worst man in the world. I am sadlie affraid of
the conciconce of this, soe doe intreat you will writ
a leter to my Lord Lovat or any other freind, and doe
me justice. I would likways heav you writ to Mr.
Dunbar, and send your leters with the bearer, my
servant, whoe comes directely after me to Inverness. I
would heav you notice that my baill is given upe, and
I am impeatched for Hy treason. God is witness if I
be guilty. I am hurried of with a partie, soe shall say
noe mor, only my humble duty to yourself and lady,
and belive me that I ever am, Sir, your most obedient and humbel servant,   WILL. DAWSON."

Forage was charged at the rate of eight shillings
per boll of "single oats," and three halfpence per stone
of straw. Each horse was allowed daily half a peck
of oats and a stone of straw.

"*March* 22d, 1716.—Accompt of straw and oates
delyvered out by William Douglass, keeper of the
Magazine at Elgin, to the regimentile officers and
troups of Generall Carpinter's Dragouns, conform to
their particular receipts and otherwise, preceiding the
twentie second inclusive.

" Imprimis, to the Generall's troup, per receitt from
John Parquett, sergant :—

	Stons of Straw.	Oates.		
		B.	F.	P.
The number of . . .	259	08	0	1
Item, to Collonell Guest's troup,	235	07	1	1½
With ane peck of malt.				
Item, to the said Collonell, for the } use of his own horses, . }	132½	08	0	2
With ane boll of malt.				
Item, to Collonell ffolley's troop, .	220	07	3	1
Item, to Collonell ffolley's own horses,	124	04	2	0
Item, to him, ane ffirlott malt.				
Item, to Captain Broun's troup, .	234½	07	1	1
Item, to the said Captain, one peck malt.				
Item, to Captain Mullen's troop, .	267½	09	3	2
Item, to the said Captain, ffyve pecks one lipie of malt.				
Item, to Captain Reid's troop, . .	247	07	2	2½
Item, to Livetenant Dupoyes's horse,	016	00	2	0
Item, to Quartermaster Kelly's horse,	002	00	0	3½
Item, to Coronett Henly,	002	00	0	2
	1739½	61	2	0½ "

A " GROAN " from the Presbytery of Elgin :—

" *Att* ELGEN, *September* 11, 1716.

" The which day, the Presbytery of Elgen, taking
to their serious consideratione the many illegal and
oppressive incroachments made upon their ministry

by Episcopal preachers, and that upon —— day of
May —— they had appointed tuo of their number to
represent to the Lifetenant-deputs of the shire of
Murray, some of those grievances the Presbytery lay
under, and that nothing could be then got done, the
Presbytery did unanimously agree and appoint that
an Informatione be given in to the Lifetenant-deputs,
that are to meet at Elgen on the accompt of the Toun
Elections ; and likewais that a copie of the said Informatione be given to the Advocate-depute, as followes :—

" MAY IT PLEASE,—It is with a depth of sorrow we
behold that after such a signal delyverance as God
wrought for us of late, when we expected law should
take place and we should be rescued from oppres-
sione, their ar so many open violations of law, to the
prejudice of the interest of the gospel, and the cherish-
ing of disaffectione to his Majesties just ·and lawfull
athority in our parishes, without restraint ; and conceave we cannot discharge the duty incumbent upon
us without acquainteng you with some of these things,
which ar in your pouer to redress.

" *Primo,* Mr. John Stewart, who preaches in a meeting-house in the parish of Duffus, did never befor the
late Rebellione, pray for his Majestie King George and
the royal family, in terms of law, but in October last,
did pray in publick for the Pretender (under the name

and designatione of our gracious Soveraign King James)
and severall of the heads of the Rebells, such as the
Duke of Marr, Lifetenant-General Gordon, Brigadeer
M'Intosh, etc., and continued this his practise untill
the Rebells wer driven from Perth ; as can be wit-
nessed by all who were his ordinary hearers, such as
Mr. Archibald Dunbar of Thoundertoune, Justice of
Peace and Provost of Elgen; Thomas Sutherland, fewer
in Kame ; William Sutherland of Roshach ; Alexander
Petry, fewer in Starwood; Alexander Andersone, tenant
in Burnsyde ; Andrew Naughty, tenant ther ; John
Rin, tenant in Inskeel ; James Rin, tenant in Kame ;
William Rin, tenant in Rosyle ; etc.

"Secundo, Mr. Beroald Innes, who lives in Instelly,
in the parish of Alves, for ordinary keeps public worship without praying for King George, Prince or
Princess of Wales, in terms of law ; frequently marries
and baptises, which shall be made evident by competent witnesses, when required.

"Tertio, Mr. Alexander Smith, in the parish of
Belly, kept a meeting-house in the toune of Focabus,
and officiat as chaplain to the Marqueness of Huntly,
every Sabboth, but did not pray for King George,
Prince or Princess of Wales, in terms appointed by
law ; and did frequently marrie and baptise in that
and other neighbouring parishes ; and, about the beginning of the late unnaturall Rebellione, did intrude
openly into the kirk of Gartely, which was settled by

a minister of the present Establishment, and continowed so to do, animating and encurageing the
people to rebellione; and, when they took arms, went
with them and preached to them in the church of
Cupar of Angus, where he prayed in express terms
for the Pretender, under the name of King James, and
continowed with them till after the Rebells were de-
feate at Dumblane; and since his return, is employed
as chaplain to the Marchoness of Huntley, but prays
not for King George, *ut supra;* all which can be
proven by famous witnesses, when required.

" *Quarto*, Alexander Robertsone, who kept a meeting-house, dureing the time of the late Rebellione, in
the toune of Focabus, did intrude into the church of
Raphane, and, both ther and at Focabus, prayed in
express terms for the Pretender, under the name of
King James; and continowes yet to keep meeting-
house at Focabus.

" *Quinto*, Mr. James Gordon, brother to Classtirum,
Mr. Patrick Frazer, Mr. ———— Reid, Mr. ———— Duglas,
Mr. John Irvine, priests, doe keep publick meetings
for worship in the toun of Focabus, in the said Mr.
Irvin's house, which can be proven by competent wit-
nesses, when required.

" These ar some of the grievances we groan under,
and we lay them before you, as persones not only
clothed with authority to give us redress, but whom
we suppose to have a due regard for the support of a

gospel interest, the maintinance of his Magesties law
and authority, and a simpathy with us ; and intreat
your effectuall interpositione for our relief."

The Presbytery mind their own affairs : —

" To Mr. ARCHBALD DUNBAR of Thundertoun.

" ELGIN, 24*th December* 1717.

" MUCH HONOURED, — Mr. Alexander Anderson,
minister of Duffus, wrotte a letter to this Presbitry,
bearing that about the beginning of the late Rebellion
he gave you, by the hands of Mr. James Tower, the
silver bason and two silver cups belonging to the
parish of Duffus, and that for more safe custody ; and
though he hade at severall times since, written to you
and required those pieces of plate back again, you
hade not honoured him with any returns. Withall
he entreats the Presbitry may concern themselves in
that matter and entreat you may return that plate to
him again. The Presbitry thought his desire reasonable, and they have appointed me, in their names, to
entreat you may deliver up these Church utensils,
that are now in your hand, to Mr. Alexander Anderson. This, in name and by the appointment of the
Presbitry, is subscryved by, Much Honoured, your
most oblidged humble servant,

" THO: MACCULLOCH, *Moderator.*"

So early as 1722, a second rising in favour of the Stuarts was expected.

"For the LAIRD of THUNDERTOUN, Sherive Principall of Murray, and the rest of the Deputy-Lievtennants of the said County. For the King's speciall service.—Elgin.

"HOLYRUD HOUSE, 15*th of May* 1722.

"GENTLEMEN,—The King having nothing more att heart than the good and weelfare of his subjects, having receaved repeated and unquestionable advices that severall of his subjects, forgetting the allegiance they owe to his Majestie, as weel as the love they ought to bear to ther country, have entred into a wicked conspiracie in concert with traitors abroad, for raising a rebellion in this kingdom in favour of a Popish pretender, but without the concurrance or aid of any fforign power. It is therefor necessary for all his Majesties dutifull and faithfull subjects to take care to disapoint the designs of his enimies, by having a watchfull eye over them, and sufering noe raballings or meetings amongst such as ther is reasin to belive are disaffected, and to disarm them; and if any attented persons come now into the country, or any strangers, that they be immedeatly secured, with ther papers, and the Lord Justice Clarke and Mr. Dundas, his Majesties Advocat, aquanted of the same, that they may be disposed of according to ther order. Your ready complyance in this, as it will bee a mark of your zeal and affectione to the King and Government, is not only expected, but earnestly entreated by, gentlemen, your most humble servant,

" SUTHERLAND."

Sir John Cope commenced his useless march to the Highlands on the 20th August 1745, and arrived on the 27th at Inverness. The defenceless state of Edinburgh demanding his immediate return to the shores of Lothian, he marched to Aberdeen, embarked his troops on transports, and, under escort of a ship of war, sailed on the 10th September.

" To the SHIREF-DEPUTE or SUBSTITUTE of the
    " Shire of Elgin and Forres.   Per express.   Haste !

" INVERNESS, Sept. 2, 1745.

" SIR,—As his Majesty's troops are to march through the county of Murray, you will immedeatly upon recept of this, give the proper orders for horses and carriages to be in readiness to perform that service. As the troops are to march from this on Wednesday, they will probably get your length on Thursday, so that they must be all in readiness to perform that service. They are to be payed conform to the Instruc-

Y

tions[1] herein enclosed. As this is a matter that will admit of no delay, I do not doubt of your assiduity. I have wrote to my chamberlain to have all my people in the Forestry of Darnway in readiness, and likewise to acquaint the Lyon, that they may be ready to meet them upon the confines of Murray. Your diligence in this affair will greatly oblige, Sir, your most humble servant,   MORAY.

" The original Instructions I keep, signed by the Crown lawiers."

_____

Two letters from the Lord Lyon—Brodie of Brodie —the first unsigned, but in his handwriting. Cope's army was then encamped at Merrytoun, on the estate of Boath :—

" To WILLIAM KING of Newmill, Esq.,
    " Shirrieff Deputy of Elgin and Forres.   Haste ! haste !

"NAIRN, _Tuesday, Septr. the 4th,
in the Evening._

" SIR,—This is by order of Sir John Cope, Commander-in-Chief of his Majesty's Forces in North Brittain, to acquaint you that he is to encamp with the troops under his command, to-morrow's night, in the neighbourhood of the town of Elgin, and that he

_____

[1] According to the " Instructions" enclosed in the Earl of Moray's letter, the Sheriff had to provide " horses and carriage, for the transport of baggage, at three halfpence per mile ; straw for the tents, and firing for the soldiers' kettles, at the ordinary rates," etc. etc.   His Lordship was then Sheriff Principal of the county of Moray.

will have occasion for four hundred horses and carts
to carry his baggage ; which horses and carts must be
in the camp to-morrow's night, because they will begin
their march next morning by daylight.

"You are also, immediately on receipt of this, to
order the bakeing of as much flour and meal into
biscuit for officers and soldiers, as your town can
possibly bake on so short advertisement, for which
you will be paid in ready money; so let me beg of you
to set all hands to work in publick and private houses.

" You are also to provide one hundred and fifty load
of straw for the men to lye on, as they all lye in camp;
of all which you are to acquaint the Magistrates of the
town, that they may be aiding and assisting to you.

" You are also to provide fireing for the troops to
make ready their meat in the camp.

" The straw to be provided must be two hundred
and fifty load, I haveing mistaken it on the other page.

" Beds will be wanted in the town for the General
and some of the officers.—I am, Sir, your most humble
servant,   ."

" To WILLIAM KING of Newmill, Esqr.,
            " Sherrieff-Deputy of Elgin.
                    " BRODIE-HOUSE, *half-an-hour past six.*

" SIR,—Yours I did not receive till this moment,
directed to the Earl, who is not yet come from Inverness. Meantime, I answered your letter before I received it.

"They will encamp probably on this side of the town, near the water of Lossie ; and Major Caulfield, the Quarter-Master-General, will be with you before the troops, and will mark out that piece of ground he likes best, whether it be corn or heath ; and some field of corn must be sacrificed for the maintainance of their own and baggage horses ; but then they give an order for the value of the field, upon the Collector of Supply, or rather the Sherrief Deputy gives it by their direction, according as four sworn birley men shall apprise it. This was done at Inverness, and last night at Nairn.

"You and the Provost, or some of the Magistrates, must attend the Quarter-Master Caulfield and the Adjutant Loudon (who go before the General), as well as the General, to receive his directions. Beef and mutton will be wanted, but what quantity I know not, only they have a butcher that goes before to provide for the officers.

"This, with my letter last night by my Lord Findlater's servant, is all, till meeting, necessary from, Sir, your most humble servant,

"ALEXR. BRODIE.

"P.S.—Enquire at Robert Inness and the rest of the merchants in your town, what money they can give Lord Loudon, for bills on his agent at Edinburgh."

From the Earl's secretary :—

" To Wm. King, Esqr. of Newmiln.

"*ffrom the Armie at* ffORRESS, *5th September* 1745.

" SIR,—It is my Lord Moray's desire that as·many boats, as can possibly be got, be had together, to carrie over Sir John Cope and the armie, at the Boat of Bog.[1] You will, therefor, immediately upon receit of this, take all the necessary measures to effectuate it. Your diligence in this will much oblige my Lord Moray and your most humble servant,   JOHN STUART."

His Excellency ought to have written *Forres* and *Cullen* :—

" By the Honble. Sir John Cope, Commander-in-Chief of his Majesties Forces in Scotland, &c.

" These are to certify, that his Majesties forces under my command halted at Forrest, the 5th September 1745, where some small damage was done. I therefore recommend it to the Sheriff of the county and his Deputys to have an estimate made of that damage, according to the directions given by the Lord Advocate and Solicitor-General thereon.—Given under my hand, at Collen, this 7th day of September 1745.   JNO. COPE."

---

[1] The ferry at the Spey near Fochabers.

" By the Honble. Sir John Cope, Commander-in-Chief
of his Majesties Forces in Scotland, &c.

" These are to certify, that his Majesties forces
under my command lay encamped at Elgin, the 5th
of September 1745, at night, where damage was necessarily done to corn, &c. I therefore recommend it
to the Sheriff of the county and his Deputys to have
an estimate made of those damages, according to the
directions given by the Lord Advocate and Solicitor-
General thereon.—Given under my hand, at Collen,
this 7th day of September 1745.   JNO. COPE."

So soon after Cope's defeat and the occupation of
the capital of Scotland by Prince Charles Edward,
Mr. Sutherland, an Edinburgh lawyer, considered it
prudent not to add his signature :—

" To ARCHIBALD DUNBAR of Newton, Esqr..
     " at Duffus, near Elgin.
                              " EDINBURGH, 13th Novr. 1745.
" SIR,—Receive inclosed this day's Currant. We
have, thir ten .or twelve days bygone, been quite free
of the Highlanders, who have marched towards England ; and this day the Lord Justice-Clerk and several
others of the Lords of Session and Justiceary, who had
been at Berwick, came to town with a good many
attendants, and the Governour of the Castle did them

the honour to fire a round of the great guns as a token
of their welcome. Whether we shall have a Session or
not this winter, is uncertain, because it will depend in
a great measure upon the success of the King's armies
against the Highlanders and others in the Rebellion;
for it is said they are endeavouring to shun General
Wade and his army, and so pass by him the western
road further up into England, where they expect
——[1] to join them; and, on the other part, no question but General Wade and the King's army will endeavour, all they can, to meet and attack them. We
know little here of both armies, only what is in the
Courrant, and we have little to expect untill a battle
happen, which, it is probable, will be very bloody and
obstinate.

" You will know what the postage of this will be.
Each print is, of prime cost, three halfpence. The
Mercury is not yet come out this day.—I am, Sir,
your most humble servant,   ———.

" You are happy to have peace and quiet in your
country so long continued, whereas we in this town
(while the Highlanders were among us), and the coun
try round us, have been greatly distressed by them
and their roberies, and we have been frighted by frequent canonading from the Castle, used for dislodging
them from sundrie houses where they kept guard,

---

[1] Torn out in opening the original letter.

which have been demolished by cannon-ball, and there-after burnt ; and, particularly, the west side of the Weyhouse is demolished down to the ground, and I have been obliged to remove my papers, for fear of fire, which now I have brought back."

Ludovic Brodie, W.S., announces that the snuff is to be sent, and that Carlisle has surrendered :—

" For ARCHIBALD DUNBAR of Newton, Esq.,
        " Elgin.
                        " EDINBURGH, 22d Novr. 1745.

" SIR,—I shall take the first opportunity to send the snuff you desire. If you have this day's Mercury sent you, it contains an account of the surrender of Carlile to the Rebels. It is thought, if the bad weather and roads have not hindered, Marshal Wade's army will be by this time near that country, and that the Rebels will offer him battle, which, if it happen, will certainly be a very bloody one. The bulk of the Rebel army being Highlanders, are resolved to overcome or die in the battle, because they reckon it a more ignominious death to die by a judicial sentence for rebellion, and be hanged, which they have just reason to expect in case they should escape and be afterwards taken. I have nothing more to write you, but am, Sir, your affectionate and humble servant,
                        " LUD. BRODIE."

Sent from Elgin to Duffus, about 10th December
1745 :—

" Ther has been no beef in toun since this day
fortnight, except one cow of Linkwood's, which was
dear and not very good. I believe ther will be none
this day neither, at least I see no appearence of any.
Ther is not one word of news ; the post that came
yesterday could tell nothing, not so much as if Lord
Lewis was at Aberdein, but that ther is a great many
of his men at Strathbogie.

" They say the Maclouds, with Louden and a great
many more men, are to be here this week, but their
intentions are not known, and some does not believe
that they are comming.

" You are obliged to Lady Newmiln for the candle-
wicks, for if she had not had them they were none in
toun."

From Mr. Brodie of Windyhills :—

" To ARCHBALD DUNBAR of Newton, Esqr.,
        " at Duffus.

" ELGIN, *Decr.* 13*th*, 1745.

" SIR,—Receve, inclosed, Mr. Brodie's bill discharged
on the back. As for news, I chuse to deal little in
them, as I think little credite is to be given to most
things told. One side tells us of landings, every day ;
and, this day or two, we are amused with a defeat of

the Brest squadron (though I do not beleive it), and
Lord John Drumond prisoner at Leith, with two
hundred French.   The first part of that I suppose
false, the last may be true.

"Macload came here yesterday with four hundred
of his men, and Gineas the day before with his men.
How long they remain here, or what there intent is, I
know not, though it is supposed they are to visite
Aberdeinshire.   One of there Captains, lodged with me,
says there rout is here to remain till further orders.
He tells me also that eight hundred men went to visit
Lovat the same day they came from Inverness.   I
think we know little of the result of this visite as yet,
only it is said Lovat is to give security for the peace
of his people, and give up all there arms.   So you have
it as I have it, which, with compliments, is all from
yours,   ALEX. BRODIE."

From Mr. King of Newmiln :—-

"ARCHBALD DUNBAR of Newtoun, Duffus.

"ELGIN, 14*th* *Decr.* 1745.

"DEAR SIR,—My wife was at church Sunday last
in the afternoon, but has not been abroad since, being
troubled with rheumatick pains.   She was expecting
the pleasure of seeing you and your lady here, in this
fine weather, where you would had the opportunity of
seeing a fine little armie of five hundred Mackleods,

commanded by their Chief and Macleod of Guineas :
and I hear wee are to have eight hundred more with
Loudon, on Munday, who went out with these men
and Lyon with him (as the MacLeods marched here),
and apprehended and brought in your friend, Lovat,
prisoner to the castle of Inverness, and fourty stand
of armes. I hear they are all to march towards Aberdein nixt week, and that the Grants are at Milnben,
ready to join them in their march. The men that are
here seem to be very good discreit civill men, and
behave very discreitly where they are quarterred in
town, and the people reckon themselves very happy
they are civill ; and this is all I can tell you, which,
with our compliments to you and lady, I am, &c.

" W. KING.

" I hear the Lyon and Sir Harrie march with them,
as volentiers, to Aberdein ; how far farder they goe
I know not."

From the Sheriff-clerk :—

" To ARCHBALD DUNBAR of Newtown, Esq.

" ELGIN, 16th Decr. 1745.

" SIR,— I shall try to get a man to take the bill on
Edinburgh, and wryte you therof betwixt and Thursday
night, if I get a good hand to take it. As for news,
we have none certain but that the Laird of M'Leod,

with his men, about five hundred, past Spey yesterday without oposition.   Culkern and Bailie William
M'Intosh are just now come in heir with two hundred
men more, and Lord Loudon is expected with five
hundred more the morow.   He also is to bring in
three field-peices.

   " I am told Lord President's son and the Master of
Ross are come by sea to Inverness, and bring some
great news ; but as neither time nor place, nor any
particular, is told, I look on it as a fable till I heir
more certainly.   I offer my compliments to your self
and lady, and remain, Sir, your most humble servant,

                               " JOHN DUFF."

                ————

   Two letters, chiefly relating to the battle of Falkirk.[1]
To the first there is no signature ; but the other,
signed " Read and Burn," is from George Cumming of
Altyre, lieutenant in Naizon's Dragoons, who, in consequence of his horse falling, was taken prisoner by
the victors.   Both letters were written on the 13th
February 1746, and probably at Altyre, where Cumming seems to have been, on parole :—

" ARCHIBALD DUNBAR, Esqr. of Newton.

   " DEAR SIR,—I am just now favoured with yours,
which contains more queries than is in my power to

                ─────
[1] Fought in January 1746.

solve, nor am I much wiser, or but little more learned in history, than when I saw you last, for the best accounts of the late battle seems to agree in substance with the short narrative I carried with me from your end of the country. The Highlanders were certainly the agressors, as they marched seven miles that morning with a design to attack the regular troops, who had no intention to engage till next morning by daylight; only when they saw the Highland army comeing on, they were then obliged to draw up in form, and the horse ordered to march in front and attack the Prince's army. As to the numbers on both sides I cannot truley inform you. Some says the Highlanders in the field were about nine thousand strong, but not one-half of them engaged. The other side, I am told, were eleven thousand regular troops, besides militia. It is agreed that the numbers killed on the Government side were not under six hundred, but not so many prisoners. The siege continued until they were forced to abandon it upon the Duke of Cumberland's comeing with a powerful army to its relief; by which it would appear their comeing to the North was rather force than choise. What succours they hope for God only knows, but I shall refer what I have heard for a conversation; but you know I am an infideal.

"We are informed (only by common report) that the Prince with his army are within seven miles of

Inverness ; and, though you tell me nothing of it, part of the horse and foot comeing to this country, under the command of Lord John Drummond, are expected this night in your nighbourhood. A friend of mine who accompanyed the prisoner[1] to this place, will be readie (as far as in his power) to oblige, if there is occasion. He is gone from here this day to Elgin. I shall not trouble you with any history of the Captain,[1] as he has wrote you himself. As to young Keam,[2] I am told he is well, but still a prisoner.

" It is expected and lookt for that the Duke of Cumberland is to follow the chase hot to this country ; but it is believed, before he can possibly come up, Inverness yields. What your politicians and Cabinet Councilemen are a doing, I know not. The M'Leods and all others att Forres got a sudden call from the west, Sunday evening last, and they marched early next morning, so that there is no body to hinder letters from being delivered. I am, with real regard, dear Sir, yours,   ——.''

————

" Archibald Dunbar of Newton, Esqr.

" *The* 13*th.*

" Dear Sir,—As the unfortunate person to whom you wrote to-day is deprived of the use of pen, ink,

[1] George Cumming of Altyre.
[2] Mr. Sutherland, younger of Keam.

and paper, as well as of every other necessary or comfort of life, he is oblidged to answer your kind letter
by an amanuensis. In the first place, it is not till
now that he has been convinced of the sincere ffriendship of you and your good lady, whom, though he
desires to see as much as any on earth, yett he can
not hope for that pleasure at present, it being absolutely necessary you remain at home, till the Prince's
army passes, and where, if occasion require it, I have
begged a ffriend to attend you for the preservation of
your house, &c., in case of moraders, which is all my
situation can permitt me to do were you my ffather;
but I hope you are so farr from all roads that there
will be no occasion for it. My unfortunate and cruel
story must be the subject of a conversation which 1
am as anxious to give so real a ffriend, as you are to
hear it, but common prudence, nay, my own safety,
absolutely debarrs my ventureing on it any other way.
What you have allready heared is so far true, that, in
less than five minutes, your ffriend, with about fifty
broadswords and daggers at his breast, ready to cutt
him in pieces, was stripped of his cavalry arms, furniture, baggage of every sort, and field-equipage, to
above three hundred and fifty guines value; nay, of
the very things and cloaths about himself, down to
his hatt, perwigg, and spurrs; since when he has been
mostly in a dungeon, without fire, light, or straw,
among the comon prisoners, oblidged to ease nature

where they satt or lay ; nor has he mounted a horse
since his unfortunate fall in the battle, the cause of all
his woe. After beeing taken from gaol, upon hard
and unheard of conditions, he came on foot here, over
mountains of snow and rivers of water, at the rate of
twenty-five or thirty miles a-day, subsisted only on
whisky and tobacco—for nothing else could mony
purchass—and only straw or heather to ly on. It is
certain, from undoubted authority, that Ligonier's
Dragoons begun the attack a great deal too soon, and
charged with their swords in their hand at a full trott,
till they came to the muzles of three thousand of their
enemy, by which means, and Hambelton's regiment
flying and breaking in on their flank, the former was
cutt to pieces. The occasion of this precipitate charge
and over heasty attack was to wipe off the dust and
odium of Gladesmoor, which their enemys allow they
did with great honour. The prisoner is confined here,
lyable to be recalled at a moment, though in great
distress of body, and in want of every necessary thing
—the smalest regrete of those that want freedome.
The rest of your ffriends here are ffaithfully yours,
and, thank God, as well as can be expected. When
the crowd is past, by you a visit will be charity, if I
am allowed to stay ; but come not without the worthy
goodwife, whom I am most anxious to see, and then
I shal promise you the most amazeing history you
ever heard or read. Young Keam I saw often, who

is as well and happy as any person ever was in confinement. I can say no more; but God bless you and your's. You will guess from whom this comes. Adiu.

" READ AND BURN."

The measures adopted by the followers of Prince Charles Edward were most oppressive. Gordon of Carnousie and Maclachlan of that Ilk were not to be trifled with :—

" To James Robertson, Groom to Sir Robert Gordon of Gordonstown.

" *Gordonstown, 23d ffebry.* 1746.—I have seized for his Royal Highness' service, and for his own proper use, from Sir Robert Gordon of Gordonstown, a young large black horse, switch tailed ; a bay mare, rel back'd ; a large black draught horse, short dock'd. You will care for, and keep, these three horses, and deliver them to no person untill called for by me, under the pain of military execution against Sir Robert Gordon, his person and effects, besides what punishment his Highness may think proper to cause inflict upon yourself for disobedience.

" ARTHUR GORDON."

" To all officers, Civil and Military, &c., employed in
his Royal Highness's service.

" By Collonell Lauchlan M'Lachlan of that Ilk,
Commissary-General of his Royal Highness the
Prince Regent's Army.

" These do order and require the heritors, and their
ffactors, tacksmen, and subtenants of and on the lands
of Duffus (belonging to the Duke of Gordon and Mr.
Dunbar of Newton), Sir Robert Gordon of Gordonstown, Brodie's lands of Kinnedder, the lands of Find-
rassie, the lands of Westfield, Coutfield, and Ardgy,
forthwith to send into the granary at Forres one
thousand bolls of wheat, flour, oatmeal, and bear, less
or more, that may be presently stord up in girnels,
houses, barns, or milns ; and, for ascertaining the
number of bolls the said lands can presently afford,
these do authorize and impower you, Captain James
Stewart, Commissary, to call for and march a partie of
fourty men, with their proper officers, to the grounds
of the said lands, and throw open all girnels, houses,
barns, milns, and other places of store, and make up
an exact account of the number of bolls of each kind
may be found in the said places, and give the samen,
duely subscribed, to the commanding officer of the
said partie, who is to lodge on free quartering untill
the full of any such accompt be transported and carried to the granary of Forres : And, in case of not

compliance within fourteen hours after making up the said accompt, these do impower and strictly charge the commanding officer of the partie to begin and go through the severest military execution, by burning their barns and barn-yards, and making the proprietors prisoners to the town of Inverness. All which you are to do, as you shall be answerable to his Royal Highness or his General Officers.—Given at Elgin, this sixth day of March 1746. L. M'LAUCHLANE."

"To Donald Macklauchlane, Serjent.

"You are to march immediately to the house of Sanchor and lands of Burdsyards, there to remain in free quartering till the above sum[1] be paid to his Royall Highness's receiver at this town of Forres. With certification, in case of contempt or refusall, you are to begin the severest military execution, by burning their houses and driving away their cattle, but still allowing discompt for what victuall is already payed ; and in case of not payment of the above sum before ten of the clock this night, you are to force the tennents to load and carry to the granary at the foot of Lochness, one hundred bolls bear and thirty bolls meall, and that by ten of the clock to-morrow.—Given at Forres, the twenty-sixth day of March 1746.

"L. M'LAUCHLANE, C. G."

[1] The sum demanded was "two terms' cess" with £60 on each £100 of valued rent, amounting in all to £689, 4s., Scots money.

The Baronet of Gordonston had cause of complaint :—

"*Memoriall for Sir Robert Gordon of Gordonstown.*

" Upon 16th ffebruary 1746, the Rebells came into the shire of Murray, where great numbers of them remained until the 11th Aprill thereafter, both inclusive.

" During this space severall outrages were committed by them ; most people were harrassed and oppressed, but none so signally as I and my tennents.

" Upon the very day of their coming, I had ane order upon me, signed by ffrancis Gordon, for no less than one thousand stone weight of hey, twenty cart loads of straw, and ten bolls of oats.

" I had a very large pease-stack in my corn-yard, and it was the practice of the Rebells, when they brought their horses to carry away loads from Gordonstown, to put their horses to eat at this pease-stack ; and as above sixty horses could have conveniently eaten at this stack at one and the same time, and that they were at different times put to, and did eat at the stack, it necessarily follows that I thereby suffered damages.

" The Rebells not only signally harrassed my tennents by free quartering upon them, &c., whilst their officers quartered within the house of Gordonstown, but also they locally quartered within that house above thirty privat men, besides their commanders, and who remained within that house for ten or twelve days.

" The Rebells destroyed my pigeons at Gordonstown, by shooting the doves; and, in the evening, when it was to be presumed the doves had entered the dovecott, they first stoped the dovecott that the pigeons could not get out, then broke open the door, and entering the dovecott destroyed the doves within.

" They also destroyed my dovecott of Bellormy.

" The Rebells carried myself prisoner from Gordonstown to Elgin, where I was detained for ten days, and from thence carryed prisoner to Inverness.

" The Rebells forced Lady Gordon and her children and ffamily to leave the house of Gordonstown, after my being carried away prisoner.

" After the ffamily were obliged to leave the house of Gordonstown, and that the doors were shut, the Rebells entered the house at the windows, threatened to destroy the servants who were about the town, as they had also threatened my officer before, and carryed away pork, hams, dry ffish, books, &c., out of the house.

" As my servants were threatened, and I was obliged to secrete my labouring horses,[1] so a part of the lands in my natural possession suffered damage by

---

[1] The stable where Sir Robert concealed his horses may yet be seen at Covesea. It is a natural cave in a rock facing the sea, and was then probably within flood-mark.

being mislaboured, and other parts by not being at
all laboured, which damage is ascertained to amount
to forty-four bolls.

" They also carryed away from me, out of Dollas,
ffive mares with ffoal, and two horses.

" The Rebells broke open the doors and windows
of my house of Rininner, and carryed away and destroyed severall things within the house.

" The Rebells killed and carryed away a large sow
from Dollas.

" They tied my herd at Dollas, and kept him prisoner untill a cow was drowned.

" The Rebells exacted from Lady Gordon a term's
cess, being one hundred and thirty-two pounds sixteen
shillings Scots.

" The haill particular damages above mentioned
were done to myself personally; and, besides those,
my tennents were severely harrassed. They were not
only obliged to maintain numbers of the Rebells, for
the far greatest part of the time they were in the
country, in bed and dyet gratis, but were also robed
of money and other effects, bodily abulziements, corns,
carts, sacks, and horses, whereof they can bring evidence. One tennent was, without offence, beat in his
own house, and afterwards carried to Elgin, and made
prisoner, where he was detained untill he paid money
for being put at liberty; and the servant of another
tennent was causless shot to death, without any pro-

vocation given, and, though the criminal was apprehended and the murder represented, no redress was had.

"The Rebell officers who put up at the house of Mr. Dunbar of Newtown, my next neighbour, sent their horses from thence to be maintained in my stables at Gordonstown, though, samctime, it is ffact true that Mr. Dunbar had aboundance of corn, straw, and hey of his own ; whence it may be presumed the horses were not sent to my stable but out of pique, and very probably upon Mr. Dunbar's recommendation.

"But Mr. King of Newmiln did not act so much behind the curtain ; ffor two witnesses declare, that about the beginning of March 1746, Newmiln, in a conversation with a company of Rebels in his own Close (particularly one called Captain Wood of Glasgow), said to the Rebells 'That they would find horses for their purpose at Gordonstown, and failling that at Drainy, for that I had thirty horses very fit for their hussars.' Thus far one of the witnesses declares, and the other says somewhat further, 'That he heard Newmiln order a party of the Rebells, who were going out to seize horses, to go to Gordonstown and Drainy, where they would find good horses, for that I never wanted thirty horses fit for their hussars ; and that he heard Newmiln caution the Rebells whom he informed, not to let him be seen in the matter.'"

Sent from Elgin to Duffus, on Sunday, 13th April 1746 :—

" The Rebels went from here last night. The Duke with his army came past this day ; did not stop here. They say they are to encamp near Alves.

" I don't know if they will need forrage, but they have prodigious quantities of that and all provisions along with them. We saw the Master of fforrbes here, and spoke to him; and I saw the Lyon, Kinstery, Spynie, and Sir Harrie, on the street. Nobody can tell their numbers, but certainly they are very numerous—they say eighteen thousand."

The list is in the handwriting of the Master of Forbes :—

" List of Rebell Officers and men killed at the Battle of Cullodden, April 16th, 1746.

" *Killed.*

" Mr. Macgillewrey of Drumnaglass, Colonel to the Macintoshes.

Mr. Macbain, Major to do., and twelve more of their officers.

Mr. Maclachlan, Chief of the clan Maclachlan.

Macdonald of Keppoch, ⎫

Macdonald of Clanronald, ⎬ These three we are not sure of their being killed.

Stuart of Ardshiel, ⎭

Lord Strathallen.

Mr. Fraser, young Inveralachy, Lieutenant-Colonel to the Frasers.

Captain Farquharson of the Farquharsons.

And a great many of their officers whoe's names are not known.

" *Wounded.*

" Cameron of Locheil and Gordon of Blelak, with several more.

" *Taken.*

" Lord Cromartie and Lord McLeod his son ; Lord Kilmarnock, Lord Balmirino, Major Glasgow of Lord Ogilvie's, Major Stuart of Perth's, Colonel Farquharson of Monaltrie, Colonel Cuthbert, and many more of the Rebell officers.

" All the French, both officers and privates, surrendered at Inverness ; twenty-four piece of cannon, ten set of colours, and two standards ; above three thousand muskets ; two thousand five hundred of the Rebells killed ; and, including the French, about two thousand prisoners in all.

" The King's army lost,—

" Four Captains, viz., Lord Robert Kerr of Barrells, Captain Simpson and Captain Grossett of Prices, Captain Campbell of Lord Loudens ; and two subalterns, viz., Ensign Dally of Monroes, Ensign Campbell of the Campbells ; forty-nine or fifty killed on the spot ; and about two hundred wounded, including officers ; and twelve since dead of their wounds."

From the Lord Lyon :—

" To ARCHIBALD DUNBAR of Newton, Esq.,
                    " att Duffus.
      " *Free.*—A : BRODIE.
                              " INVERNESS, *Sunday's night.*

" DEAR ARCHIE,--I have yours, and as to a pass
to Mr. Inness, mine cannot carry him over the ferrys ;
and if I should ask one of General Hawley, who alone
gives land passes, his only question is this, ' Do you
know the man to be a Whig (that is an honest man),
and will you answer for him ?' and if I answer in the
affirmative, then the pass is granted.   But as I cannot
say Mr. Inness is a Whig, nor can I answer for his
loyalty, since I do believe him to be a Jacobite, I
neither can nor will ask a pass for him, and I do
think he may be satisfied to be allowed to stay at
home with his liberty ; for if it had not been for my
informations of the loyalty of Murray, all the suspected persons had been in jayl long before now ;
therefore, if they are not taken notice of, I beg you
may not interest yourself for any of your Jacobite
friends ; for I know Mr. Inness to be one, and therefore I must not burn my fingers with improper applications for such people.   As to our friend, George
Cumming, he has egregiously misbehaved in not
attending the Duke at Forres or Nairn, and if he
suffers at present, he has his own imprudence alone to
blame, for he was so self-sufficient that he would not

take my advice in comeing here, or going to the regiment, or attempting to do it. You have only heard his story, but not the strong allegations against him, which I wish he may clear himself of.[1]

"William Fraser is with you before now about your forage. Tell William to write a note by each boat, directed to Mr. Laurenc Dundas, signifying the quantities of hay sent, &c., which will serve for a pass or permit to come through the fleet. Your answer to Ancrum was a right one. All our compliments to Nellie.—Adieu, dear Archie, yours faithfully,

"ALEXR. BRODIE.

"*P.S.*—For Godsake help us to some hens, capons, or chickens; for the Duke and our mess &c. have no fowl of any sort; we grudge no price."

———

Commissariat arrangements :—

" To the SHIRREFF-DEPUTE
      " of the County of Murray.
                              "ELGIN, 27 *April* 1746.

"SIR,—It will be necessary, ffor the service of his Majesty's fforces, that a small magazine of fforrage be laid up in your place, wherefor I beg you may meett with the Justices of the Peace and others concerned, about your place, and concert measures with them so

---

[1] He was, by order of the Duke of Cumberland, tried by a court-martial, at Stirling, but was acquitted.

as to get brought into some proper place in the town,
about a thousand stones straw, and twenty bols oats ;
and when any part of that is made use of by the
troops, cause as much more be brought in, that the
above quantity may be always ready on hand. You
may also secure five hundred or a thousand stones
more straw, and about twenty bols more oats, so
that, if it is wanted, it may also be brought on any
emergency. Please cause inform the country people
that they shall be honestly paid ffor all they send in,
and if they are backward in doeing it, they will have
themselves to blame if it is taken ffrom them without
weight, measure, or price. I am, Sir, your most
humble servant,

" ROBERT GARDINER,
Deputy-Commissary."

From the Lord Lyon :—

" Upon His Majesty's Service.
" To SIR HARY INNESS of Inness, Baronet,
" at Elgin.
" Free.—A. BRODIE.
" INVERNESS, May 4th, 1746.

" DEAR KNIGHT,—Though you was angry for my
recomending my Lord Ancrum to where he could get
forage, I hope you will not be angry if I intimate to
you the Duke's orders anent sending him five hundred baggage horses to carry straw to Lochend, to be
put on board the galley ; and all sorts of provisions,

to Fort Augustus. There are two hundred called for from the county of Nairn, five hundred from Ross-shire, and five hundred from this neighbourhood.

" Tullybardin is taken or surrendered att Dunbar-toun. I send you Newmills letter, inclosed, that you may assist him as a Justice of the Peace, and I do think you should send directly for Sir Robert, and Archie Dunbar, to assist you.

" My family join in compliments to my Lady, and I am, yours, &c., ALEXR. BRODIE.

" *P.S.*—I would really be glad to find out the use of sending me an express to tell me the inconveniency of sending back forage to Fochabers, after that neighbourhood had been drained of it ; since you could not think you would have rheterick enough to persuade Ancrum to obey you rather than the Duke."

" To the SHERIFF-DEPUTE
    " of the County of Murray.

" INVERNESS, *the 3d May* 1746.

" SIR,—I am ordered to acquaint you that the service of his Majesty's troops, under the command of his Royal Highness the Duke of Cumberland, will require from the county of Elgin and Forres five hundred carrige horses, with such carrige graith as they carry their straw. You will therefore order the above number of horses to be at the shoar of Inverness on Thursday the eighth currant, without faile. I am, Sir, your most humble servant,

"Laur. Dundas,

Commisry."

Mr. Hall was probably the Quartermaster of the troop :—

" To the Honble. Sir Henry Innes, Bart.,

" at Elgin.

"Gordon Castile, *May the* 9.

" Sir,—As I am informed by the Duke of Gordon, you sent an order to Mr. King to send forrage to Focabers for the troop of dragoongs, beg you will be so good as deliver the enclosed to him. We have not forrage to serve the troop till to-morrow night, so must depend upon relief from your goodness. I am, Sir, your most obedient homble sarvent,

" G. S. Hall."

" To William King, Esqr.,

" Sheriff-Dept.

"Gordon Castile, 9.

" Sir,—After an order sent you to provide the troop of dragoongs at Focabers, it surprises us much that you have had no regard to it ; but asure you, if you do not imediately comply with it, shall aquaint his Royal Highness that your assistance has been desired, but you did not honour us with due obedience as we have not forrage for to-morrow ; expect you will send a sufficient quantity to sarve for some time, to-morrow night. I am, Sir, your obedient sarvant,   G. S. HALL."

Answer to the above :---

"ELGIN, 10th May 1746.

"SIR,—I received yours of yesterday's date this forenoon, and was surprised that you acquainted me, thereby, that there was an order sent me for providing the dragoons at ffochabers, there having never any such order come to my hand, either by word or write. It is true I had ane order from Mr. Gardiner, Commissary-Depute to the troops under his Royall Highness the Duke of Cumberland's command, desireing me to lay in a magazine of fforrage at Elgin, for the use of the troops as they passed and repassed here, which I accordingly did, to the extent of eight or nine hundred stone of straw, and some small quantity of corn ; and secured the quantity of straw, you have in the inclosed list, for the use of the troops, which was to be brought in to Elgin as the magazine there turned empty. There being litle or no other fforrage left in this county, who have severely suffered by the Rebells in corn, fforrage, and otherways, except what was carryed to ffindhorn to be transported to Inverness, for the use of his Majesty's troops there ; and as there is no part of the county of Murray on the other side of the water of Spey (except the town of

ffochabers, belonging to his Grace the Duke of Gordon,
and the lands of Mulben and Mulderie, belonging to
the Laird of Grant, and the lands of Cairnty, from
which there was no forrage demanded to this county
where these lands ly), it has always been the practice
that the Sheriff of Banffe supplyed the troops that lay
at ffochabers, with fforrage and other provisions; and
much more ought it to be so at this time, when they
suffered so litle, in these commoditys, by the Rebells,
in respect of the part of the county of Murray on this
side the water of Spey.

"However, to show my willingness and readiness
that the troops should be served, I have sent an
order (the copy whereof you have inclosed), and caused
intimate the same by a shirriff officer this day, that
you may be served accordingly; which I hope you
will be this night, in terms of the order; tho' I could
have wished that, as wee are scarce of fforrage in this
country for serving his Majesty's troops, you could
have been provide by the Sherriff of Banff, where, as
I am told, there is plenty of corn and straw in severall parishes that are within that county in your
neighbourhood, such as the parish of Boharm, Bo-
triphney, and Aberlour, Keith, Grange, Belly, and
Raffin. And if you have not occasion for the quantity
in the list I have sent you, I begg you will be so good
as acquaint me of the quantity thereof you have use
for, that I may secure the remainder for the use of

his Majesty's troops, as they shall have occasion for
it, att this place or any where else ; which is all from,
Sir, your most obedient humble servant,

"W. KING."

———————

Sir Robert Gordon gives his sentiments :—

" To The LORD LYON.
                              " GORDONSTOWN, *May* 14, 1746.

" My LORD LYON,—You may be sure I would very
gladly contribute my best endeavours towards settle-
ing the peace of the country, by giving you any hints
which I could imagine would be of use ; but I can
hardly think what to say on such a subject, unless
that I had some hint of the scheme proposed.   In
generall it was, and still is, my oppinion that the
Highland dress should be absolutely forbid ; that no
Highlanders should be allowed to have or use arms ;
that no man should be suffered to live in the thieving
countrys, but such as are registred by heritors, who
should be oblidged to produce such registred persons,
under proper penalties ; that a body of the regular
troops should be stationed in proper places, to apprehend such persons as shall dare to disobey the laws, or
interrupt the course of justice ; that the Crown should
be at the expence of prosecuting criminals, at least
before the Court of Justiciary, and the expence of all
criminal prosecutions should be regulate and made
very moderate, and high penalties put on witness who

do not appear.   Forts in many places will, I dare say, be found necessary.

"I wish your Lordship a good journey to London, and shall be extreamly glad to find that such measures are taken, as may effectually prevent the Highlanders having it in their power for the future to disturb the peace of the State or of their neighbours; though in our parts Lord Pitslego, with the Aberdeen and Bamffshires Lairds (a very few excepted) and their people, did more harm since this Rebellion, than all the Highlanders put together.—I am, my Lord Lyon, your most humble servant,   ROBERT GORDON."

From the Commissary-General :—

"To WILLIAM KING of Newmill, Esq.,
    "Shieriff-Deputy of the County of Murray.
            "INVERNESS, the 20th May 1746.

"SIR,—The troops here begin to be in want of straw, for the supplying of which, I am ordered by his Royall Highness the Duke of Cumberland to acquaint you that it will be absolutely necessary to send through the different parts of your county ; that what straw is may be furthwith sent to the shoar of Findhorn, where proper persons are appointed to recieve and pay what is delivered there.

"You will signifie to me the recieving of this letter, and that you are to comply with the above order, that

I may make a report of what is to be expected from your county.—I am, Sir, your most humble servant,

"LAWR. DUNDAS, *Commissry.*"

On the morning of the 22d of May 1746, the Duke of Cumberland, with the whole army, except four regiments (left encamped), marched from Inverness to Fort Augustus :—

" To the SHIRRIFF-DEPUTE of the County of Murray.

"INNERNESS, 23d *May.*

"SIR,—It is absolutely necessary for his Majesties service that you send ffrom your county to this place, by Monday's morning next, five o'clock, at least two hundred horses, to transport provisions ffrom this to Lochend, which is to goe from that by watter to ffort Augustus, for the army's use. And it is expected that no stop or delay will happen in this demand, as it is of the greatest consequence to the army.—I am, Sir, your humble servant,

"ROBERT GARDINER,
Deputy Commissary."

Answer to the above :—

"ELGIN, 25th *May* 1746.

"SIR,—Yours of the 23d current came only to my hand, between seven and eight o'clock this morn-

ing, desireing to send up to Inverness two hundred
horses, to be there again the morrowe morning at
ffive o'clock, a thing morrally impracticable, as it
would take up all this day and the morrow, before
they could be acquainted, or the gentlemen of the
county conveened for ordering out their respective
quotas of horses; besides that, I had an order from
Commissary Dundas, Thursday last, and had, in consequence therof, issued out orders for carrying any
straw that was in this county to ffindhorn, yesterday
and the morrow, to be transported from thence to
Inverness, for the use of the troops there; and any
horses that could be ordered from this county, upon
so short advertisement as yours, are the horses from
the towns of Elgin and fforress, which are but few in
number, and the only horses at hand for transporting
the troops' bagage in their marches, and are to be
employed this night, or by two of the clock the
morrow morning, for carrying from this the baggage,
&c., of Collonell ffleeming's regiment towards Aberdeen.

"I sent you up formerly from this county five hundred horses for transporting bagage, &c., from Inverness to Kilmhuiman, and at that time the horses were
so low and weak that it cost them two days journey
before they got to Inverness, and some of them were
keept only one day ther, and others of them ten, and
some of those horses never returned; and complained

they got no hire for their labour or horses, as was promised

" The only gentleman in this county that is at hand, and that I had time to communicate yours to, before writting hereof, is Sir Hary Innes of Innes, and he was of opinion, as I am, that unless there had been time for conveening the gentlemen of the shire, as there was formerly, when the horses were last sent up, it was impossible to send up horses to Inverness to-morrow morning, to be there again ffive o'clock, as you appoint, which they could not have done had they been all ready yoaked in their carts when yours came to hand ; and the horses here are now much weaker than when last with you, occasioned by their frequent carriages and labouring, which is not over here, and the most of them employed in other carriages for the benefite of the troops every other day; and they have scarcely meat to support them, the straw being almost quite out here, and the grass not got up by reason of the great drought; and severalls of them in this county have forty-two miles to travell to Invernes, so that when you want any horses and carriages from this, you would need to acquaint, three or four days at least before, for it took up the most of that time before they were all acquainted, the last time the horses were sent up.

" The gentlemen of this county have always, on all occasions, shown their willingness and readyness to accommodate and serve his Majesty's troops in every thing, as far as in their power, as they are still willing and ready to doe ; and there is none more willing and ready, as far as in my power for serving and accommodating them, than I am ; but have wrote you honestly and plainly the state and condition of the county, as it presently is, and how the horses in it are just now employed ; which is all from, your most obedient humble servant,   W. KING."

Government enlisted the services of the Established Church. Andrew Fletcher was Lord Justice-Clerk :—

" Rt. Honble. the EARL OF MORRAY,
    Sheriff of Murray, and his Deputys.

              " EDINBURGH, *May* 3*rd*, 1746.

"MY LORD,—I have subjoined such a letter as I desire your Lordship would write to every minister within your bounds. As this is for his Majesty's special service, and by direction of his Royal Highness the Duke of Cumberland, I am perswaded you will use all dispatch possible in forwarding these letters, geting and returning the answers.—I have the honour to be, my Lord, your Lordship's most obedient and most humble servant,

           " AND. FLETCHER."

Copy of the letter which was subjoined :—

"*May* 1746.

"REVEREND SIR,—As you must be best acquainted with those in your parish who have not been connected in this wicked and unnatural Rebellion, that none of them from any unjust suspicions may suffer any hardships, I am ordered by the Lord Justice-Clerk to desire you will make up lists of all those in your parish who have not been concerned in this Rebellion, either by carrying arms or otherways ; including in that list not only residenters of all ranks, but likeways heritors and liferenters though not residing.

"Send under my cover two several copies of such lists, sealed up, one directed to the Lord Justice-Clerk, the other to the Honourable Sir Everard Fawkener, Secretary to his Royal Highness the Duke of Cumberland. As you have lists of your parish, an answer will be expected in a few days."

Some of the answers sent by the clergy to the Sheriff-Depute at Elgin :—

"ALVES, *May* 26*th*, 1746.

"SIR,—In answer to yours of this day's date, I received inclosed a print signed by his Royal Highness the Duke of Cumberland, the desire of which shall be honestly obeyed by me when required ; and, with respects to the lists in my parish of those who have not been concerned in this wicked and unnaturall Rebellion, by riseing in arms, I must give almost a whole list of my parish, there not being a husholder in the parish, but one poor grassman, that took up arms against the Goverment in any time of this Rebellion, and a very few young thoughtless servants who ingaged in this wicked attempt. I shall in a few days, send ane answer as desired.—I am, Sir, your most obedient humble servant,   GEO. GORDON."

" RAFFORD, May 26th, 1746.

"SIR,—I had your's, and, inclosed, his Royal Highness's order concerning the Rebels, &c. Whatever is proper to be done by us as ministers, I dare say will not be wanting, and more than that I hope will not be expected. I wish every minister had as little to do as I. If that was the case, the matter would be soon ended, and little disturbance or confusion in their parishes.—I am, Sir, your most humble servant,
" ROBT. LOGAN."

"DYKE, May 27th, 1746.

"SIR,—I have just now yours by Lord Justice-Clerk's order, with the Proclimation by his Royal Highness the Duke of Cumberland inclosed, and shall soon sett about makeing the proper return, though, our situation with the Rebels not allowing me to make the ordinary course of visitation and examination, it will take some days to do it exactly ; though I have reason to be thankful that, so far as I know, there will be no place for giveing any one resedenter within my parish trouble. —I am, Sir, your very humble servant,

"ROBERT DUNBAR."

"KNOCKANDO, *May* 28*th*, 1746.

" SIR,—I have just now received yours requiring lists of all those not concerned in the wicked and unnatural Rebellion; with ane enclosed print. Though I am immediately much distrest with the gravel, I shall lose as little time as possible in making up these lists, and transmitting them to you as you direct.—I am, Sir, your most humble servant,   HUGH GRANT."

"CROMDALE, 28*th May* 1746.

" SIR,—Yours of the 26th instant, requiring lists of all those in my parish who have not been concerned in this wicked and unnatural Rebellion (with a print inclosed), came to hand this day. I shall, how soon my health will allow, send two copies of said lists under your cover, as directed. It is with great difficulty I write you this, being at present confined to my bed.— With compliments to your lady, I am, Sir, your most humble servant,   FRANCIS GRANTT."

From the Revd. Lauchlan Shaw to an Episcopalian. The Historian of Moray was a large-hearted Christian and a true gentleman :—

" To Archibald Dunbar of Newtoun, Esqr.,
      " Duffus.

                        " Elgin, *June 6th*, 1746.

" Dear Sir,—I have writen to Aberdeen for this year's magazines to you, but have not as yet got them ; their posts go no farther than to Dundee, and they cannot get home books or pamphlets but by carriers, who are not frequent.

" The Lord Justice-Clerk's letter is so general and undetermined, that we cannot but differ about the meaning of it. We in this town, and others around us, send up the names of all our own hearers, who, upon conversing with our elders, we have ground to believe had no concern in the Rebellion. We omit and leave out the names of some of our hearers, because their character is not clear, and they ly under suspition ; and we leave out all the hearers[1] in the meeting-house, because they are no part of our proper charge ; their attachment to these meetings makes them to be reputed Jacobites, and we have not had that access to know their conduct, which we have had with respect to our own people. All this we wrote as a docquet to our lists; if it answers the design, it is good, if not, the general terms of the letter must

[1] Episcopalians.

be blamed. It cannot be justly inferred, that all who are not in our lists are guilty ; the natural infer- ence from it is, that we are not proper judges of the moral conduct of those who do not submit to our ministry. What methods shal be used to discover the guilty I know not. Sheriffs and magistrates are re- quired to send up lists, and so, I think, are the officers of the Custom and Excise.

"You have no doubt heard of M—j—r G——t's doom, and that he now lives at home. The Rebels in Strathavin and Glenlivat are delivering up their arms, and casting themselves on the Royal clemency. If others were wise they would do so. I have received one man's arms this day. The money, brandy, and arms landed in Moydart, make the unhappy men there backward to submit, which will provoke the Duke to destroy their countries. Glengarrie's and Lochiel's houses are burnt, and all that country, houses and woods, will soon run the same fate, if they submit not. Glenbucket and John Roy are in the braes of Strath- avin. The Strathspey hostages went south last week. The loss done to the wood of Abernethie is very great. —I am,   L. S.

"*P.S.*—If I get not your magazines, I shal send per next my own, which are now lent out."

We suspect that the solemn Fast was, in the Highland parishes, but a solemn mockery :—

" To the SHERIFF and his DEPUTS
        " of the Shire of Elgin.

"EDINBURGH, 12th December 1746.

" SIR,—Some days ago there were transmitted to
you a few copies of proclamations by His Majesty in
Council, for keeping a solemn Fast on the 7th day
of January next to come; and it being necessary
that a copy of the said proclamation be transmitted
to each parish, I send you inclosed ten copies, de-
siring you to transmit one of them to each parish
minister within your jurisdiction, with your con-
veniency, in such time however that they may reach
the ministers so as to be read from the pulpit on the
Sabbath before the Fast is to be observed.

" It is likeways desired, that when you send these
proclamations, you will take the trouble to acquaint,
by a letter, each minister, that a good many persons,
of the lower rank, who served in the Rebel army,
upon their having been lately taken up, have produced certificates from ministers in different places
in the country, bearing that they had delivered up
their arms to the ministers to whom they surrendered ; and that the Earl of Albemarle desires that all
ministers who received any such arms, may forthwith
deliver them up to the commanding officer of the army
who is quartered nearest to them, and to take a receipt

from such commanding officer, expressing the number
and quality of the arms so delivered, and transmit the
said receipts, severally, to the Right Honourable the
Earl of Albemarle at Edinburgh. I am, Sir, your most
humble servant,   PAT: HALDANE."

Concluding part of a letter from the Lord Lyon :—

"LONDON, *March* 14, 1747.

" Lovat's tryal you will see accounts of in the news-
papers. His own secretaries, and the Pretender's, have
said enough to hang him without any other evidence, of
which you shall have particulars in my next ; but this
has been a heavy week of fatigue upon us of the two
Houses of Parliament, attending this trial, insomuch
that I have no time to write any letters this week, for
we have been kept four days of this week, in Westminster Hall, till six or seven at night.—My kind
compliments to Nelly, and believe me, dear Archie,
yours faithfully,   ALEXR. BRODIE."

The clergy and members of the Episcopal Church
of Scotland, who refused to take the oaths to Government, were designated Nonjurors.

" To the SHIRRIFF-DEPUT OF MURRAY.

" EDINBURGH, 17*th October* 1747.

" SIR,—His Majesty having lately received accounts
of the insolent behaviour of the Jacobites, and that in

many parts of Scotland, the true friends of the Government, and those who have most meritoriously distinguished themselves in the support of it, have been
on many occasions oppressed and insulted by the
Jacobites and their adherents ; and that some of the
persons attainted of high treason have returned from
abroad ; and that many of the most notorious Rebels
are known to be lurking about in different places; and
that the acts for suppressing Nonjuring meeting-houses
have not been duly executed by the officers of the
law, at least that they have not been diligent in
observing and discovering the attempts that have been
made to defeat the intention of these wise and necessary laws.

" Whereupon I have had the honour to receive his
Majesty's commands, by a letter from his Grace the
Duke of Newcastle, his Majesty's principall Secretary
of State, to desire and require that you would immediately make the strictest enquirey into these matters,
and exercise the utmost force of the law for suppressing all practices whereby the quiet of his Majesty's
government may be in danger of being disturbed, and
for bringing to punishment those who are concerned
in such treasonable proceedings; and, particularly, that
you would use your utmost endeavour to discover and
secure any persons that may be lurking within your
bounds, who either were attainted of high treason or
were concerned in the late Rebellion, and are either

excepted by name or under some general description
in the late Act of Indemnity ; and that you would
make particular enquiry into the conduct of the
Jacobites, and whether there are any indications of a
design to give any disturbance to the Government ;
and that you take particular care that the Acts
for suppressing Nonjuring meeting-houses be complyed with, according to the true intention of the
same, and for that purpose that you enquire carefully
into all attempts that have been made to elude the
design thereof ; and it is his Majesty's particular
orders that you should transmitt to me constant accounts of what you shall do in consequence of these
orders.

"Give me leave, on this occasion, to advise you not
to show or communicate the orders you have now
received, to any person whatever, except so far as is
necessary for putting them in execution, lest it may
be interpreted by some persons to be done to disappoint the execution of them ; and, in the next place,
when you get information that any of his Majesty's
good subjects, who have meritoriously distinguished
themselves in support of his Majesty's Government,
have been, or may be, oppressed and insulted by the
Jacobites and their adherents, you are not to give
over your enquiry upon hearing that the matter is
transacted by the privat partys, because it is not in
the power of any privat subject to remitt the injury

done to the publick ; and lastly, that in searching for
Rebels you are not to confine yourself to suspected
places, because it is not impossible that in some of his
Majesty's subjects, not disaffected, an ill-judged tenderness may have got the better of their duty to their
king and country.—I am, Sir, your most humble
servant,   AND. FLETCHER."

Answer to the above :—

"ELGIN, 4th Novr. 1747.

"MY LORD,—I was honoured with your Lordship's
commands of the 17th past, and have the pleasure to
acquaint your Lordship, in answer thereto, that wee
have the happiness in this county, to have neither
attainted or excepted person within the same ; or doe
I hear, or can I learn, upon the narrowest inquirie, of
any insolent behaviour from Jacobites, dissafected persones, or their adhearants, to his Majestie's duitfull
subjects within our bounds, but all quiet and in good
neighbourhood; or can I learn, after the strictest
inquiry, of any Rebels being returned from abroad, or
sculking in this county, or is there any such thing as
a Nonjureing meeting within the samen ; or can I discover that ever any of the Nonjureing ministers have
atempted to preach since the batle of Culloden, but
that some of them, as they happened to be in a private family on Sundayes, have read prayers to that
family and four single persones, and noe more ; but for

publick places of worship, they have none, they being
all formerly burnt and distroyed, and noe new ones
set up.

"My Lord, if any thing worth your Lordship's
nottice, as to either of the subjects which were mentioned, happens in this county, or as far as I can
learn from any other, I shall obey your Lordship's
commands, and acquaint you thereof, from tyme
to tyme; but wee have reason to be thankfull to
Almighty God, that this county had litle or noe
concern in the late wicked and unnaturall Rebellion,
which few counties in the north can boast of except
ourselves.

"Wee, indeed, in this place mett with a great insult
in the begginning of October last, from a pairty of St.
George's Dragoones that were quartered here, who were
werie civillie used all the tyme they lay att this place,
but upon the Saturday att twelve a'cloack att night,
the night imediatly before they marched, they comitted
great insults by breaking with stones severalls of the
windows of the inhabitants, and the publick schoole-
house windows, and some of the magistrates' windows,
and our worthy good minister, Mr. Shaw's windows,
where they threw so many and big stones, that not
onley the glass but the haile timber of his windows
was driven in, so that it was onley the good providence
of God that preserved his braines from being knocked
out, for they drove in the stones with such furie that,

hard by him, they knocked a cadge to pieces, and killed a maves in it, and broke the plaister of the wall on the other syde of the room, and severall of the stones fell on his wife in her bed sleeping, untill her husband awoake her, and desyred her get up for fear of her life ; and they marched of only on the Sundayes morneing. The magistrates took a precognition of some of the facts next day, and put it after their Lieutennant-Collonell, who was very angry at his men's conduct, and ordered the payment of damnadges done by breaking the windows, so that the prosecution intended for such an insult is droped, but then I thought proper to acquaint your Lordship thereof, that in caice that corps should be guilty of any such prac-tises in any other place where they lye, your Lordship may give them a caution, for I can assure your Lord-ship they would need it from their conduct here, for they were suspected mostly of being Popish—the pri-vate men of them—and therefor it seems they poured out a great deal of their wrath, att their way-going, upon our worthy pastor, without any manner of pro-vocation ; and such insults upon his Majesties best subjects are insuferable from any sort of people.—Which is all from, my Lord, your obedient humble servant,

" WM. KING."

Verses which were printed, and privately circulated among Jacobite families :—

"The Birthday Ode.

" How long shall Rage o'er heav'n-born Truth prevail,
  And stern Oppression hold Astræa's scale ?
Must Charles's name, to ev'ry Briton dear,
  Be still remembered with a sigh or tear ?

Air.

" Sprung from kings in story great,
    For thee we hope, for thee we mourn ;
  To thy throne and ancient state,
    Royal Exile, soon return.

" Ah ! to see that happy day
    May each loyal Briton burn ;
  Tune, ye bards, the lofty lay,
    Royal Exile, soon return.

" When on Culloden's plains, in William's form
  Inhuman Slaughter led the rising storm,
  The murder'd infants sunk beneath his rage,
  And mangled Beauty fell with hoary Age,
  How 'scap'd my Prince the fury of the day
  What God, what angel, led thee on thy way !
  Yet new Affliction points her viper's stings,
  Disloyal subjects, and unfaithful kings,
  Alas, you found, nor sunk beneath the weight,
  Tho' wrong'd, triumphant, and in bondage, great.

Air.

" We'll brace the drum, the clarion sound,
And, starting from our trance profound,
In shining mail appear ;
While France shall, at our squadrons nigh,
Faint, tremble, drop her arms, and fly,
And own an Edward near.

" Can aught thy just resentment charm ?
Can aught resist thy conqu'ring arm ?
Can aught thy strength withstand ?
Yes ; when you see a prostrate foe,
You turn aside, nor strike the blow ;
Hear this, proud Cumberland."

" MERLIN.

" When a sharper shall fly from his merit, a cord,
And see his son swell with the title of lord ;
When a *Pelham* shall end what a *Walpole* begun,
And, excising the earth, lay a tax on the sun ;
When a peer, in his dotage, the privilege claims
Of bellowing for *George*, as he hollow'd for *James ;*
When possess'd of vast wealth, and abundance of spite,
A scribe is made out of a thing that can't write ;
When Episcopal lords are all aw'd with a nod,
And for *Brunswick* do more than they'd do for their God ;
Then Justice, indignant, shall snatch up her sword,
The times shall be changed, and the King be restored."

XL. CORONATION OF GEORGE III.: SUBMISSION TO HIS GOVERNMENT.

THE gentleman who "seed" his Majesty "annointed with the holy oill," held a situation in the Lyon Office :—

" To ARCHIBALD DUNBAR, of Newtoun, Esquire,
    at his House at Duffus, per Elgin, North Brittain.

                    " LONDON, 26th Septr. 1761.

" DEAR SIR,—You will be surprised to read a letter from me in this city. I was called by the Lords Commissioners of the Court of Claims to walk at the procession of his Majesty's Coronation, and was appointed grand new robes from the wardrop, with gold collar and chains with the Order of St. Andrew in gold, sett in azure and green ribben ; and accordingly I have performed that service, and had a full view of the glory that this world can afford in its perfection. It would take some sheets of paper to describe you the glory of that day. I neither know how to begin or how to end. Wee surrounded the throne in the quire of Westminster Abbey, and, as I was upon the third step of it, and so near his Majesty that I took hold of his robe with my hand, I seed him annointed with

the holy oill, taken, from the golden eagle, in a golden
spoon, and after this the crown putt upon his head
with shoutings inexpressable, and then invested with
the scepter and orb. But what I thought was the
solemnest part of the whole ceremony, and what took
my fancie most, was, immediatly after he was crowned,
the whole Peers of Great Brittain putt on their crowns
and immediatly went and laid their crowns at the
King's feet, and paid their hommage to him by kissing
the scepter, which when done, he allowed them all to
kiss his hand. Never was there a greater exhibition of
earthly glory.   Tho' the Peeresses were not allowed
any diamonds in their crowns, they fell upon a method
to supply this defect, by filling their heads so full of
them that their crowns disappeared amongst them.
The grandeur f the ladies in the gallery, both in
Westminster A   ey and in the Hall, as well as on all
the scaffoldings   the streets, with the innumerable
diamonds they   re decked with, is past description.
—I am, respectfully, dear Sir, your obedient humble
servant,   Jos. Strachane."

After the death, in January 1788, of Prince Charles
Edward, whose brother and representative, Cardinal
York, could leave no lawful descendant, the Bishops
felt that they could conscientiously recognise the
Hanoverian government :—

" INTIMATION

" To the Clergy and Laity of the Episcopal Church in Scotland.

" The Protestant Bishops in Scotland having met at Aberdeen, on the 24th of April 1788, to take into their serious consideration the state of the Church under their inspection, did, upon mature deliberation with their clergy, unanimously agree to comply with and submit to the present Government of this kingdom, as vested in the person of his Majesty King George the Third. They also resolved to testify this compliance by uniformly praying for him by name in their public worship, in hopes of removing all suspicion of disaffection, and of obtaining relie´ from those penal laws under which this Church has so long suffered. At the same time they think it th duty to declare, that this resolution proceeds fi ~ principles purely ecclesiastical ; and that they are moved to it by the justest and most satisfying reasons, in discharge of that high trust devolved upon the in their Episcopal character, and to promote, as far a s they can, the peace and prosperity of that portion of the Christian Church committed to their charge.

" For obtaining of this desirable end, they therefore appoint their clergy to make public notification to their respective congregations, upon the eighteenth

day of May next, that upon the following Lord's day,
nominal prayers for the King are to be authoritatively
introduced, and afterwards to continue in the religious
assemblies of this Episcopal Church ; and they beg
leave to recommend, as to their clergy whose obedience they expect, so likewise to all good Christian
people under their Episcopal care, and do earnestly intreat and exhort them, in the bowels of Jesus Christ,
that they will all cordially receive this determination
of their spiritual fathers.

"If any of them wish for farther information on
this subject, the Bishops hereby direct them to apply
to their respective pastors ; and conclude this address
with their hearty prayers to, and stedfast dependence
upon, their gracious Head and Master in Heaven,
that He would be pleased to bless, sanctify, and
prosper the pious resolutions and endeavours of His
servants upon earth, to the advancement of His glory,
the edification of His Church, and the quiet and wel-
fare of the State in all godliness and honesty.

> " ROBERT KILGOUR, *Bishop and Primus.*
> JOHN SKINNER, *Bishop of Aberdeen.*
> ANDREW MACFARLANE, *Bishop of Ross
> and Moray.*
> WM. ABERNETHY DRUMMOND, *Bishop
> of Edinburgh.*
> JOHN STRACHAN, *Bishop of Brechin.*"

APPENDIX.

In many cases in this Volume, persons are designated by territorial appellations. An Explanatory List is therefore given :—

Designation.	Surname.
Achnagern,	Fraser.
Arundele,	Grant.
Asleisk,	Brodie.
Barmuckatie, .	Dunbar.
Birdsyards,	Urquhart.
Bishopmiln,	Dunbar.
Boath, .	Dunbar.
Bracco, .	Duff.
Brodie, .	Brodie.
Burgie, .	Dunbar.
Cadboll,	Macleod.
Classtirum,	Gordon.
Clava,	Rose.
Cloavs, .	Dunbar.
Connadge,	Mackintosh.
Coulbin,	Kinnaird.
Coxton,	Innes.
Culkern,	Munro.
Dalrachanie,	Grant.

Designation.	Surname.
Lady Drummelzier, .	Mrs. Hay.
Drummond,	Mackintosh.
Duffus, .	Sutherland.
Dunkentie,	Innes.
Earnside,	Mackenzie.
Easterbin,	Dunbar.
ffaskin, .	Gordon.
Lady Force,	Mrs. Sutherland.
Fowls,	Sir Robert Munro.
Glenbucket,	Gordon.
Glengarrie,	Macdonell.
Grange,	Dunbar.
Grangehill,	Dunbar.
Grant, .	Grant.
Guineas,	Macleod.
Lady Hemprigs,	Lady Dunbar.
Innernity, .	Stewart.
Innes, .	Innes, Bart.
Kilboyak, .	Dunbar.
Lady Kilcowie,	Mrs. Mackenzie.
Kilravock,	Rose.
Kincorth,	Falconer.
Kinstery, .	Sutherland.
Kirkton,	Spense.
Knockando,	Grant.
· Leathen,	Brodie.
Leuchars,	Innes.
Linkwood,	Anderson.
Lochiel,	Cameron.
Logie,	Cumming.

Designation.		Surname.
Macleod,	.	Macleod.
Macintosh,		Macintosh.
Milntoune,		Brodie.
Muirton,		Calder, Bart.
Lady Muirton,		Lady Calder.
Myrland,	.	Dunbar.
Lady Newhall,		Mrs. Forbes.
Newmiln,	.	King.
Lady Newmiln,		Mrs King.
Newtoun,		Dunbar.
Lady Newtoun,	. . .	Mrs. Dunbar.
Pitfour,		Ferguson.
Pitgaveny,		Bremner.
Roshaugh,	.	Sutherland.
Skene,	. .	Skene.
Spyni (at page 48),	.	*Doubtful.*
Spynie,	.	Brodie.
Tanachi,	.	Tulloch.
Thundertoun,	. .	Dunbar.
Lady Thunderton,	. .	Mrs. Dunbar.
Woodhead,	. .	Spense.

The signature of each of the two Baronets of Innes, several of whose letters appear, was *Harie* Innes—not *Harrie*, as printed by mistake.

"The Lyon" was the usual designation of Alexander Brodie of Brodie, Lord Lyon King-at-Arms. By Lord Lovat, however, who disliked him, this very popular Laird was called "The King-of-Beasts."

The Vignette on the title-page is copied from a sketch taken before the tower was pulled down.

INDEX.

ABERCROMBY, Alexander, hopes that the Sheriff of Moray will allow the Duke of Gordon to settle T. Miller's case in his Grace's Court of Regality, 81.

Aberdeen, John Sinclair collecting for Lossie Harbour at, 168, 170; King's College, 1-5; Old Town preferable to New for student, 10; plaiding exported, 144.

Abernethie, wood of, messenger attacked in, 293; loss done to, 379.

Abjuration, oath of, how received at Aberdeen, 168.

Abstinence, total, for six days, 23.

Achnagern, Laird of, 244.

Achtirtyre, 87.

Adair, William, Esq., army agent, London, 322.

Adam, Isobel, Pittenweem witch, 264; her confession, 267.

Adamson, Mrs. Rebecca, her marriage in 1703, 200.

Addresses, complicated before streets were named or houses numbered, 33.

Adjutant for troops joining Duke of Gordon, in 1685, 311.

"Advice," a poetic exhortation, useful in revolutionary times, 233-235.

Advocate, Lord, in 1709, letter on quarantine, 49.

Advocate to Sir Robert Gordon, yearly pension paid to, in 1697, 193.

Advocates, Faculty of, refuse to assess themselves for poor's-rates in 1749, 103.

Ale to be taken with gilded pills, 20; price of, at Elgin in 1742, 277; at Inverness in 1654, 308.

Alexander, Mr., a portrait painter, 116.

Allacants, a kind of drink, 161.

Allan, John, in Mostowie, 87; fined, 89.

Almonds and raisins, price of, in 1689, 160.

Allyhore, Majorca, 320.

Altyre, 348.

Alum imported, 148.

Alves parish, 48, 49; letter about rebels, 375.

America, the reduction of, in 1759, 104.

Ancrum, Lord, 363; forage for, 364.

Anderson, Rev. Alexander, minister of Duffus, secures communion plate during rebellion of 1715-1716, 335.

—— Alexander, tenant in Burnsyde, 333.

—— Christian, master of a ship, 151.

—— Deacon, 170.

—— John, writer in Edinburgh, 236.

—— John, armourer, Elgin, 325.

—— Rev. Hugh, of Drainie, 241.

—— Robert, Clerk of Elgin Town Council, 160, 163, 165, 236.

—— William, Bailie of Elgin, 173.

Anise seeds imported, 148.

Anodyne, price of, in 1720, 21.

Anstruther, Captain Philip, of New Grange, lives near the Fountain-well, Edinburgh, 34.

—— General, Lieut.-Governor of Majorca, 321.

Antimony, tincture of, its price in 1720, 21.

Antonius, John, an Edinburgh undertaker in 1732, his account, 274.

Apples, Flanders, 191.

Aquavitæ, burnt, price of, in 1700, 39.

Araskine or Askine, Sir Charles, of Cambo, Bart., Lyon King-at-Arms, 74.

Archbishops of Canterbury and York written to by King James II., 313.

Ardgy, 93; tenants of, to send in provisions, 354.

Argyle, Duke of, influence of, at an election, 217.

Arndilly or Arundele, 96, 97 : laird of, 116.

"Art of Love," a book sent to a young lady by Duchess of Gordon, 109.

Ashhurst, Henry, merchant tailor, London, 192 ; Henry Ashhurst, junior, 192.

Asleisk, Laird of, also Laird of Brodie, 317.

Assemblies for dancing, etc., at Edinburgh in 1723, particulars about, 118.

Association of freeholders in Moray to annul " paper votes," 225, 227.

Aughteendales, 148.

Bacon, price of, at Inverness in 1654, 308.

Badenoch, 49 ; braes of, 296.

Badham or Badhame, William, dancing-master in Edinburgh, discharge and obligation from, in 1704, 14.

Badon, John, Findhorn, 152.

" Baron, The " (Mr. Gordon of Cluny), 223.

Bail for Laird of Thunderton in 1716, 299.

Baillie, Mr., of Inverness, 246, 250.

—— Lieut. A., letter from, 61.

—— Evan, 304.

—— George, his marriage, 103.

—— William, letter to Bailie Dunbar of Inverness, 179-181.

Bailly, Mr., Sheriff-depute to Lord Lovat, 301.

Baily, Rev. Mr., Inverness, 300.

Bajans, students of first year, 1, 3.

Baker's land and mill, 190.

Balantir, Laird of, his funeral, 281.

Baldic (contraction for Archibald), 10, 12.

Balfour, Captain, 161.

—— Sir William, of Pitcullo, his daughter, wife of fourth Earl of Moray, 279.

Ballichastell belonging to Laird of Grant, 294.

Balls (pills), masticatory, price of, in 1720, 21 ; box of small, sent by Dr. Walker, 26.

Balmerino, Lord, a prisoner at Culloden, 361.

Balsam, price of half an ounce in 1719, 20.

Baltic sea-ports, ships from, under quarantine in 1709, 50.

Banks of Edinburgh in 1756 send Glasgow notes to get specie for them, 103.

Banff, servants' wages in county of, in 1760, 97 ; Magistrates of, interested in Lossie Harbour, 170 ; plenty of corn and straw in, for use of King's army, 368.

Baptism of a natural daughter, 240.

Barmuckatic or Barmukety (also spelt Belmukedie and Bermucktere), Laird of, his

daughters' board and education, 16 ; his wife's death, 280 ; serves as a volunteer, 315-318 ; made an officer, 319.

Barnhill, 87.

Baronius, Annals of, and other books, bequeathed by the Dean of Salisbury to the Library of the Cathedral, 290.

Batavia, Governor of, pays £120,000 to the British, and begs pardon, 104.

Batchen, John, feus grounds of Thunderton House, 282.

Batesson, Na., Bailie of Perth in 1652, 307.

Bath recommended, 24.

Bawer, Alexander, 168.

Bean, Mr., 131 ; made fortune in India, 132.

Bear, price of, for Elgin in 1699, 30 ; meal, price of, for Elgin in 1699, 31 ; five bolls of, given for a dog, 46 ; a boll of, its price in 1708, 55 ; bear and malt exported from Elgin to Bordeaux and Drontone in 1676, 144 ; and to Rotterdam in 1685, 145.

Beaufort, seat of Simon Lord Lovat, 243, 246, 247, 248 ; Thomas Fraser of, 310.

Beef, price of, at Elgin in 1710, 32 ; barrels of, in 1694, 147 ; sent to Zealand, 150 ; price of, in 1742, 277 ; price of, at Inverness in 1654, 308 ; scarce in Elgin in December 1745, 345.

Beekworth, Capt., 124.

Beer, price of, at Inverness in 1654, 308.

Belcher, William, of Elgin, 188.

Bell, Peggie, Queen at Lord Crighton's ball, 118.

Bellenden, William, Lord of Broughton, Lord Treasurer Depute of Scotland, 75.

Bellie or Belly Parish, 193, 333.

Bellman, Langbryde, son of, his certificate, 99.

Bellormy, dovecot at, destroyed by rebels, 357.

Benefices to be given only during pleasure of Bishop, 314.

Benzion, 22.

Berwick, Earl of Deloraine visited there by Laird of Brodie, 111 ; Lords of Session and Justiciary return from, to Edinburgh on its evacuation by the Highlanders, 342.

Bill of Lading in 1694, 150.

Billiard-table at Elgin in 1732, price of, 99.

"Birley men," 340.

Biscuit, sugar, sent from Elgin, 19 ; why sent, 17.

Bishopmill, Laird of, 33, 223, 317, 326.

Bishops of Episcopal Church in Scotland submit to Government, 391.

Bitters, charge for a bottle of, in 1719, 20.

Blackstob, 190.

Blackwood or Blaikwood, Robert, merchant in Edinburgh, a son of Sir L. Gordon, Bart. apprenticed to, 138, 142.

Blak, James, 3.

—— Wil., Professor at King's College, Aberdeen, letters from, 1-4; some things sent to his care, 280.

Blantyre, Lord, married to Lady Catherine Cochrane, 119; his sister married to Mr. Hay of Drummelier, 121.

Bleeding for a cough, 216.

Blennshell, Wm., tailor in Elgin, his account in 1719-1720, 195, 196.

"Blode," two dogs to have, 43.

Blubber of whales, charges for procuring and carriage, 57.

Board of young ladies in 1709, 16; of students at King's College, Aberdeen, in 1755, 7.

Boat of Bog, a ferry on the Spey, 341.

Boath, Laird of, younger son of, 130; brother of, an ensign, 318.

Boerhaave's, Dr., receipt for pain in head, etc., 22.

Bogg, 49.

"Bogsie," William Sutherland, merchant in Elgin, so called, 153.

Bogtoun, Alex., in Khieclchik, 294.

Bole (a bolus), price of, in 1719, 20.

Books wanted by Bailie Innes of Elgin, 18; lent by Duchess of Gordon, 108, 109, 113, 114; bequeathed to Library of Salisbury Cathedral, 290.

Bordeaux, 64; export to, of bear and malt in 1676 by an Elgin firm, 144.

Bottles in salt-cellar at Duffus in 1708-1709, 213.

Bower, Rev. John, presented to Duffus Kirk, 241, 248; becomes minister of Duffus, 249, 250; letter from, 254; his death, 255.

Boyes, Admiral, pursuing Thurot, 104; his anchoring, Oct. 1759, in Leith Roads, 104.

Bracco or Braco, his reported marriage to Lady Mary Montgomery, 117; Lord, 223.

Brander, James, elder in Miltown, 87.

—— James, younger, 88.

Brandy not to be had at Fortrose in 1723, 187; price of, in 1714, 195; in 1742, 277.

Brass, old, 144.

Bread, prices of, at Inverness in 1654, 309.

Breeches, leather, price of, in 1720, 196.

Brest fleet pursued by Admiral Hawke, 104; squadron defeated, 346.

Brewhouse at Duffus, its contents in 1708, 212.

Brodie, Alex., of Brodie (Lord Lyon), whale speculation, 57; gossip about his being married, 111; letters on politics, 216, 217; recommends an obedient fellow as a preacher, 258; on funeral of Duchess of Buckingham, 277, 278; letter to Sheriff about furnishing baggage-horses and provisions for the use of Cope's army, 338, 339; a volunteer, 347; will not ask a pass for Mr. Innes after battle of Culloden, 362; letter to Sir H. Innes, Convener of the county of Moray, to send 500 horses, 364; at Lovat's trial in Westminster-Hall, 381.

—— Miss, of Brodie, her yellow gown, 123; to be married to the young Laird of Macleod, 124.

—— Alex., of Tillieburies, 146.

—— Alex., of Windyhills, letter from, 345.

—— Capt., at Dijon, 318; his letter from Werwick, 319.

—— Col., in Brussels, 318.

—— George, of Brodie, letter from, about the training of hawks, 42.

—— James, son of J. Brodie of Windiehills, 318.

—— Rev. James, recommended for Duffus Kirk, 257.

—— John, of Windiehills, 318, 324.

—— Joseph, of Milntown, 16.

—— Laird of, 49, 134.

—— Lewis Dunbar, of Burgie and Grange, 71.

—— Ludovic, W.S., drinks to excess with Mr. Eyre, 67; letters about succession to Westfield, 86; about settlement of vacancy of Duffus Kirk, 249-254; about surrender of Carlisle in 1745, 344.

—— Major, his company in Tullibardine's regiment, 316.

Brodie, William, ensign in Sir James Wood's regiment, 318.
—— William, merchant, Elgin, an account rendered by his wife in 1700, 38.
Broun's, Captain, troop at Elgin in 1716, 331.
Broune, Mr., 161.
Brown, Provost George, of Elgin, his letter about grain for the inhabitants, 174.
—— Thomas, with Pittenweem witches, 264.
Bruce, Mr., of Kinross, 269.
Brulet, Mr. John, a French master from neighbourhood of Rheims, 12.
Buchan, Earl of, in 1619, his letter to Sir Robert Gordon for a falcon, 42.
—— Earl of, in 1770, his note to Earl of Errol, 228.
Buckingham, Duchess of, account of her funeral, 277, 278.
Bugdaline, nails and deals for, 56.
Bulkes-head, 56.
Bulson, Francis, master of ship " Susana," 59.
Burdsyards or Birdsyards, Laird of, 251 ; and family, 124; lands of, to be quartered on, 355.
Burges, James and John, gunsmiths at Elgin, 325.
Burgess of Elgin, entertainment at making of, 160.
Burgh-head, or Burghsea, quarantine at, 50 ; letter from fishermen at, 54; whales stranded at, 57, 58 ; threatened by a lieutenant of the Navy, 63 ; complaint against fishermen of, 173.
Burgie sold to Dunbar of Grange, 71 ; house of, seized in 1668 by young Burgie, 72 ; and Grange, families of, 71-76.
Burnett, Miss Mary, of Kemnay, handsome, 131.
Burnside, 333.
Butcher-meat, price of, at Elgin in 1710, 32 ; at Inverness in 1654, 308.
Butter, price of, at Elgin in 1710, 32 ; at Inverness in 1741, 189 ; at Elgin in 1742, 277.
Butter-kit sent to Dr. Walker, 28.

CADBOLL or CATBOLL, Laird of, 143.
Cairn, The (one of the Grampian Mountains), 35 ; not to be crossed on account of snow, 170.

Cairngorm-stone, 97.
Calamus aromaticus, charge for 2 oz., 20.
Calder, Bailie, of Wick, beef, tallow, and hides bought from, 146, 147.
—— George, grieve at Kilcoy, 98.
—— Sir James, of Muirtown, partner of an Elgin firm, 144, 145, 148, 150.
—— William, brother of Sir James, 146.
—— Sir Thomas, of Muirton, Knight Baronet, settles prices of provisions in Elgin in 1710, 31 ; his niece, 107 ; his interest in a herring fishery, 112 ; bill on, 186.
Cambrick, two els of, 187.
Camels' hair imported, 149.
Cameron of Lochiel wounded at Culloden, 361.
Camila, Mrs. Stuart of, 111.
Campbell, Captain, of Lord London's, killed at Culloden, 361.
—— Ensign, killed at Culloden, 361.
—— Mr., of Delnies, his daughter, 221.
—— Mr. James, of Moye, 49.
Camphere, traffic with, in 1694, 148, 150.
Candles, price of, at Elgin in 1742, 277.
Candlesticks, brass, from London, 183.
Cannell imported, 149.
Cap Lacken, thirty guilders to be paid in name of, 145.
Capers imported from Holland, 53.
Capitulation of Perth in 1651, 306.
Capons, price of, at Inverness in 1654, 308.
Caption against Sir Robert Gordon, 254, 255.
Capuhins, a lady's dress in 1745, 123.
Carpenter's, General, dragoons at Elgin in 1716, 330.
Carlisle, surrender of, in 1745, 344.
Carltown, Mrs., and the new fashions in 1745, 123.
Carolina, John Dunbar of Burgie emigrates to, 71.
Carriage-horses, etc., wanted from county of Elgin for Duke of Cumberland's army, 365.
Carstairs, Alexander, merchant in Rotterdam, 148.
Casks that may be of use afterwards, 149.
Castledowney, seat of Lord Lovat, 302.
Cattle-stealing, 292-296.
Caulfield, Major, Quartermaster-General of Cope's army, 340.

Causi or Causy (now Covesea), boats of, 47, 49, 64.

Centaury, charge for two ounces of, 20.

Cephalic powder, charge for, in 1719, 20.

Certificate, of a French master, 12 ; of a grieve, 98; of a bellman's son, 99.

Chein, Jean, a governess, her qualifications and salary in 1710, 15.

Chaise had to be bespoken in Edinburgh in 1783, eight or ten days before it was wanted, 36.

Chalmer, George, clerk to Magistrates of Elgin, 238.

—— James, younger, Deacon Convener of Crafts, Elgin, 177, 178.

—— John, 38.

Chalmers, John, clerk to Magistrates of Elgin, 176.

Chalon sur Saune, Lieut. Dunbar, a prisoner at, 318.

Chanori or Chanry, 57 ; Lady Seaforth writes from, 105 ; Lady Duffus writes from, 106.

Chapin stoups from London, 183.

Chariot from London arrives at Findhorn in 1717, 185.

Charles, James, Bailie of Elgin, imprisoned by Earl of Sutherland, 300.

Charles-Edward, Prince, birthday ode in honour of, 387.

Charles IX. of France, Dean of Salisbury once Gentleman of Chamber to, 286.

Charlton, Esquire, not pardoned after Monmouth's Rebellion, 313.

Cheese, price of, at Elgin in 1710, 32 ; Cheshire, its price at Forres in 1714, 195.

"Chittock," a person in Elgin so called, 132.

Chrichton, Patrick, saddler, Edinburgh, his account in 1731, 197, 198.

Chickens, price of, at Elgin in 1742, 277.

Christie, Alexander, 168.

Chyr-aporie, Mackenzie, of Elgin (i.e., chirurgeon-apothecary), his account, 20, 21.

Cinnamon waters, 160.

Circuit Court of Justiciary had not proper accommodation at Inverness in 1786, 89-92.

Citydella, Majorca, 320.

Clanranald engaged in cattle-lifting, 292.

Claret, price of, in 1769, 40 ; in 1742, 277.

Classtirum, Laird of, 334.

Clava, Laird of, 55.

Clergy feasted by rival claimants for patronage of Duffus Kirk, 241, 250.

Cleveland, Captain, 160.

Cloavs, Laird of, 44.

Cloth, scarlet, and scarlet stockings, 186.

Clove gillifloor, syrup of, 161.

Cloves imported, 149.

Cluny M'Pherson, letter to Sir L. Gordon, Bart. in 1676, 292.

Coach, The Royal Charlotte Light Post, took two and a half days to run between Edinburgh and London in 1789, 37.

Coban, Mr., 96.

Cochran, Lady Anne, birthday, 6th Feb. 1723, her wedding dress, 117.

—— Lady Catherine, to be married to Lord Blantyre, 119.

Cock-a-leekie, 28.

Coquet, 147.

Cod-fish, price of, in 1708, 55 ; in 1710, 32.

Coffee-beans, price of, in 1712, 195.

College servants, King's College, Aberdeen, 8.

Collie, Mr. William, helper at Drainie, 241, 242.

Colme, M. Jo., poetic begging-letter from, 201.

Colt, Major, 50.

Commissariat arrangements after Culloden, 363.

Commissioners of Supply for Elgin fix prices of grain in 1699, 30.

Committee of the shire of Elgin on Quarantine, July 1647, 47.

Communion Office of Scotch Episcopal Church introduced by Bishop Gadderer, 238.

Communion-plate of Duffus Kirk, 335.

Compton, Spencer, Speaker of House of Commons, to High Sheriff of Elgin, 80.

Comrie, Patrick, Surveyor of Inverness, 152.

Confession of Faith, Mr. Robertson has scruples about subscribing to, 171.

Conqueror, John, Bailie of Perth in 1652, 307.

Controversial subjects to be avoided by clergy, 314.

Cook, Mr., 9.

—— John, in Barnhill, 87.

Cook, Robert, Advocate, and the Pittenweem witch, 270.

Cope, Sir John, his march to Highlands, 337; encamps near Elgin, 338; provisions for encampment, 339; letters about damage done by his army halting at Forres and Elgin, 341, 342.

Copper, old, 144.

Cordecitron, a sweetmeat, 160.

Corf-house, loads of whale-blubber taken to, 57.

Corn and straw for a horse, price of, at Elgin in 1700, 39.

Corphar, Janet, 268, 269 (see *Corseitt*); her miserable murder, 272.

Corseitt, Jane, Pittenweem witch, 264 (see *Corphar*).

Cosmetic, price of a, in 1719, 21.

Cottise (now Cotts), Loch of, 45.

Couban, Andrew, in Mostowie, 87.

Coubin, Laird of, 49.

Country matters, 93-100.

Couper, Mr., 170.

Coutfield, blacksmith in, 58; tenants of, to send in provisions, 354.

Courant, Edinburgh Evening, 134; of 13th Nov. 1745, with news of rebels' movements, 342, 343.

Covesea, fishermen of, complaint against, 173; cave at, where horses were concealed, 357.

Cow, Dr. Walker proposes to kill a full-fed one, its price per pound, 29; price of, at Inverness in 1654, 308.

Cowper, Rev. Mr., of Pittenweem, 271, 272.

Coxton, also Coxtoune or Coxtown, 87; Laird of, 52, 317.

Craigemur, Wood of Abernethie, 294.

Craigo, James, shoemaker, Edinburgh, his account in 1718, 197.

Crafts in Elgin, order for regulation of, in 1675, 176.

Crape, mourning, imported, 149.

Crawford, John, collector at Inverness, 151.

—— John, servitor to Mr. Dalrymple, Advocate, 193; receipt of, 194.

Creich, Kirk of, 232.

Crighton or Crichtoun, Lord, gives a ball, 118; pays his addresses to Lady Susan Hamilton, 119.

Criticism, on a tragedy, by Duchess of Gor-

don in 1722, 108; on novels, by the same, 113, 114.

Cromarty, 57.

—— George, first Earl of, 105.

—— George, third Earl of, a prisoner at Culloden, 361.

Crombie, Wm., vintner in Elgin, 65.

Cromdale parish, letter about rebels, 377.

Cromdell, Alex. Gordon of, 295.

Cromwell lays siege to Perth, 305; his troops at Inverness, 307.

Crookmoor, 45.

Crossley, 87.

Croughtly, *alias* "Croupie," his begging letter, 202, 203.

Crowns of Peers laid at feet of George III. at coronation, 390.

Cucumbers from Holland, 53.

Cullen House, 132.

Cullen, Cope writes from, 341.

Culkairn or Culkern, Laird of, sends express to London in 1723 about landing of Highlanders, 188; arrives at Elgin, 348.

Culloden, allusion to report of Rev. Mr. Murray having informed against parties who were at, 258, 259; list of rebel officers and men killed at, 360; officers of King's army killed at, 361.

"Culloden Reel," an officer in the Theatre at Edinburgh in 1749 shouts to the fiddlers to play it, 103.

Culnakyle belonging to Laird of Grant, 294.

Cumberland, Duke of, loses his sword, and trick on him, 102; his army, 22d May 1746, 371; pursuing rebels, 350; his cruelty at Culloden referred to in Jacobite verses, 387.

Cumin, Logie, son of, at Elgin school, 2.

Cuming, Rev. Alex., clerk to Synod, 233.

Cummin, Mrs., 120.

Cummine, Alex., tide-surveyor at Inverness, 65.

Cumming, Alex., of Logie, his wife's death and funeral, 283.

—— Janet, 240.

—— Capt., comical adventure caused by, 116; at Forres Church, 123, 124.

—— Lieut. Geo., of Altyre, made prisoner at battle of Falkirk, 348, 351-353; not in favour with Lord Lyon, 362; acquitted at Stirling, 363.

Cumying, Da., Sheriff-depute of Nairn, 89.

Cunningham, Miss Peggy, her runaway marriage with Col. Keith's son, 122.

Cupar of Angus, Rev. Mr. Smith preaches to rebels in church of, 334.

Custom-house charges in 1708, 56.

Cuthbert, Col., a prisoner at Culloden, 361.

DALLY, Ensign, of Monroes, killed at Culloden, 361.

Dalrachanie, Grant of, 245; writes to Lord Lovat, 248.

Dalrymple, Sir James, marries Lady Christian Hamilton, 122.

—— Hew, of North Berwick, advocate, receipt for year's pension, 193.

Damage to corn by Cope's army at Forres, 341; at Elgin, 342.

Dancing-master's discharge and obligation in 1704, 14.

Danzick, ships from, under quarantine in 1709, 50.

Darnaway, people of forestry, ready to assist Cope, 338.

Dawson, William (afterwards Provost of Forres and Laird of Hempriggs), captain of " Seven Brethren," 55; letter about a chariot having arrived at Findhorn from London in 1716, 185; his account in 1709-1714, 194; accused of importing arms for rebels in 1716, 329; imprisoned by Earl of Sutherland, 300.

Dean's manse, Elgin, 71.

Death, the punishment for breaking quarantine at Covesea, 48.

Deloraine, Earl of, Laird of Brodie visits at Berwick, 111.

Demurrage on detention of ships, 145.

Denoon, David, makes foot-mantle for Laird of Mackintosh, 215.

Deskford, Lord, reported marriage with Laird of Drummelzier's daughter, 118; like the ghost of Tenducie, 132; gives money for Lossie Harbour, 170.

Designation of estate to a person's name does not necessarily prove ownership of estate, 74.

Diack, Mr. Alexander, recommended as a tutor in 1754, his qualifications and terms, 11.

Diamonds not allowed in crowns of peeresses, how they supplied the defect, 390.

Dieppe, invoice of ship from Findhorn bound for, 56.

Diet, physical, what it was in 1713, 20.

Diet-drink, 21.

Dining-room furniture at Duffus in 1708, 208.

Dinkinty, or Dunkenty, Innes of, 300, 317.

Dipple, Duff of, 299.

Dogs, two young, to be tried at sport, 43; " Grossie " and " Spottie Boug," valuable animals, 46.

Dollas or Dollase, 292; depredations of rebels at, 358.

" Don Carlos," a novel sent by Duchess of Gordon, 115.

Donaldson, James, merchant in Edinburgh, 15.

—— Robert, writer, Covenant Close, 134.

Dornoch, 232.

Douglas, Duke and Duchess, separation of, in 1756, 103.

—— James, 88.

—— William, keeper of magazine at Elgin in 1716, 320.

—— Rev. Mr., a priest, 334.

Doune, Lord, funeral of his mother, the Countess of Moray, in 1683, 279.

Dragoons, St. George's, breaking windows at Elgin, 385.

Drainie, parish of, 241.

Drainy, horses at, kept by Sir R. Gordon, 359.

Drinking habits in 1742, curious illustration, 283.

Drinking-song in 1725, 153-158.

Droutone, traffic of Elgin firm with, in 1676, 144.

Drugs imported in 1705, by Dr. Innes of Elgin, direct from London, 17.

Drum cords from London, 183.

Drummelier or Drummelzier, Lady, a patroness of the assemblies at Edinburgh in 1723, and daughter, 118.

Drummer of Elgin, petition from, 162.

Drumnochter, Lord Strathnaver issues orders from, 311.

Drummond, Laird of, pursued by Cluny M'Pherson, 293.

—— Lord John, reported to be a prisoner at Leith, 346, 350.

Drummond, William Abernethy, Bishop of
Edinburgh, submits to Government, 392.
"Drunk at Inverness," Laird of Brodie
writes that he is to be, 218.
Duck and drake, price of, at Elgin in 1710, 32.
Dues paid by students at King's College,
Aberdeen, in 1755, 8.
Duff, Rev. Alexander, demits title to Kirk
of Creich in 1623, the reasons why, 232.
—— Provost, of Elgin, writes about scarcity
of peats, 94.
—— William, of Dipple, 299.
—— Mr., of Crombie, 253.
Duff House, seat of Earl of Fife, 227.
Duffs, at an election, 230.
Duffus, 45; Kirktown of, 48; Laird of, 48;
parish of, 49; vacancy in kirk, 240;
teinds, 242; letters from Lord Lovat about
the patronage, 243-249; Mr. Bower settled
as minister, 249; applications in 1748 for
vacant church, 255-257; letter to minis-
ter's widow from an Elgin writer, 278.
—— Alexander, Lord, possesses Thunderton
House in 1653, 282; Governor of Perth
in 1651, 365.
—— James Lord, 14; kills Ross of Little
Kindeace in 1688, 105.
—— Margaret, Lady, letter from, in 1688,
106.
Dumbrake, Alexander, his pole-money, 193.
Dumbrek or Dumbreak, Christian, 143.
Dunbar, Alexander, of Barmuckatie, serves
under Duke of Marlborough, 16, 315;
extracts from his letters, 316-318; a pri-
soner at Chalon, 318; has to sell his
clothes, 318.
—— Alexander, of Bishopmilne, Sheriff of
Moray, 326.
—— Alexander, of Westfield, 83.
—— Sir Alexander, Bart., letter to Earl of
Fife, 226-228.
—— Sir Alexander, of Westfield, heritable
Sheriff of Moray, 80, 282.
—— Archibald, of Newton, certificate in
1755 to a French master, 14; letters to
James, seventh Earl of Moray, 219-221;
letter to Henrietta Duchess of Gordon,
242, 243; rebel officers put up at his
house, 359.
—— Archibald, of Thunderton, letter to
his wife, describing a journey in 1708,

35; whale speculation, 57; countenances
smuggling, 64, 65; sold Thunderton in
1712, 74; Deputy-Lieutenant in 1722,
297, 298; imprisoned by Earl of Sutherland, 298-304; attends a meeting-house,
333; Sheriff-Principal of Moray, 336.
Dunbar, Sir Archibald, sells Thunderton
House to John Batchen, 282.
—— Bailie, George, merchant, Edinburgh,
86.
—— Captain, his writing-chamber near
the Cross, Edinburgh, 33.
—— Captain John, 316.
—— David, of Dunphail, Deputy-Lieutenant
of Elginshire, 326.
—— James, 48.
—— James, what he said to Lord Lovat,
303; gets information about W. Dawson
having assisted rebels, 329.
—— James, merchant, Inverness, letters to,
179-183; answer to first letter, 181;
could have been a witness, 300.
—— James, of Inchbrok, his undutiful wife,
77; funeral letter from Lord Doune to,
279.
—— James, of Westfield, his three daughters
possessed Thunderton House in 1601,
282.
—— James, Sheriff of Moray, 82.
—— John, of Burgie, emigrates to Carolina,
71.
—— Ludovic, of Grange, his horse, etc., required for Government, 325; value of
arms received from, 327.
—— Ludovic, of Westfield, sells jurisdiction of Sheriffdom of Moray to the Earl
of Moray, 82; his death, 86.
—— Robert of Burgie, 49, 73.
—— Robert, of Grangehill, commander of
the Moray Horse in 1716, 324.
—— Robert, of Newton, settles price of
provisions in Elgin in 1710, 31; two
notes to his brother Archibald, 43, 44;
letter about funeral of wife of Laird of
Barmukaty, 280.
—— Robert, younger, of Burgie, cited by
Lyon King-at-Arms, 74.
—— Rev. Robert, wants to get a book pub-
lished in London, 184.
—— Rev. Robert, of Dyke, letter about
rebels, 377.

Dunbar, Thomas, of Grange, 71.
—— Rev. Thomas, D.D., Vicar of Little
Bustead, Essex, letter about the sale
of the Sheriffdom of Moray, 82-85.
—— William, Adjutant, letter from, dated
Port Mahon, 320, 322.
—— William, of Kincorth, account ren-
dered to him for entertainment at Elgin
in 1699-1700, 38.
—— William, W.S., letter from, 130-133.
—— Sir William, Bart. of Durn, 38.
—— Sir William, of Hemprigs, 86, 124, 221,
222.
—— Mrs. Ann, letters from, 122, 123.
—— Mrs. Elizabeth, letters to, from
Duchess of Gordon, 107-116.
—— Mrs. Elizabeth or Bettie, how she is
to take pills, 20; receives a fan from the
Duchess of Gordon, 115; her funeral ex-
penses, 274.
—— Mrs. Peggy, an active partisan, 250,
254.
—— Janet, gets £2 sterling, as quarterly
board for two young ladies, 16.
—— Meg and Ket, daughters of A. Dunbar
of Belmuckedie, their board and education
in 1709, 16.
Dunbar's Hospital, Inverness, founded in
1668, 319.
Dundas, Mr., Lord Advocate in 1722, 337.
Dundas, Laurence, Commissary-general,
363; order from, for carriage-horses, 365;
for straw, 370.
Dunibristle, Fifeshire, seat of Earl of Moray,
117.
Dupoye's, Lieutenant, horse at Elgin in
1716, 331.
Duradounes, or cross dollars, current at
Liege and in Scotland in 1705, 316.
Dutch ships taken in 1760, 104.
Dyke, parish of, 48; Countess of Moray
buried at, in 1683, 279; letter about
rebels, 376.
Dykeside, Lady, or Mrs. Anne Dunbar, 122.

EARNSIDE, Laird of, his son dies at Rheims
in 1712, 318.
Ecclesiastical matters, 232-260.
Edinburgh, gossip in, 101-104; dancing assemblies in 1723, 118; Guild Court, books
of, 141; John Sinclair collecting for Lossie

Harbour, 169; gallant defence of Castle
in 1686, by Duke of Gordon, 314.
Education in former days, 1-16.
Eggs, price of, at Elgin in 1710, 32; in 1742,
277; at Inverness in 1654, 308.
Elches or Elchies, Lord, 249; his sister
married to Grant of Dalrachanie, 248.
Election, for county in 1747, and election
trick, 216, 217; correspondence, 218-228;
song, 229-231.
Elecuary, an, for Lady Thunderton, 21.
Elgin, school of, 1; High-Sheriff of, written
to in 1721 about representation of shire,
80; plaiding exported in 1692, 144;
Town Council, tavern account in 1693,
159-161; town-officer's petition for fees
due, 164; Presbytery of, and Mr. William
Robertson, in re Confession of Faith, 171,
172; Greyfriars Kirk, repair of, 176, 177;
church vacant in 1689 and 1694, letters
about, 235, 236; jail used as lunatic
asylum, 281; exactions on, in 1715 by
Earl of Sutherland and Lord Lovat, 323;
Sir John Cope encamps near, 333; rebels
at, in April 1746, 360.
"Elizabeth," a tender at Speymouth in
1761, why there, 61.
Elphinston, Master of, his son's tutor passes
as factor, etc., 11.
Episcopalians, after Rebellion of 1745-1746,
reputed Jacobites, 378.
Episcopalian ministers complained of by
Presbytery of Elgin in 1716, 331-335.
Errol, Countess of, her death in 1723, 119.
Erskine, Alexander, Collector of Customs at
Inverness, protests against the Provost of
Elgin for converting wine into water, etc.,
65, 66.
—— Major, magnificent marriage of, 121.
Esterbin, Laird of, 49.
"Etmullerus, his Works Compendised and
Englished," a book wanted by Dr. Innes
of Elgin, 18.
Exactions on Elgin during Rebellion of
1715-1716, 323.
Excise, on wine and salt in 1695, 151.
—— Inverness disjoined from Ross in, 214.
Express, to be sent to Edinburgh, 129.
Eyes, pain in, receipt for, 22.
Eyre, Charles, Solicitor for H.M. Customs
in Scotland, 66; a hard drinker, 67.

FAIR drops, price of four bottles, 195.

Falcon, Earl of Buchan writes for one, 42; Laird of Brodie sends two to be " bredd," 43.

Falconar, William, Bishop of Moray, letter from, about a pedagogue, 10-12.

Falconer, Hon. Captain George, 61; his printed circular about men for the navy, 62.

Fare from Aberdeen to Edinburgh in 1789, 37.

"Farms," Provost of Elgin writes about, 174.

Farm-servants' wages in 1760, 97.

Farquharson, Colonel, of Monaltrie, a prisoner at Culloden, 361.

—— Captain, killed at Culloden, 361.

Fascan or Faskin, Laird of, 35, 38.

Fashions in 1745, ladies' caps, etc., 123.

Fast, solemn, January 17, 1747, ordered by Government, 380.

Faun (Fan) sent by Henrietta Duchess of Gordon, 115.

Fawkener, Sir Edward, Secretary to Duke of Cumberland, 375.

Fees of a French master in 1755, 13; of a governess in 1710, 15; of servants in 1760, 97.

Fenton, James, Bailie in Findhorn, 146.

Festivities of Town Council of Elgin in 1693, 159, 160.

Fiddich, 49.

Field-sports, 42-46.

Fife, James, second Earl of, M.P. for Moray, 225; created an English Peer, 228.

—— Mrs., an Edinburgh milliner and dressmaker, 125.

—— Bailie of Elgin, 159.

Figs and prunes imported, 148.

Findhorn to be secured from infection, 48; letter to skippers of, and their answer, 54.

Findlater and Seafield, Earl of, 133, 340.

—— Anne, Countess of, 38.

Findlay, Thomas, skipper in Findhorn, 54.

Finrassie, lands of, to send in stores, 354.

Fish, exported to Continent, 52; price of salted, in 1713, 54; price of, at Inverness in 1654, 308, 309.

Fishermen, protections for, 61, 62.

Fish-market of Elgin, Magistrates would have fishermen of Burghsea, etc., first offer their fish in, 173.

Fishings, records of, 52-60.

Fitch, Colonel Thomas, Governor of Inverness, his order about price of provisions in 1654, 307-309.

Flambeaux at funerals, 275.

Flanders, news of battle in, July 1711, 130.

Fleet, English, off Majorca in 1742, 321.

Fleming, Colonel, baggage of his regiment, 372.

Flesh, license granted in 1665 to eat it in Lent, 75.

Fletcher, Andrew, Lord Justice-Clerk, letter from, in 1746, 374; letter to Sheriff-depute of Moray about the Jacobites, 381.

Flock of whales, 60.

Flowers, artificial, 127.

Fly, The, fare from Aberdeen to Edinburgh by, in 1789, 37.

Flying Post, a newspaper in 1700, 33.

Fochabers, 132.

Folley's, Colonel, troop at Elgin in 1716, 331.

Forage in 1716, price of, 330; to be laid up at Elgin in 1746, 363.

Forbes, Alexander, gunsmith, Elgin, 325.

—— Dr., of Elgin, son of, 3.

—— Duncan, of Culloden, Lord President, letter to local Justices against smuggling, 68-70; alluded to, 216, 217; Lord Advocate, 299.

—— John, of Culloden, called " Squire Bumper," 129, 299.

—— Master of, 124; list of rebels killed at Culloden, in his handwriting, 360.

—— Rev. Mr., would not accept call to Elgin, 236.

—— William, cannot attend funeral as he has been drinking all day with Magistrates of Elgin, 283.

Force, Lady, her new cap, 123.

" Force of Friendship," a novel so called, recommended by Duchess of Gordon, 113.

Fornella's Castle, Majorca, 320.

Forres, Commissioners of Supply for Elgin, meeting at, 30; parish of, 48; Bailies of, 49; Presbytery of, consulted, 237; Cope's army at, 341.

Forsyth, John, 278.

Fort Augustus, 301, 365, 371.

Fountainwell, Edinburgh, 34.

Foxes, winter, in demand at Rotterdam, 144.

Frasers, influence of, at an election, 217 ; of Stratherrick, 310. See Lovat, Lord.

Fraser, Captain, his son goes back to Bajan class, 6.

—— Lieutenant-Colonel, younger of Inveralachy, killed at Culloden, 361.

—— James, Sheriff-clerk of Elgin and Forres, 81 ; his certificate, 251.

—— Major James, cf Culduthel, receipt of, 328.

—— Mr., 246, 247.

—— Rev. Patrick, 334.

—— Thomas, of Beaufort, 310.

—— William, his instructions about forage after Culloden, 363.

—— William, merchant in Inverness, letter from, 188, 189.

Free trade in fish, Magistrates of Elgin in 1738, will not allow, 174.

French master, certificate in favour of, 12 ; his terms in 1755, 13.

French surrendered at Culloden, 361.

Frigge, John, letter from, offering a price for grain, 190, 191.

Funeral charges in Edinburgh in 1732, 274 ; funeral letters, 279-283.

Furniture of Students' rooms, King's College, Aberdeen, in 1755, 7 ; Dr. Thomas Reid suggests it should be their own, 8 ; inventory of household, in 1708, 205-213.

GADDERER, Bishop, of Aberdeen, his beautiful seal, 238 ; letter from, 238-240.

Gaelic, want of knowledge of, causes Mr. Duff to resign the Kirk of Creich, 232.

Gallan, James, in Insharnach, 87.

Gambo, governess can play on, 15.

Gardiner, Robert, Commissary-Depute, order for forage, 364-369 ; for horses, 371.

Gargarism for Lady Thundertoun, 21.

Garmouth, 52.

Gartely, Rev. Alexander Smith, intruded into parish of, 333.

Gazette, Edinburgh, for 1700-1701, 33.

Geddes, Mr., 249.

—— skipper, Burghead, 58.

—— Thomas, Deacon of Square Wrights, Elgin, 177.

—— William, fisherman, Burghead, 54.

General of Artillery for troops joining Duke of Gordon in 1685, 311.

Genial letters, 123-137.

George III., his coronation, 389 ; Scotch Episcopalians recognise his authority after the death of Cardinal York, 391.

Gibson, Robert, of Linkwood, became insane, letter from, in 1701, 281.

Gilchrist, Rev. Messrs., 244.

Gilzean, Alexander, 88.

—— William, tenant in Ardgy, 93.

Gimp, Countess of Moray does not want, 125

Ginger, green, imported, 148.

Girds, 147.

Girnels, 31, 354.

Gladesmoor, how the odium of defeat was wiped off, 352.

Glasgow, city of, bank notes in 1756 and the Edinburgh Banks, 103 ; John Sinclair collecting at, for Lossie Harbour, 169.

—— Major, of Lord Ogilvie's, a prisoner at Culloden, 361.

Glass, Alexander, 88.

—— Alexander, musician, 165.

—— Mrs., 127.

Glenagies, Laird of, 269.

Glenbucket, Laird of, in braes of Strathavin, after battle of Culloden, 379.

Glengarrie's house burnt, 379.

Glenlivat, rebels in, delivering up arms, 379.

Glenmoristoun, Grants of, 310.

Godsman, Rev. Alexander, Roman Catholic priest, was in distress after Culloden, 258.

Goolhouse at Duffus, its contents in 1708, 212.

Goose, price of, at Elgin in 1710, 32 ; at Inverness in 1654, 308.

Gordon, Alexander, first Duke of, order for men to join his army in 1685, 310 ; his gallant defence of Edinburgh Castle, and fees of Commission, 314, 315.

—— Alexander, second Duke of, pays deference to Sheriff of Moray, 81 ; did not agree with the Duchess, 119, 120 ; his funeral, 282.

—— Cosmo-George, third Duke of, 241.

—— Henrietta, Duchess of, letters from, 107-116, 241 ; did not agree with her husband, 119, 120.

—— Jane, Duchess of, her approaching confinement, 132.

—— Lord George, 229.

—— Lord, breaks his thigh, 301.

Gordon, Sir Robert, of Gordonston (1st Baronet), letter to, from Earl of Buchan, 42 ; President of Committee of Supply, Elgin, 49 ; son-in-law to Dean of Salisbury, who leaves to him the care of publishing his works, 286 ; order to join Duke of Gordon in 1685, 310.

—— Sir Ludovic, of Gordonston (2d Baronet), binds his son George apprentice to an Edinburgh merchant, 138 ; letter to, from Cluny M'Pherson, 292.

—— Sir Robert (3d Baronet), entertained by Elgin Magistrates, 159, 160 ; yearly pension paid to his advocate, 193 ; some of his cattle stolen, 293, 295.

—— Sir Robert (4th Baronet), whale speculation, 57 ; projected marriage of, 111 ; feasts clergy, 250 ; tells a clergyman that he is a liar, 254 ; thrashes a woman, 260 ; damage done to him by the rebels in 1746, 356-359 ; letter to the Lord Lyon after Culloden, 369.

—— Sir William, of Gordonston (6th Baronet), letter from, 134.

—— Louise or Lucy, wife of Sir Robert Gordon of Gordonston, 284, 289.

—— Alexander, Bishop of Galloway, 284.

—— Alexander, of Cromdell, 295.

—— Alexander, of Ardoch, 298.

—— Arthur, seizes horses for use of Prince Charles Edward, 353.

—— Mr. Charles, 252.

—— Charles, of Buthlaw, buys Thunderton from Archibald Dunbar in 1712, 74.

—— Cosmo (younger of Cluny), 131.

—— Francis, order for 1000 stone weight of hay, 356.

—— Rev. George, of Alves, 250 ; his speech, during which he " sweat heartily," 252 ; letter about those engaged in rebellion, 376.

—— George, son of the Premier Baronet of Scotland, becomes apprentice of R. Blaikwood, merchant, Edinburgh, 138, 142.

—— Rev. James, a priest, 334.

—— Sir John, advocate, 315.

—— John, of Auchinereath, his widow, 25.

—— John and William, merchants in Camp hire, 148.

—— Lodovic, brother of Sir R. Gordon, letter to, from Macdonald of Keppoch, 295 ; answer by, 296.

Gordon, Ludovick, merchant, Elgin, 275.

—— Robert, landlord of " British Arms," Elgin, his bill, 40.

—— Robert, brother to Sir L. Gordon, 142.

—— Mr. Thomas, W.S., 315.

—— Thomas, merchant, Edinburgh, letter from, 186.

—— Thomas, 214.

—— William, master of ship "Betty," runs a cargo of smuggled goods into Speymouth, 67.

—— Rev. Dr., Dean of Salisbury, his will, 284-291.

—— Rev. Mr., of Leuchars, and Pittenweem witch, 270.

—— Rev. Mr., Episcopalian minister, Elgin, his salary incompetent, 239.

—— Rev. Mr., of Alloa, 250.

—— of Blelak, wounded at Culloden, 361.

—— Mr., of Haughes, 22.

Gordonstown, rebels at, their conduct to Sir Robert Gordon and his family, 357.

Governess in 1710, qualifications and salary of, 15.

Gow's, John, wife thrashed by Sir R. Gordon, 260.

Gowns, night, in 1722, quantity of satin to make two, 108.

Grafton, Duke of, interferes with election of Peers of Scotland, 228.

Graham, Dr. James, letter from, 23.

Graham's regiment in Majorca, 322.

Grahame, Major, entertained by Town Council, Elgin, 159.

Grain, price of, in 1699, 30-31 ; in 1741, 190.

Grangehill, Laird of, 49.

—— Robert Dunbar of, 324 ; letter from, 323.

Grange, Dunbars of, 71.

—— Laird of, 124, 221, 222, 317.

Grant, Alexander, in Coxtown, 87, 89.

—— Sir Alexander (of Dalvey), 223.

—— An., Provost of Perth in 1652, 307.

Grant, Castle, 119, 224.

—— Duncan, in Green of Manbean, 87.

—— Rev. Francis, of Cromdale, letter about rebels, 377.

—— General, 226.

—— Captain George, 300.

Grant, Rev. Hugh, of Knockando, letter about rebels, 377.

—— John, captain of guard for transport of Jean Mill, 88.

—— John, merchant, Elgin, 325.

—— John, wigmaker, Elgin, a jack-of-all-trades, 199.

—— Laird of, his children made burgesses of Elgin, 160; at General Assembly, 253; cited by Hugh Thaine, messenger, 294.

—— Major, at home after rebellion, 379.

—— Major, votes for M'Leod, 217.

—— Mr., younger of Grant, elected for Moray in 1741, 218.

—— William, merchant, sent by magistrates of Perth to Lord Duffus in 1652, for the deed of capitulation signed by Cromwell, 306.

—— Mrs. Jean, of Arndilly, letter from, returning thanks for the use of a stallion, 96.

Grants of Glenmoristoun, 310.

—— at Milnben, 347.

—— of Urquhart, 310.

Greek, lessons in, 3; New Testament, 4.

Greek-regent, a small compliment to be given to, by students entering Semie class, 4.

Greens, boiled and raw, recommended by Dr. Graham, 24.

Gregson, Nicholas, merchant-tailor, London, 192.

Grey, Henry, magistrate of Perth in 1652, 307.

Greyfriars, near Elgin, 94, 95; crafts of Elgin permitted to repair kirk of, 176-178.

Grieve's wages at Kilcoy in 1767, 98.

Grilses and salmon, 52, 53; price of, at Banff in 1716, 53; exported, 55, 56; price of, at Inverness in 1654, 309.

Grossett, Captain, of Price's, killed at Culloden, 351.

"Grossie," a valuable hunting dog, 46.

Grote, Andrew, 63.

Guadaloupe, a place of banishment in 1759, 103.

Guard for conveying Jean Mill to Nairn, 87.

Guest's, Colonel, troop, at Elgin in 1716, 331.

Guineas or Gineas, Macleod of, 143, 346, 347.

Guthrie, Robert, Cullen, his wife very plain, 227.

HADDOCKS, price of, at Elgin in 1710, 32; at Inverness in 1654, 309.

Haldane, Mr. Patrick, a lawyer, his fee, 252; sends proclamation of solemn fast to Sheriff of Elgin, 380.

Hall, G. S., writes to Sir H. Innes, Bart., and to W. King, Esq., about forage for horses, 366.

Ham, price of a, at Elgin in 1712, 277.

Hamilton, Duke of, married, 6th February 1723, 117.

—— Duchess of, in family-way, May 1723, 119.

—— Lady Christian, her marriage to Sir James Dalrymple, 122.

—— Lady Susan, courted by Lord Crichtoun, 119.

—— Walter, 111.

Hamilton's regiment, misconduct of, at battle of Falkirk, 352.

Hair-dressing in 1753, charges for, 198.

Hats imported in 1694 by an Elgin firm, 149.

Hatton Lodge, 131.

Haughes, Mr. Gordon of, 22.

Hawke, Admiral, pursuing Brest fleet, 104.

Hawking a favourite sport in the North, 42.

Hawks, training of, for falconry, 42, 43.

Hawley, General, only person who could grant land-passes after Culloden, 362.

Hay, George, town-drummer of Elgin, his petition, 162.

—— John, waiter at funeral of minister of Duffus, 278.

—— Lieutenant R., letter from, 63.

—— of Drummelier, Mr., marriage to Lord Blantyre's sister, 121.

—— Rev. Mr., of Crimon, 250.

—— Provost, of Aberdeen, 250.

Headache, receipt for, 22.

Head-suits dressed in 1710 by a governess, 15.

Hempriggs, W. Dawson of, 300.

Hemprigs, Lady, 86.

Henly, Cornet, at Elgin in 1716, 331.

Henry III. and IV. of France, Dean of Salisbury once Gentleman of Chamber to, 286.

Hens, price of, at Elgin in 1710, 32;

in 1742, 277 ; at Inverness in 1654, 308.

Heralds, power of, in 1668, 74, 75.

Herdman, Mrs., clergy feasted at her house by Sir Robert Gordon, 250.

Herring-casks for floating whales, 57.

Herrings, price of a last, 55 ; of a barrel, 53 ; of red dried, at Inverness in 1654, 308 ; of salt, 309.

Herring-fishery, overseeing of, by Sir Thomas Calder, 111, 112.

Hides in 1694, price of, 147.

Highland dress to be prohibited, Sir R. Gordon's opinion, 369.

Highlanders, obedient only to their chieftains in 1685, 310 ; commence attack at battle of Falkirk, 349 ; their march from Edinburgh, 342, 343 ; take Carlisle, 344.

Holster-tops and hose proper for mourning in 1700, 280.

Holland, oil and spermaceti command a better price there than in London, 59 ; merchant's apprentice in Edinburgh to go to, 141.

Home, Lady Jane, 126.

Horse, seventeen days' keep of one, in 1700, 39 ; sale of, in 1705, 129.

Horses, breeding and rearing of, part of duty of lady, 96 ; for use of Government in 1716, 324 ; of rebels, sold for little, 327 ; concealed in a cave at Covesea, 357.

Houme, 87.

Howstone, John, younger of Howstone, 151, 152.

Hume, skipper, arms imported in his ship, 329.

Humour, piece of, said to be by Duke of Montague, 101.

Hungary water camphored, 21.

Huntly, Earl of, killed at Corrichie, 284.

—— Marquis of, in 1707, at sport, 45.

—— Marquis of, in 1728, his letter about getting a house in Elgin, to entertain company, at funeral of Duke of Gordon, 282.

—— Marchioness of, her chaplain, 333, 334.

Hypnotic for Lady Thunderton, 21.

IMLACH, George, 88.

"Imperial Captives," a tragedy sent by Duchess of Gordon, 108.

Impressing for the navy, 61-63.

Incorporated Trades of Elgin in 1675-1676, 175.

Indigo, rock, 122 ; imported, 149.

Inerlochty or Inverlochty, 87, 88.

Infection, measures taken to prevent, 47.

Inglis, Thomas, servitor to Mr. Dalrymple, advocate, 193 ; receipt of, 194.

Inhibition against wife of James Dunbar of Inshbrok, 77.

Innernighty, or Innernity, Laird of, 111 ; his daughter marries the Master of Stormont, 121.

Innes, Laird of, 49, 317.

—— Alexander and George, letter from, 45.

—— Bailie, 237.

—— Rev. Beroald, in Instelly, does not pray for King George, etc. in 1716, 333.

—— George, of Dunkinty, imprisoned by Earl of Sutherland, 300.

—— Sir Harie, of Innes, letter about shooting, 44 ; letters about salmon-fisheries, 52, 53 ; genial letters, 128, 130 ; bail for Laird of Thunderton, in 1716, 299.

—— Sir Harie (son of above), letter about supply of peats for Elgin in 1747, 94 ; opinion about demand for horses, 373.

—— James, Provost of Elgin, 173.

—— James, son of Dr. Innes, Elgin, 18.

—— J., 131.

—— Mr., cannot get a pass after Culloden, 363.

—— Dr. Robert, physician, and bailie of Elgin, memorandum from, in 1705, 17 ; letters from, 18-20.

—— Robert, Elgin magistrate, 161, 162.

—— Robert, merchant, Elgin, expenses for wine at funeral of Robert Dunbar of Newtown, 276 ; Lord Loudon wants him to cash his bills, 340.

—— William, writer in Edinburgh, 193, 194.

Inns, New Black Bull, Edinburgh, 37 ; Black Bull, Glasgow, 37 ; New Inn, Aberdeen, 37 ; George and Blue Boar, Holborn, London, 37 ; Turk's Head, Newcastle, 37.

Insharnach, 87.

Inskeel, 333.

Instelly, 333.

Inverness, 52, 56 ; memorial from magistrates about condition of court-house and jail, 89-92; escape of prisoners, 133; prices of provisions when held by troops of Oliver Cromwell, 307-309; Dunbar of Thunderton prisoner in the Castle, 303; Lord Lovat prisoner, 347.

Iron not to be had at Fortrose in 1723, 187.

Irvine, Rev. Mr., 251.

—— Rev. John, a priest, 334.

JACK, Margaret, Pittenweem witch, 264.

—— William, price for apprehending, 199.

Jacobites, Andrew Fletcher on, 381; verses privately circulated by, 387.

Jailer's fees exacted at Elgin in 1780, 203.

"Jannet of Belfast," a ship chartered for Dieppe, the invoice, 56.

Jango, a sort of drink, price of, in 1700, 38.

Jeffrey, Francis, wigmaker, Edinburgh, in 1753, 198.

Juices, a bottle of, 21.

Julep, a hysteric cordial, one for Lady Thunderton, 19; a bottle of, 21.

July flowers (jelly-flowers) sent by Duchess of Gordon, 108.

Justices of Peace, meetings of, at Elgin, 49, 68.

KAME or KEAM, 333; young Laird of, 350, 352.

Kames, Lord, 133.

Kear, Robert, Elgin town-officer, 164.

Keith, town of, 35.

—— George, writer in Edinburgh, 15.

—— James, 2.

—— Mr., and Miss Peggy Cunninghame's runaway marriage, 122.

Kellie, Earl of, 269.

Kelly's, Quartermaster, horse, at Elgin in 1716, 331.

Kemnay, 131.

Ker, Mr., of Kippilaw, and the Pittenweem witch, 270.

Kerr, Robert Lord, of Barrell's, killed at Culloden, 361.

Kessock, 188.

Kid, price of a, at Inverness in 1654, 308.

Khieclehik, 294.

Kilbyoak, Laird of, 149.

Kilcowie or Kilcoy, Lady, 97, 98.

Kilgour, Robert, Bishop and Primus of Epi-

scopal Church in Scotland, submits to Government, 392.

Kilmalies, kirk of, 232.

Kilmarnock, Lord, a prisoner at Culloden, 361.

Kilmhuiman, 500 horses sent to, 372.

Kilmuir, Wester, 99.

Kilravock, Laird of, 43, 55, 222.

Kincorth, Laird of, 49.

—— W. Dunbar of, his tavern account in January 1700, 38.

Kinach, Robert, 21.

Kindeace, Little, 104.

King, William, of Newmiln, Provost of Elgin, and member of a firm there, 144-152; converted Greyfriars Kirk, Elgin, into a mausoleum, 176.

King, William, of Newmiln (son of above), Sheriff-Depute of Moray, warrant for removal of prisoner, 88; political letters to, from Brodie, 216-218; instructions from the Earl of Moray and the Lord Lyon as to Cope's army, 338-341; letter from, about forces in Elgin in December 1745, 346, 347; directs rebels to where they could find horses belonging to Sir R. Gordon, 359; answer to Mr. Hall about forage, 367-369; to Deputy-Commissary about horses, etc., 371-374; to the Lord Justice-Clerk about Jacobites, 384-386.

King, Mrs., and her infant son Alexander, 238.

King, Magdalen, her baptismal regeneration, 240.

King-Edward (now Kinnedar), parish of, 49; village of, 116.

King's College, Aberdeen, 1.

King's House; Thunderton House, Elgin, supposed to have been so called, 282.

Kinkine (small cask) of tarmaluk for dyeing, imported, 148.

Kinneder, widow of Dean of Salisbury, buried there in 1643, 284; tenants of Brodie there, to send in provisions, 354.

Kinsteary or Kinsterie, Laird of, 55, 360; and family, 124.

Kirktown, Laird of, 48, 223.

Kitchen furniture at Duffus in 1708, 211.

Knives for flensing whales, 58.

Knockando, young Laird of, 131; letter from minister of, about rebels, 377.

Kyligo, for mantle to Laird of Macintosh

when Member of Parliament in 1685, 215.

Kynnoch, George, in Inerlochty, 87.

Lac, tincture of, 23.

Ladies, of rank, letters from, 105-127 ; young, expenses of board and education of, in 1709, 16.

Laing, Beatrix, a Pittenweem witch, 262, 264 ; her confession, 265.

—— John, tenant in Ardgy, 93.

Lamb, price of, at Inverness in 1654, 368.

Langbryde, minister of, amusing certificate from, 99.

Latin must be understood before students can enter Semie class, 3 ; students should be well advanced in, before entering a University, 9.

Lawson, Nicolas, Pittenweem witch, 264 ; her confession, 266 ; her treatment, 272.

Leathen, Laird of, 221.

Leather alarmed, 144.

Lemon peel, 160.

Lent, license granted to eat flesh in, 75.

Leslie, Colonel, 160.

—— Rev. William, minister of Langbryde, 99, 100.

Leuchars strong ale, 46.

"Leusden's Collections of the New Testament in Greek," a book written for by Dr. Innes of Elgin, 18.

Levingston, Dr., of Aberdeen, 132.

Lewis, falcons of the, 43.

Lewis Gordon, Lord, supposed to be at Aberdeen early in December 1745, 345.

License to eat flesh in Lent, 75.

Liege, letter from a volunteer there in 1705, 316.

Ligonier's Dragoons, Col. Whitney of, his marriage to Meg Dunbar, 16 ; the regiment began attack at battle of Falkirk too soon, 352.

Lillie, Mr. John, Hague, 319.

Liniment, pot of, charge for, in 1719, 20.

Linkwood, Laird of, 223 ; beef from, 345.

Linlithgow, Earl of, in 1723, his death, 119.

Lisbon, "Seven Brethren" chartered for, 55.

Lisbon-wine, price of, in 1769. 40.

Lisle, letter from an officer there in 1708, 317.

Lochiel's house burnt in 1746, 379.

Lochness, granary at, for use of Duke of Cumberland's army, 355.

Logan, Rev. Robert, of Rafford, letter about those engaged in rebellion, 376.

Logie, Laird of, 2, 237.

—— Alexander Cumming of, his wife's funeral, 283.

London, merchant's apprentice in Edinburgh, to go to, 141.

Longacre, London, 34.

Lord Justice-Clerk in 1722, 337.

Lord's-day to be strictly observed in 1686, 313.

Lossie, Runns of, 43.

Lossiemouth purchased in 1698 by town of Elgin, from Brodie of Brodie, 166.

Lotion, price of, in 1719, 21.

Loudon, Adjutant, 340.

—— Lord, arrests Lord Lovat, 347 ; expected at Elgin, 348.

Lovat, Simon, Lord, letters about patronage of Kirk of Duffus, 243-249 ; letter and examination as to imprisonment of Dunbar of Thunderton, 300-304 ; letter in 1716 for horses, 327 ; thanked and rewarded by the King for services in 1715-1716, 328 ; brought as a prisoner to Inverness, 341 ; to give security for the peace of his people, 346 ; his trial, 381.

"Ludovick and William" of Findhorn, ship, 145, 150.

Lumsden, Professor, 250.

Lyon, Lord, 124, 250, 254, 269. See Brodie.

Mace, price of half an ounce of oil of, in 1719, 21 ; imported, 149.

Macbain, Major, killed at Culloden, 360.

—— Evan, messenger, 255.

M'Bean, Mr. H., 246, 247.

Macculloch, Rev. Thomas, Moderator of Presbytery, Elgin, letter from, 335.

Macdonald of Keppoch at Culloden, 360.

—— of Clanronald at Culloden, 360.

—— Coll., of Keppoch, letter from, in 1693, 295.

M'Edwart, John, Glenrinnes, 294.

M'Ever, Charlie, at King's College, Aberdeen, 6.

Macfarlane, Andrew, Bishop of Ross and Moray, submits to Government, 392.

M'Gillivray of Drumnaglas killed at Culloden, 360.

Machattie, Peter, letter from, about blubber and spermaceti, 59, 60.

Mahon, Majorca, 320.

Mackintosh or Macintosh, Laird of, his Parliamentary expenses in 1681 and 1685, 214.

—— William, Provost of Inverness, 92.

—— Bailie William, at Elgin with men in 1745, 348.

M'Kay, Major Eneas, made a burgess of Elgin, 160.

Mackean, John, schoolmaster, Elgin, 159.

Mackenzie, of Suddy, skilled in hostile encounters, 106.

—— George and Rod., certificate to a grieve, 98, 99.

—— Sir John, of Tarbat, his daughter the Countess of Seaforth, 105.

—— Sir Kenneth, of Cromarty, 187.

—— Kenneth, Bailie of Elgin, his account for spirits and wine to Town Council of Elgin, 159-161.

—— Kenneth, surgeon-apothecary, Elgin, his account in 1719-1720, 20, 21 ; bailie in 1733, 275.

—— Katharine, wife of James Dunbar of Inshbrok, 77, 78.

M'Kimmie, Alexander, in Overtown, 87.

Maclachlan, chief of the clan, his peremptory order for provisions to be stored at Forres, 354; another order, 355; killed at Culloden, 360.

—— Donald, serjeant, order for him to quarter at Sanchor, 355.

Macleod or M'Leod, Lord, son of Earl of Cromarty, a prisoner, 361.

—— Laird of, a candidate for the county of Inverness, 217 ; with his men at Elgin in 1745, 345-347 ; passed the Spey, 348 ; sudden march from Forres in 1746, 350.

—— young Laird of, very plain, intended marriage to Miss Brodie of Brodie, 124.

—— William, a carpenter in Inverness and brother of Macleod of Geanies, 143.

Mackmichan, John, master of ship " Janet of Belfast," 56.

M'Pherson, D., of Cluny, letter from, in 1676, about cattle-lifting, 292.

Macqueen, Donald, clerk, 304.

Magazines for year 1746, difficulty of forwarding, 378, 379.

Magistrands, students of fourth year, 1 ; Professor Reid's class in 1755, 5.

Mail, mistake in sending, 34.

Majorca in 1742, 321.

Manbean, Green of, 187.

Manicords, governess can play on, 15.

Mantle worn at opening, etc., of Parliament, 215.

March of troops joining Duke of Gordon in 1685, rules for, 312.

Maraken shoes, price of, 197.

Margaret, Princess, daughter of King Robert the Bruce, married fourth Earl of Sutherland, 138.

Marischal College, Aberdeen, Dr. T. Reid educated at, 4.

Marlborough, Duchess of, refuses sight of the Duke's pall to Duchess of Buckingham, 278.

Marnoch, John, skipper, Findhorn, 55.

Marriage-dress, magnificent ones described in 1725, 122.

Marrow-tarts at funeral, 277.

Marseilles, quarantine at, 322.

Marshal, the, of Elgin, flogs a woman, 102.

Martinique, a place of banishment in 1759, 103.

Master of Arts, Professor Blak makes a student, 4.

Masticatory balls (pills), price of, in 1720, 21.

Mastich, 22.

Mathews, Admiral, burns five Spanish galleys, 321.

Matricalis, Bynlis, spirit of, 23.

Matrimonial alliance projected in 1676, correspondence regarding, 179-182.

Maxwell, Earl of, not pardoned after Monmouth's Rebellion, 313.

Medical practice in former days, 17-29.

Meeting-houses of non-jurors to be put down, 382.

Menzies, Colin, 21.

—— Mr. Michael, 252.

Merchant-Company, Edinburgh, and poor's-rates in 1749, 103.

Merchants, wholesale, 144-152.

Merchants' letters, 185-191.

Mercury, Caledonian, referred to in November 1745, 343, 344 ; sent to Duffus in 1749, 101.

Merrytoun, Boath, place where Cope's army encamped, 338.

" Mess John," episcopalian clergyman, 128.

Milk, price of, at Elgin in 1710, 32; at Inverness in 1654, 308.

Militia, Elgin, men pressed for, 164.

Mill, Jean, accused of child-murder, escorted from Elgin to Inverness, 87-89.

Miller, Thomas, sues for an assault, 81.

Mills, rights of, in olden times, 94, 95.

Miln, Rev. Mr., 253.

Milnben, Grants at, 347.

Milntoune, Laird of, 16, 317.

Milton Brodie, formerly Windyhills, 324.

Miltown, 87, 88.

Minister wanted for Elgin, 335, 336.

Ministers in 1723 preaching against Edinburgh dancing assemblies, 118.

Mixture, stomachic, its price in 1719, 21; morning, 21.

Moncrief, Mr., 161.

Monmouth Rebellion, episode in, 310; general pardon after, 313.

Montague, Duke of, trick devised by, 101; crowd angry at, 102.

Montgomery, Lady Mary, 117.

Moray, youth of, frequented King's College, Aberdeen, 1; office of Heritable Sheriff of, 80-86; Brae of, 292.

—— Alexander, fourth Earl of, letter in 1668 about Lairds of Grange and Burgie, 72; to be Commissioner in 1686, 314.

—— Charles, fifth Earl of, 116-120.

—— Francis, sixth Earl of, 117.

—— James, seventh Earl of, letters from, political, 218-223; on death of his brother, 224; to Sheriff of Elgin to supply horses to Cope's army, 337.

—— Countess of, in 1683, her funeral, 279.

—— Countess of, in 1725, bad health of, 120, 121.

—— Margaret, Countess of, wife of James seventh Earl, letter from, 125.

Mordaine's, Lord, regiment, 316.

Morison, Peter, Fochabers, 294.

Mortoun, Patrick, Pittenweem, under influence of witchcraft, 261-268.

Mostowie, 87.

Mourning clothes borrowed, 281.

Moydart, men at, unwilling to submit to Government, 379.

Muir, Sir Archibald, of Thornton, 151, 152.

Muirfowl and partridges, price of, at Elgin in 1710, 32.

Muirsone, John, clerk to the crafts of Elgin, 178.

Muirtown, Laird of, 55.

—— Lady, July flowers sent to by Duchess of Gordon, 108; loses a child, 110.

Mulben, 368.

Mulderie, 368.

Mullen's, Captain, troop, at Elgin in 1716, 331.

Multures paid at mills, 95.

Mumbire, a kind of drink, 160.

Munro, clerk, 237.

Munto (Minto), Lord, waited on by Lord Lovat, 301.

Murdoch, Alexander, in Achtirtyre, 87; fined, 89.

—— Thomas, in Westhill, 87.

—— William, in Crossley, 87.

Murray, county, Sheriff of, 48, 49. See Moray.

—— Rev. Alexander, 258; letter on Sir Robert Gordon's health, 260.

—— Mr. Archibald, 252.

Musical accomplishments of a governess in 1710, 15.

—— treat given by Elgin Magistrates, 165.

Muslin, Holland, 53; imported, 149.

Mutchkin stoups from London, 183.

Mutton, price of, at Elgin in 1710, 32; in 1742, 276; at Inverness in 1654, 308.

Myrland, Laird of, 50.

Myrrh used for teeth and gums, 23.

Nairn, county, Sheriff of, 216.

—— Mrs., account for baking and cooking, 277.

Naizon's dragoons, G. Cumming of Altyre, a lieutenant in, taken prisoner, 348.

Napkin, silk, price of, in 1710, 194.

Naughty, Andrew, tenant, Burnsyde, 333.

—— William, Burghead, 58.

Naughtie, John, miller at Oldmilns, 95.

Needles, a hundred thousand imported by an Elgin firm in 1694, 149.

Neilson, James, 63.

Ness, bridge over, commenced in 1681, 319.

Newcastle, Duke of, Secretary of State, 381.

Newhall, Lady, a patroness of the assemblies at Edinburgh in 1723, 118.

Newmiln, Lady, sends candle-wicks, 345.

News in 1749, 1756, 1759, and 1760, sent from Edinburgh to a gentleman in Moray, 101-104.

Newton or Newtown, R. Dunbar of, 38, 43.

Nicholson, Alexander, at Dyke, receipt for a quarter's college-fee for two young ladies in 1709, 16.

Nisbet, John, 315.

Nonjurors, Episcopal clergy and laity who would not take oaths to Government, 381.

North College, Elgin, became the chief seat of the Dunbars of Burgie, 71.

Novels, sent by Duchess of Gordon, 113, 114.

Nuckell, James, Elgin town-officer, 164.

Nuid, M'Pherson, laird of, 292.

Nuptials of A. Dunbar and Rebecca Adamson, Epithalamium on, 200, 201.

Nursery furniture at Duffus in 1708, 209.

Nutmegs imported, 149.

Oak planks, price of, in 1712, 195.

Oatmeal, price of, for Elgin in 1699, 31.

Oats, price of, for Elgin in 1699, 30.

Œconomy servants, King's College, Aberdeen, 8.

Ogilvie, Bailie, 160.

—— George, advocate, 132, 133.

—— George, in Houme, 87.

Oil, from whale blubber, 59 ; holy, at coronation of George III., 390.

Oldmilns, to which Elgin was "thirled," 94.

Olibanum, 22.

Ombrdd mather imported, 148.

Oppressive measure of rebels in 1746, 353.

Orange peel, 161.

Orton, Dumbreaks of, 143.

Oseburne, Mr. James, 237.

Overtown, 87.

Oxycroceon, price of two ounces, 21.

Panmure, Earl of, Miss Stuart in mourning for, 119; his age and cause of death, 119.

—— Countess of, a patroness of the assemblies at Edinburgh in 1723, 118.

Pann brass imported, 148.

Panton, Master, musical treat given to, by Elgin magistrates, 165.

Paper, writing, price of a quire in 1712, 195.

Pardon, conditions of, after Monmouth's Rebellion, 313.

Parish ministers to give in lists of such as were not engaged in rebellion, 375 ; some of their answers, 375-377.

Parliament of 1721, representative for Elgin, summons to, 80.

Parliamentary, Laird of Mackintosh's expenses in 1681 and 1685, 214, 215.

—— Commission for visiting Universities, and the practice in 1708 of all the Colleges, 3

Parquett, Sergeant, a dragoon, 331.

Partridges, price of, at Elgin in 1710, 32.

Paterson, Margaret, mother of James Robertson, 182.

—— William, was at Culloden, 259.

Patersone, John, Bishop of Ross, 176.

Patronage, right of, to Kirk of Duffus, 241 ; curious case in 1748, 256, 257.

Pease, price of, for Elgin in 1699, 30.

Pease-stack used by rebels, 356.

Peats, horses of Sir Harie Innes at hill for, 53 ; burned on shore at Burghead during whale-blubber getting, 58; supply of, by tenants of farms, 93 ; distress at Elgin in 1747 for want of, 94 ; price of, in 1742, 277.

Peddie, Leonard, Deacon of the Shoemakers, Elgin, 177.

Pellem bridle, its price in 1731, 198.

Pepper, black, imported, 149.

Perth, invested by Oliver Cromwell in 1651, 305; demands made on, in 1652, by the English, 366.

Peterborough, Earl of, his daughter the Duchess of Gordon, 107.

Petaw, Dame Geneviev, widow of Dean of Salisbury, 284, 289.

Petrie, Alexander, 73.

Petry, Alexander, feuar, Starwood, 333.

Petticoat, crimson velvet smoke, 122 ; from London, 183.

Philp, Alexander, writes for men and arms to keep boats, of ships under quarantine, from landing at Burghead, 50.

Phlebotomy, charge for, in 1719, 20, 21.

Pigeons at Gordonstown destroyed by the rebels, 357.

Piliegrest imported, 148.

Pills, gilded, to be taken with ale, 20; charge for a box of, in 1720, 21.

Pint stoups from London, 183.

Pipes imported, 149.

Pirrie, Thomas, writer in Edinburgh, 141.

Pitcalnie, Ross of, letter from his widow, 76.

Pitcullo, Sir William Balfour of, 279.

Pitfour, Lord, 133.

—— Laird of, lines on, 229.

Pittgaveny, Graystone of, a place of rendezvous, 45 ; Laird of, 223.

Pittendreich, Col. Stuart of, 218, 219, 223; his death, 224.

Pittenweem, Magistrates and Minister of, disgraceful treatment by, of so-called witches in 1704-1705, 261-273.

Pitriken, Alexander, 88.

Pitsligo, Lord, Sir R. Gordon's opinion of his conduct in the rebellion, 370.

Plaid, Highland, wanted by a volunteer at Liege in 1705, its price, 316.

Plaids, three pair of white ones, sent from Inverness in 1678 to be sold, 183.

Plaidings, Aberdeen and Elgin, exported in 1692, 144.

Plaster, charge for a, in 1719, 20; a stomachic one, 21.

Plumb-cakes sent from Elgin, 19; why sent, 17.

Pluscardine, Oldmilns belonged to prior of, 194.

Podesoy, blue, part of marriage dress, 122.

Poetic effusions and begging-letters, 200-204.

Polwarte, Captain, 161.

Poor's-rates, hubbub about, in Edinburgh in 1749, 103.

Pork, price of, at Inverness in 1654, 308.

Port, price of, in 1769, 40.

Porter, price of, in 1769, 40.

Portmahon, Majorca, 320.

Post at Aberdeen in 1723, dilatoriness of, 119.

Postage to and from Bordeaux and Drontone in 1676, 144.

Postal arrangements in former days, 33, 34.

Postmaster-General's obligation to send Flying Post and Edinburgh Gazette in 1700, 33.

Pott, a celebrated pool in the Spey, 52, 53.

Poultry, price of, at Inverness in 1654, 308 ; wanted after battle of Culloden, 363.

Powder, gun, imported, 148.

Powders, morning, price of thirty in 1719, 21.

Precognition in case of smuggling, 67 ; Lord President Forbes on, 68.

Presbyterian, dominie not approved of by Bishop of Moray, 12 ; minister of Elgin an enemy to holidays, 128.

Presbytery of Elgin, their complaint in 1716 of encroachment on their parishes by Episcopal preachers, 331-335.

President, Lord, his son, 348.

Pretender, rising in favour of, expected in 1722, 336.

Price's regiment at Culloden, 361.

Primrose, Viscount, 269.

Prince Charles-Edward and his army reported to be near Inverness, 349.

" Princess of Cleaves," a novel recommended by Duchess of Gordon, 114.

Printers, poverty of, in Scotland in 1695, 184.

Printing a book in London, Rev. Robert Dunbar writes about, 184.

Prisoner, transport of, from Elgin to Nairn, 87 ; G. Cumming of Altyre taken by rebels at battle of Falkirk, 350-353.

Proclamation at market-crosses of Elgin and Forres, about an extravagant wife, 77-79.

Professors' and masters' fees, King's College, Aberdeen, 8.

" Prophet Jonas," a ship, in which twenty-nine tuns of claret, etc., were imported by an Elgin firm in 1695, 151.

Prot, John, fisherman, Burghead, 54.

Prott, Alexander, his boat, 188.

Protections for fishermen against impressment, 62.

Protestants, Gordon ducal family become, 107.

Provisions, prices of, in Morayshire in former days, 30-32 ; in Inverness during occupation by Cromwell's troops, 307-309; to be stored at Forres, March 1746, 354.

Prunes, imported, 148.

Psaltery, 137.

Psaltero-violin, a musical instrument, 137.

Punch, price of, in 1769, 40.

Purse, John, Deacon of the Weavers, Elgin, 177.

QUARANTINE, in former days, 47-51 ; at Marseilles in 1742, 322.

Quartermaster-General for troops joining Duke of Gordon in 1685, 311.

Quebec, reduction of, in 1759, 104.

RAFFERT or Rafford, parish of, 48 ; letter about rebels, 376.

Raick, a celebrated pool in the Spey, 52, 53.

Raisins, imported, 148 ; and almonds, price of, 160.

Randerston, Laird of, 269.

Ranes, Huntly, letter of a governess from, 15.

Raphane, church of, Mr. Robertson prays for the Pretender in, 334.

Ratterie, Mrs., 126.

"Read and Burn," letter so signed by Lieut. George Cumming of Altyre, giving account of his being made prisoner at battle of Falkirk in 1746, 350.

Reay or Rae, Lord, sends a letter with two prescriptions in 1727, 22 ; at Inverness in 1715, 300.

Rebellion of 1715-1716, 323-335.

—— of 1745-1746, 336-388.

Receipts and accounts, 192-199.

Recruiting in Scotland for Low Countries, 317.

Red wine, smuggling of, 65.

Reid, Dr. Thomas, Professor of Moral Philosophy, King's College, Aberdeen, 4 ; letter from, 5.

—— Rev. Mr., a priest, 334.

Reid's, Capt., troop at Elgin in 1716, 331.

Rent of room in King's College, Aberdeen, in 1755, 7.

Revell, The Iron, part of address on a letter, 33.

Rhind, William, merchant in Elgin, 145.

Rice imported, 149.

Riding cloathes for ladies, fashion of, in 1763, 126.

Rin, James, tenant, Kame, 333.

—— John, tenant, Inskeel, 333.

—— William, tenant, Rosyle, 333.

Rindes, mouth of the, a place of rendezvous, 45.

Rininner, depredations of rebels at, 358.

Roasting and broiling meat recommended by Dr. Graham, 24.

Robb, John, 88.

Robertson, Rev. Alex., prays for the Pretender in churches of Fochabers and Raphane, 334.

—— James, seeking Lilias in marriage, questions and answers as to his means and character, 179, 182.

—— James, groom to Sir R. Gordon, receipt for horses taken by rebels from his master, 353.

Robertson, J. and Co., Edinburgh, innkeepers and coach proprietors, rate of travelling in 1789, 37.

—— Bailie Thomas, of Inverness, cousin to Lord Lovat, 246, 300.

—— Wm., master of the grammar-school, Elgin, compelled by the Presbytery to resign, 171.

Rogues, or able-bodied vagrants, wanted as recruits, 317.

Rose, Rev. Mr., of Nairn, 244.

—— William, Treasurer and Dean of Guild, Elgin, 161, 162, 164, 165.

Roses, the family visits Forres, 124.

Rose-water, distilled, 23.

Roshach or Rosehaugh, Laird of, buying fish, 54 ; attends a meeting-house, 333.

Ross, Bishop of, John Patersone, 176-178.

—— Master of, in 1745, 348.

—— Alexr., W.S., 298.

—— Naomi, widow of Ross of Pitcalnie, 76.

—— Pa., magistrate of Perth in 1652, 307.

—— William, of Little Kindeace, killed in 1688 by Lord Duffus, 105, 106.

—— Wm., burgess and drummer in Inverness, his memorandum in 1687, 182, 183.

Rosyle, 333.

Rothes, 6th Earl of, Chancellor of Scotland, order for apprehension of R. Dunbar of Burgie and A. Petrie, 73.

—— 7th Earl of, returns south, 109 ; Sheriff of Fife, 268.

—— 8th Earl of, reported marriage to Lady Isabella Scott, 117.

Rotterdam, traffic between it and Findhorn in 1685, 145 ; commission to merchants at, 148 ; bill of lading printed at, 150.

Roxburgh, Duke of, direct male descendant of Sir Haric Innes, 128.

Roy, John, in Braes of Strathavin, after battle of Culloden, 379.

Russell, Jo., Elgin magistrate, 162, 163.

Sabin, General, 109.
Sack-possets, price of two, 39.
Sack wine, imported, 149 ; price of, 160.
Saddler's account in 1731, 197.
Salary of Episcopalian clergyman at Elgin in 1726 was incompetent, 239.
Salisbury, Dean of, in 1618, his will, 284-291.
Salmon, 144 ; price of, at Inverness in 1654, 309; and grilse, great take of, 52 ; relative prices in 1708, 55 ; in 1717, 56.
Salt, 36 ; horses to carry to Badenoch, 49 ; for curing fish, 52 ; price of peck in 1713, 55 ; excise on, 151 ; Spanish, 187.
Salvonsvall, Richard, 192.
Sanchor, house of, to be quartered on, 355.
Sarum, Close of, house of Dean of Salisbury in, 289.
Satin, flowered painted, sent by Duchess of Gordon, 107.
Scarcity of grain at Elgin in 1783, 174.
Scots-Tarves, Laird of, 269.
Scott, Lady Isabella, her dower in 1723, 117.
Scurvy grass, spirit of, 23.
Seafield, Countess of, bill on, in 1705, 18.
Seaforth, Kenneth, 4th Earl of, sends Laird of Brodie two hawks from the Lewis, 43 ; at London in 1688, 106.
—— Isobel, Countess of, widow of 3d Earl, her letter to Lord Duffus, 105.
Seal of Bishop Gadderer, device on, 238.
Semies, students of second year, 1-3; how they may enter the University at once, 4.
Serge, dyeing of red, 196.
Servants' wages in 1760, 97.
" Seven Brethren," a ship chartered at Findhorn for Lisbon, the invoice, etc., 55.
Shaw, Sir John, of Greenock, 151, 152.
—— Rev. Lauchlan, the historian of Moray, letters from, 9, 378, 379 ; certificate from, 251 ; his mavis killed, and his windows broken, 385.
—— Professor, 10.
Sheepherd, Mr. Edmund, druggist, 17.
Sheriff of Elgin, instructions for, 338.

Sheriff of Moray, office of, heritable, 80-86.
Sheriff's House ; Thunderton House, Elgin, so called in 1601, 282.
Sheriffmuir, battle of, allusion to, 157.
Sherry, price of, at Elgin in 1742, 277.
Shipping, charges for, in 1708, 56.
Shoemaker's account in 1717-1718, 197.
Siddy or Suddy, Mackenzie of, skilled in hostile encounters, 106.
Signal to be made by a smuggler, 64.
Sim, James, 88.
—— or Syme, Rev. William, of Mortlach, 244, 245, 253.
Simpson, Captain, killed at Culloden, 361.
—— Mr., was at Culloden, 259.
Sinclair, Mr., at Forres church, 123.
—— John, collects money for Lossie harbour, 166.
Skeen, John, 88.
Skene, Laird of, M.P. for Aberdeen in 1786, lines on election of, 229-231.
Skeoch, Gavin, his letter to Sir A. Dunbar to get him out of Elgin tolbooth, 203-204.
Skinner, John, Bishop of Aberdeen, submits to Government, 392.
Skirdastan, 49.
Slye, Mrs., gossip about her being married to Laird of Brodie, 111.
Smith, Alexander, Postmaster-General, obligation in 1700 to send *Flying Post* and *Edinburgh Gazette*, 33.
—— Rev. Alexander, did not pray for King George, etc., 333.
—— Walter, Deacon of Hammermen, Elgin, 177.
—— William, letter from, about his violin, 136.
Smookes, 45.
Smuggling in former days, 64-70.
Snuff, Lady Thunderton to take, 19 ; purpose of, 17.
Soap, importation of, 148 ; price of, in 1712, 195.
Solebay man-of-war in 1759, 104.
Soldiers in Elgin, very riotous, 164.
Speck, or blubber of whale, 57.
Spence, Robert, Elgin town-officer, 164.
Spens, Alexander, his letter about a borrowed suit of black clothes, 281.
Spermaceti, 58 ; sent to London, 59.

Spey, water-mouth of, 49; harbour of, 67; a ferry at, called Boat of Bog, 341.

Speymouth, "Elizabeth" tender at, and why, 61.

Spinle moore, a hunting-ground near Alves, 44.

"Spottie Boug," a dog, his price, 46.

Spynie, Laird of, 48, 257, 360; parish of, 49; Loch of, 44, 45; attempt to prevent drainage of, 134.

Squair, Rev. Mr., 251; speech in Assembly, 252.

"Squire Bumper," name applied to John Forbes of Culloden, 129.

St. Abastins, ship from, 151.

St. Andrews, University of, Greek more studied than Latin, 10.

St. Andrew Street, London, 34.

St. Phillips, the only fortification in Majorca in 1742, 321.

Starwood, 333.

Stays, stitched, price of, in 1719, 196.

Steel imported, 148.

Stelline, deals and nails for, 56.

Stephen, James, Bailie of Elgin, 173.

Stewart, Bailie, 39.

—— of Blairhall, marries Lady Anne Stuart, 117.

—— James, Elgin Magistrate, 161, 165.

—— Captain James, Commissary, order to, from Colonel M'Lachlan, 354.

—— Rev. John, at Duffus, accused of praying for rebels, 332.

—— Provost, 250.

Stockings sent on venture, 187.

Stodhart, William, was at Culloden, 259.

Stone-weight, various numbers of pounds assigned to, 29.

Stormont, Master of, and daughter of Laird of Innernity, to be married, 121.

Stotfield, complaint against fishermen of, 173.

Stowel, Mrs. Mary, her direction in London in 1704, 34.

Strachan, John, Bishop of Brechin, submits to Government, 392.

Strachane, Joseph, his letter on the coronation of George III., 389, 390.

Strathallan, Lord, killed at Culloden, 360.

Strathavin, rebels in, delivering up arms, 379.

Strathbogie, Lord Lewis Gordon's men at, 345.

Stratherrick, country belonging to Lord Lovat, 301; Frasers of, 310.

Strathmore, Countess of, her death, 119.

Strathnaver, John, Lord, order for troops to join Duke of Gordon in 1685, 310.

—— Lord, minor title of Earl of Sutherland, 297.

Straw for use of Cope's army, 339.

Stronoch, Wat., a fisherman, in one forenoon catches eighteen hundred salmon and grilses, 52.

Stuart, of Ardshiel, at Culloden, 360.

—— Commissary, lines from, to Commissary Paterson in 1688, 233.

—— Dr., factor to Duke of Gordon, 241.

—— Hon. Colonel, of Pittendreich, defeated at election in 1741, 218; again proposed, 218-224; his death, 224.

—— John, secretary to Earl of Moray in 1745, 341.

—— Major, of Perth's, a prisoner at Culloden, 361.

—— four Anne Stuarts married, 121.

—— Lady Anne, marries Stewart of Blairhall, 117.

—— Miss Anne, niece of Charles, fifth Earl of Moray, letters from, 116-122.

—— Mrs., of Camila, talked of as the bride of Laird of Brodie, 111.

Students at King's College, Aberdeen, their behaviour narrowly looked to, 6.

Styræ-Calamit, 22.

Suddie, parish of, 99.

Sugar, price of, in 1700, 38; Mellis, imported, 148; fine and coarse, in loaves, 187, 188; price of, in 1709, 194; in 1742, 277.

Surnames of the Lairds and Ladies whose territorial designations are given in this work. See Appendix, 393-395.

"Susana of Burlington," a ship, the cargo and charges, 59.

Sutor, Alexander, 63.

Sutherland, John Earl of, his influence and power, 297-304; Lord-Lieutenant of six northern counties, 324; writes from Holyrood House, to Sheriff of Moray, about likelihood of rebellion in 1722, 336, 337.

—— Earl of, in 1733, expenses for torches at his grandfather's funeral, 275.

Sutherland, William, Earl of, married Princess Margaret, 138.
—— George, of the Royal Coffee-house, Edinburgh, 280.
—— Mr. James, advocate, second son of James Lord Duffus, pays his sister's dancing-master, 14.
—— Jack, 124.
—— John, an Edinburgh agent, letters from, 101-104; writes from Edinburgh in November 1745, after Highlanders had marched towards England, 342.
—— Thomas, feuar in Kame, 333.
—— Will., letter from, in 1707, 45.
—— William, merchant, Elgin, extract of letter in 1710, 64; drinking-song and humorous degree, 153-158.
—— William, of Roshach, 333.
—— Mr., younger of Keam, 350.
—— Anne, innkeeper in Burghead, 58.
—— Mrs. Elizabeth, daughter of Lord Duffus, her dancing account in 1704, 14.
Swan's skin, 44, 45, 199.
Sweden, King of, picture-frame sent by Duchess of Gordon, 115.
Swine for Lord Reay, 22.
Sword presented by Queen of Hungary to Duke of Cumberland, reward offered for restoration of, 102.

Tailors, discharge of, in 1662, 192; worked for ladies in 1719-1720, 126.
Tallow, 144; price of, in 1694, 147; sent to Zealand, 150.
" Tam," (probably) Miss Grant of Arndilly, 97.
Tanachi or Tannachy, Laird of, 49; and family, 124.
Tarbet, Laird of, his land in Alves, 48.
Tarbot, Master of, troops under, for Duke of Gordon in 1685, 310.
Tavern bill in 1699-1700, 33; at British Arms, Elgin, in 1769, 40.
Tea, imperial and green, sent by Duchess of Gordon, 108; four pounds sent to Lady Thunderton, 122; price of, in 1710, 194.
Teeth and gums, receipt for, used by Lord Reay, 23.
Teinds of Elgin, 237.
Tenducci, referred to, 132.

Tenpence, price of a letter from Nairnshire to London in 1768, 131.
Terfle falcon, sent to a friend, 43.
Tertians, students of third year, 1.
Territorial designations of persons. See Appendix, 392-395.
Thaine, Hugh, messenger, meets with hard usage in Strathspey, 293.
Theatre of Edinburgh in 1749, scene in, 103.
Thirled to mills, 94, 95.
Thom, Gilbert, skipper, Findhorn, 55.
Thompson, Mr. 248.
Thomson, Rev. Mr., called to Elgin, 237.
Thores, David, 214.
Thundertoun, also Thunderton or Thundertown, Laird of, 55; Archibald Dunbar, still called of, though he had sold the estate to C. Gordon, 74; incarcerated by the Earl of Sutherland in the Tolbooth of Elgin and the Castle of Inverness, 299; threatened to be carried in irons on board the king's yacht to London, 302.
Thundertoun, Lady, wants a governess in 1710, letter from one, 15; pleased to hear a sermon after securing her peats and harvest, 115; requested to assist at funeral of Duke of Gordon, 282.
Thunderton House, Elgin, its history, 282.
Thurot, sailing of, 104.
Tippets, new-fashioned, sent by Duchess of Gordon, 115.
Tobacco imported, 149.
Tod, Mr., schoolmaster at Elgin, 2.
Tolmie, William, merchant at Fortrose in 1723, letter from, 187, 188.
Tongues exported, 147, 150; price of, in 1742, 277.
Toothache, receipt for, 22.
Torcastell, L. Mackintosh of, 215.
Torches used at funerals of nobility and gentry, 275.
Trade, export and import, of North of Scotland, in former days, 144.
Tradesmen, incorporated, of Elgin, 175-178.
Tragedies sent to a young lady in 1722 by Duchess of Gordon, 108.
Travelling in former days, 35-37.
Treble, governess can play on, 15.
Trick upon sight-seers, a man in a chopin-bottle, 101.
Trotter, T., 142.

Tullibardine, Marquis of, his regiment of foot with Marlborough, 316.
—— taken at Dunbarton, 365.
Turkeys, price of, at Elgin in 1742, 277.
Turnbull, Thomas, Fochabers, 193.
—— Mr., 237.
Twine imported from Holland, 53.
Tyack, The, a small stream near Elgin, 162.

UMBRE ; Sir Harie Innes, though a Presbyterian, could play it on Yule-day, 128.
Urquhart, Grants of, 310.
—— James, 168.
—— Robert, of Burdsyards, 251.

VEAL, price of, at Inverness in 1654, 303.
Villa Francia, a pass in Majorca, 321.
Viol, governess can play on, 15.
Violin, praises of one offered for sale, 136.
Virginelles, governess can play on, 15.
Vomitory, charge for, in 1719, 20.

WADE, General, rebels trying to evade, 343.
Wagens, Mathijs, his widow, dwelling near the fishmarket at Rotterdam, sells printed bills of lading, 150.
Wager about sport, 44.
Waiters at funerals, 278.
Walker, Dr. James, of Elgin, letters and notes in 1778, 1779, 1780, and 1782, to Sir Alexander Dunbar, 25-29.
Wales, Mr., sells his violin, 136.
Wallace, Margaret, Pittenweem witch, 264.
Ware, and ware horse, 97.
Water-drinking recommended by Dr. Graham, 23.
Watson, John, tenant in Ardgy, 93.
—— Thomas, 251, 252.
Watsone, Gavin, Deacon of Glovers, Elgin, 177.
Watt, skipper of a smuggling ship, what signal he is to make, 64.
Weighhouse, Edinburgh, its west side demolished in 1745, 344.
Wemyss, Earl of, his daughter the Countess of Moray, 125.
Westfield, tenants of, to send in provisions, 354.
Westhill, 87.
Westminster Abbey, coronation of George the Third in, 389.

Westminster Hall, Lord Lovat's trial in, 381.
Whales stranded in November 1729, on sands of Burghead, 57 ; loss on outlay, 60.
Wheat, price of, for Elgin in 1699, 30.
Whig tutor not approved of by Bishop Falconar, 12.
Whipping John Young's wife, in 1693, 162.
Whiteacres, St. Andrew Street, London, 34.
Whitings, price of, at Elgin in 1710, 32.
Whitney, Lieut.-Colonel of Ligonier's dragoons, married Meg Dunbar, and was killed at battle of Falkirk, 16.
Whytte, William, his poetic effusion on a marriage in 1703, 200, 201.
Wife, an extravagant and undutiful, 77-79 ; minister will marry one, a friend or relation of patron, to get church, 256.
Wigmakers' charges in 1753, 198 ; for oil and for shaving in 1743, 199.
Wightman, Major-General Joseph, his order about rebels' horses and arms hidden in Elgin, 328.
Wigton, Countess of, in family-way, 119.
Will of the Dean of Salisbury in 1618, 284-291.
William III. and Mary proclaimed at Elgin, 159.
Willow-green, cockades of, an expression for " setting caps at," 119.
Wilson, George, sen. and jun., Bailies of Elgin, 173.
Winchester, Alexander, Deacon of Tailors, Elgin, 177.
—— Rev. Mr., 251, 254.
Windiehills, John Brodie of, 318, 324.
Wine, spirits of, camphored, 21 ; price of, in 1700, 38 ; in 1769, 40 ; and brandy, smuggled, 64, 65 ; Rhenish, imported, 149 ; French, 149 ; twenty-nine tuns imported by an Elgin firm in 1695, 151 ; claret and white, sent from Fortrose, 187 ; claret and sherry, price in 1742, 276.
Wiseman or Wyseman, James, Justice of Peace Clerk, Elgin, 39, 50 ; Commissary Clerk, 46 ; fond of drink, 67 ; letter of, showing the power of John Earl of Sutherland, 298-300 ; Collector of Land-tax in 1716, 327.
Witches in Scotland : Pittenweem case, 261-273.

Wood's Regiment, Lieutenant Dunbar of, a prisoner of war, 318.

Woodhead, Laird of, 49.

YELLOW clothes worn by Lord Binny at marriage, 122.

York, Cardinal, last heir-male of Stuarts, 390.

Young, Captain, his Company in Tullibardine's Regiment, a volunteer promoted to be Ensign in, 316.

Young, Alexander, Elgin town-officer, 164.

—— Andrew, inhibition signed by, 79.

—— James, master of ship " Lodovick and William" of Findhorn, his " charter party" in February 1685, 145, 150.

—— John, his wife whipped, 162.

Younger sons, 138-143.

Youngson, Rev. Alexander, 240.

ZEALAND, 150.

EDINBURGH : T. CONSTABLE,
PRINTER TO THE QUEEN, AND TO THE UNIVERSITY.

www.ingramcontent.com/pod-product-compliance
Lightning Source LLC
Chambersburg PA
CBHW032305280326
41932CB00009B/702